A GARDEN
IN LUCCA

A GARDEN
IN LUCCA

Finding Paradise
in Tuscany

PAUL GERVAIS

**WITH ILLUSTRATIONS BY
THE AUTHOR**

HYPERION
NEW YORK

From *Collected Poems* by Wallace Stevens, copyright © 1923 and renewed 1951 by Wallace Stevens. Reprinted by permission of Alfred A. Knopf, A Division of Random House, Inc.

Grateful acknowledgment is made to Sheil Land Associates Ltd. on behalf of Christopher Lloyd for permission to reprint a passage from *The Well-Tempered Garden* by Christopher Lloyd.

ISBN 0-7868-6521-0

First Edition
10   9   8   7   6   5   4   3   2   1

To Alice and Marty

A GARDEN
IN LUCCA

PROLOGUE

GIL SHRUGS AND HANDS ME THE PHONE. THE CAL-
ler introduces herself. It's Shirley Kozlowski, travel coordinator for the
Gamble Garden Center, a horticultural foundation in Palo Alto, California. "I'm lining things up for next year's tour," she says. "It's not
only monumental gardens we're after, Lante, Gamberaia and the rest. I
want to show them gardens they can imagine themselves living in.
Would you mind if my husband and I came by for a look?"

A few days later. My universe welcomes Shirley and Jan, two
mythographers with dream-filled eyes. They consider my *Ceanothus* "Trewithin Blue," ponder, with quiet ambivalence, the vermilion of Gil's Ena
Harkness rose. They step back for an all-inclusive view: an angular sweep
of hedge, a file of potted lemons, a board game of topiary shapes.

"Aren't gardens marvelous," Shirley says, "all the different aims and aptitudes we bring to bear upon a common subject." She's a woman of casual grace, of languid beauty. Her blond hair is straight and bluntly cut, her country shoes dusty, well trod. She moves haltingly along my hedged front border the way one lingers thriftily over a chef-prepared plate, only occasionally raising the fork. "And such order everywhere," she says. She's gazing at my edges—they're so crisp they almost embarrass me.

"Frankly," she admits, "I've been a bit worried about this upcoming tour. Such abandon in these famous old Tuscan gardens. The marigolds *hardly* save them. It's a trial for the soul. But here, only the magic shows."

"This is the first Italian garden we've seen that has any plants in it," Jan remarks, gazing at our *Acnistus australis*, whose diminutive blue, bell-like flowers bring to mind pendulous datura blooms—it's an uncommon plant, and Gil's proud of the fact that I grew it from seed.

"This is just the kind of personal garden I've been looking for," Shirley says. "It's marvelous."

"Well, *we* like it," I admit. "But is it good enough for a tour group?"

"Good enough? Don't be so modest! You might just win this year's Visitors' Prize!"

"Is there a Visitors' Prize?" asks Jan, leaning in with a squint of doubt.

"Well, no," Shirley says, "caught me again."

It amazes me that I have a garden I personally keep—even this need of mine to have a garden is new to me. I think it's safe to say that no matter how long I live, how diligently I study and work, I'll always be a neophyte in the world of plants; I've had far too late a start.

But more amazing still is the fact that my garden is not in North Tewksbury, Massachusetts, where I grew up, not in New England with its shallow horticultural roots and climatic extremes, but in Italy, in the cradle of a great garden tradition, in a light-filled, temperate landscape that seems, even now that it's mine, unattainable.

Villa Massei in Massa Macinaia, a small town in the province of Lucca, has been home to Gil and me since 1982. This is a book about the making of its garden: a contemporary garden, inspired by and set within the faded structure of an old, half-abandoned one. And it's the story of my becoming a gardener, a pretty unlikely development for someone who was never taught to appreciate the earth and its gifts by a guiding mother or grandpa who gestured about demonstratively with a trowel. I was never given, as a child, a mysterious seed to sow, a promise in the hand. No one ever marked off for me a few square yards of ground, saying, "This is your very own plot to do with as you please."

I came to the garden the long way around, from out of America's suburbs, where gardening meant little more than mowing lawns and raking leaves. I came here after some years in the city, where gardeners choose, sensibly, not to live, and so I'd never even known any real gardeners until recently. I came to gardening by chance, whose largess can be just as big as nature's when it wants it to be. Gardening is a credo; it matters not *how* the soul comes to be saved, only that we plight our faith. The garden is a temple. This book, a personal account, tells of what I found within its sacred walls.

But if the garden is a metaphor for all that we touch with a fervid stretch of our imaginations, then this book will describe my life, or way of life, in a place that people like Shirley Kozlowski will inevitably call, in wistful tones, "paradise."

. . .

I lead Shirley and Jan along the usual route, down the meadow's mown central strip lined with knee-high wildflowers, a watercolorist's gestural spattering of pale pinks, faint purples, warm yellows. "I'm walking in the very footsteps of Venus," Shirley says.

We double back via the cherry walk, then enter the terrace with its geometric hedgework inspired by Villa Buonacorsi in Potenza. We visit the grotto with its pagan memories, the drooling stone masks— "It's enough to inspire new fears!" she says.

I invite them in to the "Risorgimento room," as someone once called our nineteenth-century–style *salone*. Vittorio Emanuele II, Italy's first king, looks thirstily out of his gilded frame as I offer the visitors a taste of the wine we make, our Sorbus '94, the best vintage of our white.

"I'd love to include you on our tour," Shirley says, aglow. "They'd be absolutely thrilled. May I?"

"I guess that would be . . . all right," I hesitantly say. Shirley and Jan are so ingratiating, I might have agreed to an annual event.

"It's a whole year away," Shirley reminds me soothingly. "Next May. But you needn't make any special preparations. The garden is lovely as is."

My mind is a list of purloined projects: build trellis for Cooper's Burmese, repair fallen retaining wall below loquats, tie back wisteria above *cantina* door, shop for a terra-cotta destination for the cherry walk . . .

One of my worst nightmares involves an imminent, crucial final exam for which uncontrollable circumstances foil my attempts at study. Will I pass or fail the garden lovers' scrutiny? My garden pleases me enormously, but how much will it please the seasoned garden tourist who's traveled seven thousand miles just to see it?

The phrase "a whole year away" echoes in my mind. Who knows what obstacles will prevent my making the special preparations I needn't bother with, yet have every intention of seeing to?

We accompany them back outside, where they take one last look at the dolphin niche, my little collection of aquatics among volunteer ferns in the singing waters of a siren's cave.

"See you a year from now," Shirley says, headed to their old, collectable Mercedes; it's back to the Lubéron and home—big smiles, she got what she came for.

How could someone like me, so famous for saying no, have said yes to this?

Italian gardens have been open to the public since the Renaissance by virtue of *Lex Hortorum*, a law that affirmed the people's right to the pleasures of fine gardens, no matter who owned them. The house we gardeners keep is the continuum, boundlessly inclusive; I believe this. But the Elizabeth F. Gamble Garden Center tour group in *my* garden?

I must be mad.

chapter one

TRANSPLANTED

WE'D COME TO THE WALLED CITY OF LUCCA ONLY once before buying this house. I might have gone anywhere that November, 1979— restless days for me. In fact, I was ready for an all-out move. The isolation of Point Reyes, California, its fragile sun taken in for the winter, weighed heavily on my spirits then. It was as if I were stranded on an island in time. If I didn't do something about it quick, in a million and a half years (what with migrating land masses) I'd be living in the Bering Sea somewhere off the coast of Kamchatka.

The group of Lucchesi (not "Luccans") in which Gil and I found ourselves increased in number with every step we took along the city's humid stone streets. We lived for pleasure: a feast at the famous restaurant Vipore one night, a Bacchic revel at Solferino (Ari's and Jackie's favorite) the next. We were caught up in a hedonistic race for more of the region's antique tastes, for the last amber bottle of its light-bodied, tingling wines. I never adjusted to the time zone, sleeping till midday when I'd hear the rumble of *saracinesche*, shopkeepers lowering their heavy metal doors. When finally I'd venture out of our host's attic apartment, Lucca was deserted as its citizens slept off their proper lunches. What I'd learn of this place was gathered of the lingering smells of finished meals, of closed church doors, the voices and footsteps of the unseen.

I came away with only a forming sense of the place. This visit had the resonance of a dream. Its remembered details: the gentle curve of sluice-like, foggy streets filled with strolling teenagers; the gilded, crumbling light of antique shop windows; the diffuse, pungent smells of pressure-brewed coffee, fresh-baked sweet anise bread, the tobacco factory's hovering emissions.

What urged me back a year later was all that I'd clearly missed. I was after the undiscovered daily life those parties had disallowed, Lucca's buried treasures. I wondered, Is this city as lovely as its withheld secrets seemed? I wondered, Is it time to make the move we'd often imagined and discussed, time to buy a place in Italy and begin the daring journey that would change us deeply and forever?

Our friend Emanuela had heard that there was a house for sale. It was in Massa Macinaia, she said, eight kilometers from the city walls. We could see it from her brother's balcony at Belvedere, above a narrow valley people call *La Conca*, the shell,

"That's a *house?*" I said. A bleated laugh. "The only thing as big as that in Point Reyes is the ranger station, and even the ranger station's not *that* big! That's a *mansion*."

"Whatever," Emanuela said (she'd learned her English in two Americanizing semesters at San Jose State).

"That's not *quite* what I had in mind," I said. "I was looking for a *house*. That thing could put up half the surviving nuns of all the Roman Catholic convents between here and Manila."

Which is not to say that I didn't find the house beautiful—who wouldn't have?

Its low, wide facade, all mottled and molting, was streaked by the shaggy vertical shadows of a pair of three-hundred-year-old cypress trees, tufted and top-heavy. I was charmed by the tiny multi-paned windows (in Point Reyes I lived with sliding glass doors). Its louvered shutters, a nineteenth-century improvement, were the bleached green of a cabbage patch gone dry in the August sun, and its heaped roof, mossy and sagging, was like the weighty, encrusted shell of an old tortoise.

On either side of the main house were two smaller stone structures. One was built, I'd later learn, to house a unit of peasants and their families, the other to accommodate a shepherd and his flock. The hill above the villa was a dense growth of pine, chestnut, and ash, underplanted by nature with holly and myrtle and cistus. On another hill, to the north of the main house, a thousand olive trees were arrayed on half a tiered wedding cake of yellowed grass, and at the foot of these terraces, along the neatly scythed banks of a stream, grew dark jungles of bamboo and Indian cane. There was a vineyard in the foreground, rectilinear in the sun, and there were fruit trees shading meadows all around: apples, peaches, pears, apricots, figs, pomegranates, loquats, persimmons. And as for all those other trees everywhere, what were they? Oak, I'd later learn, cedar, chestnut, camphor, tulip, arbutus, linden—all full and sheltering.

Just the other day, when I showed a visitor our grotto, the garden's cynosure, she asked, "Did you know this grotto was here when
you bought the place?" And I thought, What a funny question. There
it was, big as life all around us—the frightful terra-cotta masks, the
trickling water, the simulated stalagmites, the dark, rippling, bottom-
less pools—how could I not have known it was here? But the truth is,
I knew I wanted to live at Villa Massei the moment I first entered its
ornate iron gates. And just as my visitor seemed, strangely, to have
guessed, both Gil and I had made up our minds to buy this house even
before seeing the grotto, even before seeing the garden, such as it was.

At the top of the drive, a small grove of ancient olives, sentries
to the chaotic village beyond, raised their gnarled, unpruned branches
to the sun. Ugo, the farmer, met us near the barn. He said we couldn't
possibly see the inside of the house without advance notice, but he
could show us the garden, if we liked. "The *signora* is resting now,"
Emanuela said, translating Ugo's apology. "See, he knows exactly
what her schedule is, and he protects her. I mean, he's very good, this
man. You'll be lucky to have him."

"He goes with the place?"

"Well, not like that tree does," she said. "He works the land.
Look around you. This is a farm. What do you think, you're like,
doing all this yourself?" I looked around. She was right; that neatly
trimmed grass along the driveway couldn't possibly have been the
work of a herd of goats.

We walked the "*giardino*," Ugo as our guide.

"What a mess," Gil whispered. He has an eye for overgrowth.

Beyond a pair of brick columns, and at the edge of the sweeping
front lawn, green as anything you'd see in Ireland or Virginia, stood an
American sweet gum tree cheek to jowl with a thirty-foot-tall Italian

cypress, no more than four feet of space between their thickening trunks. There was a loquat in the shade of a cedar of Lebanon whose needleless lower limbs swept the compacted clay soil at its feet. There was a yucca the size of a dinosaur smothered in its own dried leaves. There were cypress trees choked to near death by creeper, euonymus shrubs entangled with woody philadelphus callously hacked off at the top and wildly branching. There was a "pan of gold," as they call it in California, entwined with a yellow banksia rose that seemed intent on making the whole garden its host, and beneath this aerial display *Iris foetidissima* waged war with the stronger choke vine, wild clematis, self-seeded Tartarian honeysuckle, and all manner of weeds that were lost on my uninformed, busy-elsewhere eye.

There were mature box hedges so overgrown that we'd later see them collapse in the lightest rainfall, opening up ugly views into their ancient gnarled armatures. There was an arbor of wisteria that hadn't been pruned in so long that its suckers were trees; the iron trellis that supported the vines when young was now out of the ground with the force of their upward pull. In the shade of all this arcing, aggressive vegetation, which dislodged roof tiles with its grasp, were rows of red roses reaching for the scarce light—for the longest time I thought they were intentionally long-stemmed and so prized their convenient, puny buds which didn't open until you brought them into the house and put them near a window facing south.

But I noticed little or none of this neglect during my first visit here; I saw, instead, only beauty. The twin cypresses at the top of the *viale*, the swooping pedestrian access, were the largest examples of their kind I'd ever seen. Just last week, walking the Viottolone in Boboli Gardens in Florence, a cypress avenue dating back to 1637, I didn't find a single tree with anything close to the girth of even the smaller of my two. Over the years landscape designers and agricultural students have made pilgrimages to my magnificent set of twins, calibrating the widths of their trunks and measuring their heights with sextant-like instruments you raise and gaze through as if to their crowns in the stars—the result is that these trees are now listed in a national registry of monumental garden plants.

By the *limonaia*, the lemon house, a modest appendage of the farmhouse to the north, stood an unpollarded plane tree, tall and stately as any of those on the walls of Lucca which were planted in the early 1800s to transform the city's ramparts into a welcoming public park. But the most intriguing tree of all at Villa Massei was, to my mind, the cinnamomum—not the tropical *Cinnamomum zeylanicum*, whose wood is harvested for the spice, but *Cinnamomum camphora*. Though they menace the streets of Cape Town and undermine the gardens of Palo Alto, they're appreciated for their rarity here in northern Italy. This Asian native had been given its unlikely happy home more than one hundred fifty years ago within the enclosed rear garden, its position protected from the winds and cold by twenty-foot-tall battlement-like retaining walls. While life beneath a camphor's fitful cascade of debris has proven to be anything but easy, the tree's great strength is endlessly comforting, and we love to snap fallen twigs under our guests' noses, releasing the acidic aroma familiar to all.

But these are just a few examples of the plant life this purchase of ours would include, for the garden I visited that day in 1981 was "mature."

Ugo stopped at the top of the *viale* and looked down towards the fruit orchards in the lower distance. He drew an arc with his arm, describing. I understood almost none of what he said.

"There's a little stream that passes through the land," Emanuela translated. "It's like, unbelievable. It flows all year round and so you'll always have water for the garden and the crops."

"*Un patrimonio,*" Ugo said.

And just what crops were they?

Grapes, olive oil, corn, we were told. Oh, and peaches. "I sell them in the *piazza,*" Ugo explained.

The cedar of Lebanon wooed like an owl in the afternoon *tramontana* wind. Our brief visit, for now, had ended. I turned toward the house and saw a white-haired woman sitting, as if over a puzzle or a map, in a glass-walled conservatory. She fled this glimpsed troop of unexpected visitors, quickly disappearing through a doorway. Wearing an article of clothing I called, in my mind, a "dressing gown," she seemed so dignified to me. I assumed that she was Italian, and that this property had been in her family for generations. It came as an odd disappointment to learn that she was from Manchester, England, and that she and her husband had lived in the house for just fourteen years.

WE DRESSED UP LIKE SERIOUS BUYERS TO MEET Midge Oliver, to view the house and those parts of the garden we hadn't yet seen.

"Italy was my husband's idea," she told us. I was at the threshold of his bedroom. It had been two months since he'd passed away (he had a heart attack while trimming a box hedge along the farm road), but his reading glasses were still on the nightstand beside a book with its dog-eared page marker in place. His bedroom, adjoining his wife's by way of a metal simulated-wood door, had its own bath, significantly more spartan than hers.

"It was a second marriage for both of us," she explained. "My husband said, 'We're alone in life, let's be adventurous and go and live abroad.' I thought it over and said, 'Oh, why not?' "

There was a young woman from New Zealand staying with Midge as a paid companion. She was a very good sales assistant, though that couldn't have been in her job description. "Isn't it lovely," she kept saying, as she anticipated Midge's wishes, preceding her through drab, well-used rooms to fluff up cushions, push back the faded curtains.

In the study, Midge showed us a packet of photos. There was a picture of the *viale* covered with snow. Snow? I'd thought I was moving to a great natural hothouse of temperate Mediterranean bliss, the most sought-after macroclimate on the planet. There were palm trees on the front lawn. There were camellias. There were yuccas and oleanders, plants that need mild winters. Maybe I'd misunderstood.

"You mean it *snows* here?" Gil asked.

"Oh, thick as that," Midge said, showing a depth of eight inches with her gaunt, blemished hands.

"And who are all these people walking up the road?" I asked. There were ten or twelve of them, mostly women, dressed in black. The dark umbrellas over their heads were dusted with snow between the ribs. They were making their way up the formal viale which leads from the village to the main entrance of the villa. Were they coming to extend condolences, in a customary way, upon Major Oliver's death?

"There's a procession here once a year," Midge said proudly. "A *bacia' crocifisso*, we call it." Her accent seemed even more English when she switched to Italian. "Ugo puts a fresh coat of paint on the little chapel in front, and I do the flowers. It's a great village tradition. You'll enjoy it, I'm sure." She sighed.

We sat out on the balcony in white metal garden chairs, the sharp wrought-iron scroll work digging into our backs. I pictured Midge and her husband having drinks here evenings, pitched safely forward in their seats, looking out upon the village rooftops towards that elusive range of mountains in the distance which appeared and disappeared with the changing, moody sky. I comforted myself with the understanding that these white metal garden chairs weren't real estate.

We talked business. She named her price, we a lower one. We agreed on a figure closer to hers than to ours, but it seemed to make each of us happy as we smiled, all our shuffled prospects falling into place.

A woman was crossing the yard. Her soft, swollen ankles were stuffed into a pair of black high-heeled shoes. Her dark hair was neatly styled, but in a much less stately way than was Midge Oliver's.

"*Buona sera,*" Midge said to the woman, who nodded shyly before climbing the stairs to Ugo's part. "That's Ottavia," Midge explained, "the farmer's wife. Every morning she goes off to work in the thread factory. I wish she'd have helped me in the house instead, but alas."

We went out to dinner. The owner of the restaurant greeted us warmly. Midge was a regular customer, but she'd obviously not been there in months. "And where is your husband this evening?" the owner asked, holding Midge's hand. She lowered her eyes. "He is dead," she said, in Italian words that seemed all too direct somehow: *è morto.*

She drank a lot of wine that night and grew soulful and plaintive. "We had eight good years here," she told us, "and oh, I suppose I was happy then." She hardly touched her *tortelli.* "We had a dear friend, a British musicologist who lived in Pieve Santo Stefano. He committed suicide, I'm so terribly sad to say. When he died, I was ready to leave. I would have left then and there, but my husband wanted to carry on, and so we stayed. It's been six years since our friend's death." Her smile was suddenly willful and poised. Her life had resolution now. "I'm happy to be going home," she said. No more compromise.

The woman from New Zealand listened to Midge's stories as if she were hearing them for the very first time. Her face showed concerned support. "Yes, yes," she said, always agreeing, or, "Nay, nay." Her accent was thick, her tones sharp.

"I think we came here too late in life," Midge said, as if to begin listing the mistakes she and her husband had made. "I was too old to learn a second language."

"I'm looking forward to learning Italian," I said. Enough sadness for one night. Enough for endings, what about beginnings?

"Oh, but you're young," Midge said dreamily. "Everything is so much easier when you're young. I'm sure you'll keep the garden far better than we ever did." She thought for a moment, then asked, "You *are* interested in gardens, aren't you?" It was as if she'd change her mind about selling us the place if we had any doubts.

"Ahm . . ." I said. "Well, I like *looking* at them."

It was cold by the time we left the restaurant. The car windshield was opaque with dew. I had to put on the heat driving back to Midge's villa, which looked completely different to me each time I saw it, in each change of light or temperature.

When I handled well the tricky turn at the top of the driveway, Midge said "*Bravo*" as if to congratulate me upon acquiring one of the many new skills I'd need in order to manage my Tuscan life.

Midge kissed us both good night. She had tears in her eyes; they glimmered in the yellow light of the wrought-iron lantern above the *cantina* door.

"I'm so pleased you're retaining him," she said, pointing to Ugo's narrow staircase, added on to the side of the main house in an expedient, defacing way. I could hear adults talking over each other, then the voice of a small child. They were no doubt sitting around the table I'd seen earlier that day. It was laid with a checkered tablecloth whose scalloped, fringed edges made it look more suburban than rural. There was a *fiasco* of wine swathed in white plastic lattice, not in woven straw as in those quaint paintings that describe a vanishing country life. The walls above the stove were glossy with a film of fat. There were ruffled stuffed birds, Ugo's hunting trophies, on the squat, ancient refrigerator. Midge said, "He's very loyal, you'll find. I wouldn't be selling you the house if you intended to let him go."

"We'll need his help," I said.

There was a moon over the villa with a fine lace of mist all around. Bats flew across it clumsily, in and out of their roosts in the great cypress trees that had made their way to the Casa Oliver wine label, becoming emblematic of their Italian hours.

Midge laughed as if to distract us from her tears, the embarrassment she felt at being unable to stop them. "I had a discussion with him about what he should call you," she said, pointing to Ugo's window where a cartwheel chandelier dimly glowed. She looked at me and said, "We decided that you should be called Signor Paolo." She turned to Gil. "And you shall be Signor Gilberto. There. How does that sound?"

Guess we'll have to buy a few suits, I thought.

IT WAS THE KIND OF MOVE YOU MAKE ONLY WHEN you're very young, before those restraining little wisdoms of age acquire you.

For all its shortcomings, Point Reyes was a beautiful place. Our work in real estate (fixing up houses and reselling) allowed us time for the activities we loved most: my writing, Gil's volunteer work. Our friends thought we were crazy rainbow chasers risking so much for experience.

Our Lucchese villa cost a fraction of what it would today, yet we had to sell everything we owned to buy it. For this we needed time. It would take six months, we figured.

I coped, barely, with the humiliating garage sales where you learn that the things you value most are worth nothing to anyone else ("Well, I'll take it off your hands if you're getting rid of it, but not at *that* price"). I weathered the daily shiftings of heart, the sad goodbyes to friends, to the Australian tree fern I'd planted by the creek which hadn't as yet formed the hairy trunk I'd longed to see, to the much loved cutting-edge–modern house built just for us, alas, in the wrong location.

But we got through it all, more or less unscathed. It was spring of 1982 and we were gone as planned.

The villa looked so unfamiliar. Perhaps it was because the shutters were closed, because it was standing in the shadow of a cloud that paused, along its inland course, above Monte Serra.

And the garden. When I stood in this very spot last summer the lawn was freshly mown, and there weren't all these weeds in the rectangular rose beds by the driveway. I fought off a surprising sense of disappointment as I crossed the muddy yard strewn with crumbling shards of terra-cotta. Last year the knee-high fields all around were spattered with the soft colors of a late summer flowering. Wine grapes blackened in the vineyard. Bursting figs proffered their crimson contents to flocks of songbirds. I gazed up now at this disintegrating farmhouse set in its wintery, abandoned garden, and thought of my Point Reyes house, with longing, as a loss.

Ugo, the farmer, appeared in his doorway at the top of his narrow, steep staircase. There was a green oilcloth umbrella hanging from the iron and glass shelter above his head. It was lunchtime and he was chewing. He smiled as he buttoned his hunting jacket, skipping down the steps to welcome his new *padroni*.

We shook Ugo's hand. It was hard with stratified calluses, covered

with small cuts at various stages of healing. Midge Oliver once referred
to him as "my dearest Ugo." Another time she said, "Honest as the day
is long." I remembered overcoming my first impressions: Ugo seemed,
at first, disinterested and hard; it was as if his soul had gripped too
tightly the tools with which he'd built beautiful lives for others.

Ugo lived in the villa's north wing with Ottavia and their two
children: Sandra, sixteen at the time, and Fabio, three. When I first
saw this house from the garden gate I thought they occupied one of
the villa's two ancillary cottages. I didn't understand until Ugo, showing us the upstairs of the main house, pointed across a wide, unfinished space where the grain had once been stored, and said, "Beyond
that door is my part." Emanuela had said, "Oh, but you want them,
these *contadini*; they're doing everything for you." I wasn't sure I wanted
to live with people who did everything for me. I was only thirty-five
and still enjoyed doing most things for myself.

We greeted Ugo. I barely understood his welcoming remarks; the
Italian words he said out loud seemed to have very little to do with
those I'd studied on paper.

"*La vedo deluso*," Ugo said, looking at me. "*C'è qualcosa che non va?*"

"He says you look disappointed," said Emanuela, who'd picked
us up at the airport and driven us to our new home.

I clapped my gloved hands, warming them. My shearling flight
jacket was too snug, but even without it I'm often conscious of my stiff
frame. "Oh no," I said, forcing a smile. "Just tired after a long flight."

Ugo insisted on carrying our bags to the door. We all followed.
Even through two-foot-thick walls I could hear the furnace in the cellar; it rumbled, then clicked and went silent. I could smell the vegetables Ugo's wife was frying in her kitchen, whose window looked out
onto the garden.

Ugo put down one bag. He opened the door and took the key out of the lock. Without the slightest hint of ceremony, he placed it in the outstretched palm of my hand. Old-fashioned and huge, this key made me think of the ones in childhood storybooks that are just as likely to unlock coffers of gold as admit the holder to a chamber of horrors.

In the icy cold entrance hall, purged of Midge Oliver's English furniture, I almost wished we'd bought the villa contents and all: the chintz-covered lounging sofa with remnant arm guards, the mahogany sideboard with its display of electroplate, the antiqued wrought-iron grapevine sconces: green leaves, red grapes. I did the best I could to take my mind off the obvious fact that this house would require years of hard work to make it livable—if I'd known anything about gardens then, I'd have been even more distressed. When I looked the kitchen over with Midge, I thought, Well, so what if it's ugly, we'll remodel. We had lots of experience with that. But these old stone structures are different from the California houses I'd worked on in the past, pasted together with wooden studs and Sheetrock. I'd soon learn that in a stone house the slightest alteration takes months, jackhammers raising dust that settles in your every pore, between your teeth, between the pages of your books, even if you've covered them with plastic, taped down.

Gil rushed to open shutters. A small measure of comfort came in with the light. "Finally," he said, his face lit by the late winter sun.

I stood beside him and looked out. For the past few months my every act had been governed by a memory of this view. Corrugated *capanna* rooftops: terrariums of moss. The arresting black punctuation of cypresses, the rows of vines in their red clay soil, the dagger-topped pines laid tight against the hillsides like artichoke leaves. Today, the distant Apuan Alps were covered with snow. The lamb-shaped clouds butting them were agile and playful. We'd risked everything for this, and now it was ours.

My courage had briefly waned, but it was back. I went to one of the radiators and in a fearless, proprietary way put my hands on it. It wasn't cold, but you could hardly say it was warm.

Ugo explained something I didn't quite get. Emanuela translated, "There's almost no *gasolio* in the tank. He says that by tomorrow it'll be like, finished." Her words got vaporized in the frigid room, whose marble chip floor was covered with tiny cupolas of dew.

"What do you mean?" Gil asked.

Emanuela laughed. "I mean the tank is empty," she said.

Ugo explained: "The Signora Oliver moved out of the house a month early so that she would not have to buy more oil than she herself would use. The Signora Oliver turned off the heat, then went to stay with a friend in Gattaiola until her business was done and she could leave."

In my broken Italian, I asked Ugo how much it would cost to fill the tank.

"One and one half million," he said.

"That's more than a thousand dollars," said Gil. It was a thousand dollars we hadn't planned on spending our very first day in Italy.

"Welcome to villa life," Emanuela said, as if to imply that the next surprise would be far worse than the last.

I changed the subject to a happier one. "Signora Oliver wrote to say that the wine is very good this year." Midge's husband had planted the vineyard and improved the *cantina*, where a domestic quantity of red wine was made. I had tasted it only once. We sat out on the front balcony with Midge the day we agreed to buy the property, and she poured us each a sample glass of it as we watched the sun go down behind the Apuans.

"Yes," said Ugo. "Eighty-one was a very good year." He smacked his lips together gently as if tasting it even now. He turned to Emanuela and explained something quickly. I didn't understand, but noted a shade of regret in his voice, in his gestures.

"But there is no wine left," Emanuela said, translating. "The *signora* sold it all before she went away."

"Sold it?" I said. "Sold it to who?"

"To him," Emanuela said, pointing to Ugo, who cast his gaze downward.

"But she said she'd leave it for us," I said.

"She didn't," Emanuela said, the corners of her mouth rising to a smile.

Gil opened more windows as we walked together through a series of empty rooms. As he unlatched shutters and leaned out, parting them, his curly red hair absorbed light and the white walls brightened. Electric cords twisted out of crumbly holes where sconces had hung. There were black tongues of soot over the outlets, and the wires leading away from them were mounted externally. The paintings Midge Oliver shipped off to England had left behind their faint shadows.

Leaning against the wall was a stack of doors. The one on top wore a sticker with a hand-written code number beneath the printed logo of a moving company. "What's all this?" Gil asked, looking at a doorjamb where the male parts of its hinges stuck straight up longingly.

"The Signora Oliver wanted to take these doors to England with her," Ugo explained. His face didn't reveal how he felt about this. "But the movers would not allow it. They told the *signora* that this is unheard of, and so she left them there for you."

"How kind of her," Gil said through a little laugh. With his arms spread wide he picked up one of the doors and went to the closest doorjamb. Ugo and I rushed to give him a hand, aligning the upper hinge as Gil saw to the bottom one. I doubted that it was the right door for this jamb. But miraculously it was. With a gentle push, the door swung silently. The latch bolt clicked precisely into place.

The three of us stepped back to admire our good work. It was the first job we'd done together, the first of many to come, and we looked at each other now and smiled, understanding that we shared a dream for this place, assured that working together in this way, we would make the dream come true.

chapter two

HACK JOB

I WENT OUT INTO THE GARDEN. OTTAVIA'S ELDERLY cat, Stellina, walked the wall, ducking under the bare branches of a fig. Ugo's dog, Lea, a short, big-breasted she-wolf, was sleeping on a dry, dusty spot within the drip line of a young cypress tree. My eager imagination quickly recast this dismal yard into a spiffy Blenheim, Lea into a decorative King Charles spaniel.

The lawn was littered with the liquidambar's spiny fruit balls. Gil guessed this tree was a cork at first, with its thick, furrowed bark, the corky wings on its twigs, its comfortable home here in a wine-growing region—I had no guesses. But the cork, *Quercus suber*, with its ovate-oblong leaves and smooth acorns, bears very little resemblance to this curious tree, *Liquidambar styraciflua*, the American sweet gum.

The gum tree's bare branches embraced the Italian cypress that was stepping on its toes like an inept dancing partner—it was planted, by the Olivers, no more than four feet away from its companion. Ugo had voiced his sage, folkloric objections when the major dug in his spade, the potted cypress sapling by his side. The response was, "What do I care, Ugo, if they get in each other's way; I'll be dead by then." *Après moi le déluge!*

There was a rose tied against one of the brick, pinecone–topped columns which lent the garden's entrance a certain ghostly formality. Gil studied it now, gently pulling at its overgrowth with a single finger laid deftly between two viscously hooked thorns. "I wonder if there are any clippers around here," he said. He's never met a rose he didn't care to prune.

I remembered that there was a kind of garden room in the *cantina*, the half-underground basement where the wine was made and stored. *Seminterrato* is the term for this hillside building style; in front, doors and windows give to light and air; in back, the ground provides warmth in winter, coolness in summer.

I entered the cantina by a narrow wooden door under Midge's former bedroom. The door was chalky green. Its most recent layers of color were chipped away at the juncture of vertical boards, revealing dozens of other, different greens, older still. An enormous iron key leaned out of its keyhole, which was scraped wide with centuries of grinding use. When I righted the key and turned it, the well-oiled lock bolt sprang out of its hold with a deliberate clunk, and I was in the garden room.

In the half dark, I tripped over an ancient lawn sweeper. It was wide as two mowers. Its thinning wiry bristles were clogged with camphor leaves, russet brown after a year in the cellar. Its irremovable, wedge-shaped bag was in tatters, its duct-tape mendings unstuck. I remembered having seen this disreputable machine when I toured the house for the very first time. It had stood among the spring rakes, hoes, and other assorted garden implements the Olivers had stored in the grotto, the most breathtakingly beautiful garden shed in all of Italy. But I hadn't thought of this sweeper's role here until now. The machine was a wreck for a reason; a camphor tree loses all its older leaves each spring before a hail of unctuous flower pods falls, thick as advancing desert sands. Even pushing this sweeper three times daily you can't keep up with the tide of debris, for the inevitable, sudden breeze brings down more than you've just removed. Had the camphor been planted along some far-off farm road it wouldn't matter, but it's in the heart of the rear courtyard, where daily life ensues. I was once told, by a lady gardener, that only men (obsessive groundskeepers that we are) are bothered by such detritus, but it couldn't have been over a camphor-seasoned lunch under the tree's shedding limbs. When I first gave parties beneath this evergreen canopy my Italian guests would sip their camphor-mulled wine and say, with a shrug, *"Quello che non ammazza, ingrassa!"* That which doesn't kill you makes you fat. But I've since read that the once commonly marketed oil of the *Cinnamomum camphora* is now believed to be carcinogenic.

In a smaller space within the garden room a few hand tools were stored. Apparently Midge Oliver hadn't intended to make a garden in her new life on Thistle Grove in London's Chelsea, for if she had, then these quaint implements would have followed her there. Perhaps she'd thought them too old to have any value, and I myself reasoned as much until, years later, I'd come across those ads in *Gardens Illustrated* magazine: "Antique garden tools from Rachel Brand. By appointment only."

The oddest tool caught my eye. It looked like a medieval instrument of torture. It had a two-foot-long wooden handle, turned, and scored with a pair of ornamental rings. Its metal business end took the shape of a short, two-tined fork, below which the stem widened to form a kind of shallow spoon. For tasting *perugina* (liquid manure)? Skewer a meadow muffin and sip the runoff? Manure tasting was once a highly respected profession in these parts, the only reliable way to establish quality and price.

There was a hand cultivator with a dual function, a mini-hoe up, a fork down (or vice versa). There was a chestnut-handled pruning saw with a narrow, rusted, toothy blade; an ancient scythe sharpened thin; various hole punchers, perhaps for lawn aeration; a long-handled edge trimmer, one of whose handles was bent; and a pair of short ladies' Wellingtons with a wide slice through the right instep. There was a colorfully boxed Carborindum Brand scythe sharpening stone made by Czechoslovak Ceramics, section abrasives, of Benatky, and a single pair of clippers, or secateurs, made of black steel and fastened closed with a crudely fashioned leather strap.

I handled the clippers and tried them in the air. They were silvery at the cutting edge with sharpening. They seemed to work.

When I got outside, Ugo was standing under the smaller of our two giant cypresses. He was looking up at its height as if it had just sprouted there in a single surge. He spread his arms wide and smiled. "Have you seen this?" he said, still selling the property even though it was already mine. "Look how big. Can you imagine how old it is?"

"How old?" I asked.

"Oh, I don't know," he said. "Old as the house, surely. Old as the house."

Under this tree, in a nest of banksia, stood another, far smaller tree, no more than two feet away from the cypress's huge trunk.

"Did Major Oliver plant *that* too?" I asked about the cypress's odd bedfellow whose appeal, if any, was lost on me.

"Oh, no." He laughed. "This tree is as old as the one over its head. It's a *giuggiolo*."

Its branches were spiny and weeping, its gray trunk ridged and knotted. It was a *Ziziphus jujuba*, the Chinese jujube. There are two cultivated varieties of this slow-growing, drought-loving tree; mine, with its inch-long date-like fruits that ripen in autumn, is called Lang.

"They're a funny old couple," Ugo said. "The cypress and the giuggiolo. More funny than Ottavia and me." He laughed. He'd been tying vines; there was a bunch of water-softened willow shoots attached to his belt in a kind of quiver.

Gil appeared.

"It's a giuggiolo," I said, pointing to the tree. Ugo nodded. I guessed I'd said it right.

Ugo pressed three fingers to his lips as if they held a tidbit. "You should taste how sweet and good the giuggiolo fruit is," he said. He made a sucking sound. "*Sì sì, buono buono!*"

"Do you know how many roses we have?" Gil asked. "I've gone around and counted."

"How many?" I asked.

"A hundred and eleven."

"It is true," Ugo confirmed. "There are many, many roses in this garden. There was an old lady who lived here in the time of Professor Sorbi, back in the forties. She loved to plant. She planted and planted, never stopped. Roses were her passion."

I handed Gil the ancient pair of clippers I'd found. He accepted them like a passed torch whose oil he feared upsetting. He tried their weight and balance. He unhooked the twisted leather strap and tested the clippers' spring. Roses were his passion too; he was about to make a hundred and eleven new friends. "I guess I've got my work cut out for me," he said.

WE SPENT THE NEXT DAY SHOPPING FOR HOUSE-hold essentials: lightbulbs, pots and pans, detergents. I was surprised to learn that mops did not exist. The only broom I managed to find was made entirely of plastic and promised to take all the charm out of the Old World task of sweeping.

Every time we got back to the villa, Ugo's dog barked at us as if we were trespassers. There were white hairs on her snout, and she had trouble moving. "Ooooh," said Gil, his hand out to her. It's the way he greets all unfriendly dogs. "Ooooh," he repeated consolingly. "I'm sorry you're only a dog and don't understand I'm harmless."

"I'm sorry you're only a dog and don't understand we live here," I said.

Ugo informed us that a load of heating oil had been delivered while we were out. Even though the temperature inside the house had not risen noticeably, the heat was on.

As I unpacked our groceries in the kitchen, Gil went off to get the old space heater that Midge Oliver had left behind in a dusty corner of the granary. I hoped it still worked. It was the first time I'd ever slept in a room with a fire burning; I was allergic to the smoke, apparently, and then, when the fire was out, to ashes.

Ugo brought us his garden table to use until our furniture arrived from California. It was round, and there was a receptacle for an umbrella cut through at the center. He brought us a bottle of the wine he'd made and bought from Midge. He gave us some olive oil and vinegar. He said he could sell us, at cost to him, a *damigiana* of wine. He showed us, with his hands, just how big a container that was. It seemed like more than enough.

Running, Ugo disappeared again to fetch a bottle of gas for the heater. When doing errands for his *padroni*, he moved with dispatch. Keeping his feet close to the ground, he wasn't running, just walking fast. Since it was midday and he had left the fields, he was wearing, over a pair of thin socks that were stiff and discolored at the toes, blue plastic sandals with the image of a seagull on the vamps.

Ugo showed me how to install the tank of gas, and how to light the stove. It was burning in the kitchen now, giving off a suspiciously acrid smell, but at least I could remove my coat as I prepared a lunch of prosciutto, pecorino cheese, and salad. The young greens I'd bought were tender and varied, still white and juicy at the cuts. The Sicilian early season tomatoes tasted better than the excellent ones my mother grew the only year she tried to keep a garden—how heroic she'd seemed to me then, doing all the work herself; my father wasn't one for gardening. But that first taste of our own olive oil! Now, that was a special moment. Though dense as drawn butter, it's so light you can wash it off your fingertips with a gentle rinse under the tap. And its flavors of green olive complement, never dominate its supporting ingredients: in this case Ugo's own red wine vinegar, sea salt, and fresh ground pepper. It was the first time I'd ever had a salad whose condiments had been produced just a few steps away from where I now sat eating it.

I OPENED MY WINDOWS THIS SATURDAY MORNING to spring and church bells. The Blake learned in childhood we never forget: "The Sun does arise,/ And make happy the skies;/ The merry bells ring/ To welcome the Spring;/ The skylark and thrush,/ The birds of the bush,/ Sing louder around/ To the bells' cheerful sound . . ."

I swept up the fireplace ashes and brought them out to the pile of garden waste Gil aggrandizingly called the "compost heap." This rising mound of grass clippings and rose prunings stood next to the garden shed, an open-fronted squatter's lean-to, half hidden behind a viburnum bush and a starving gold dust plant—otherwise known as speckled something-or-other. I dumped the pail of ashes on the heap's steaming peak. Out with winter, in with spring! Turning quickly, I found that my right foot was tangled up in an imbroglio of snaking wisteria. I sent my hand down, to loosen its vice-like grip, straight into a bed of stinging nettle. Ouch! The burning. I don't know what possessed me to do it, but I picked up my ash pail, turned it upside down, and put it over my head. "Ooooh," I moaned, sitting there in the stinking gladwyn (*Iris foetidissima*)—it doesn't stink until you crush it like I'd just done with my whole fallen body. And then I sneezed.

"What do you think you're doing?" Gil said. "Gesundheit!"

"Thank God there's an opinion coming by," I said, my voice echoing. "This garden! Sometimes I feel like calling in the bulldozers."

"Take that thing off your head," he said. "All I got was rurrr-rurrr-rurrr-rurrr."

Off came my Byronic helmet. "The garden," I said. "Help!"

The "opinion" was Albertina Castoldi. A professional (sort of).

"*Io so tutto!*" Albertina assured me when I invited her to lunch. "I know everything, and I have the books to prove it!"

"Good thing," I said. "I know nothing."

For the first time ever we ate outside. There was a cuckoo hiding in the pines; it called in answer to the church bells when they chimed the hour and half hour (I'd never realized that it was this responding habit of cuckoos that inspired the cuckoo clock). We sat at a white metal table on a cement terrace by the kitchen door where the Olivers must have taken their warm-weather meals al fresco. At the terrace's four corners stood terra-cotta pots of calla lilies just now coming into sweet, candid bloom. Up until a month ago they'd been wintering in the grotto—Ugo and Ottavia, using a complicated rig of poles and ropes to move them out, placed them exactly where Midge Oliver had always kept them. These callas, with their thick green stalks bending gracefully out of outsized pots, were almost enough to make you believe that the old *padrona* possessed a genuine, if seldom exercised, spirit of extravagance.

But even with these gorgeous callas, my luncheon scene was a graceless tableau—I might just as well have staged it in that hovel of a tool shed. Something about the peeling modern white paint that covered the villa's rear facade, slapped up there by old Mac Oliver himself. And the confinement of this tiny cement patio; it was as if the broad garden space all around belonged to the condominium and not to us.

"So what about this?" Gil asked, gesturing widely towards a motley array of herbaceous perennials that were making their seasonal appearance in a disorder of cement-bordered flower beds.

"Well, I don't know about these plantings here," Albertina said, "we'll have to wait and see. But as for all this cement, just get rid of it."

"*All* the cement?" I said. There was *so* much. Lionel Fielden, the Englishman who'd owned the house before the Olivers, had fashioned everything imaginable out of cement. He skimmed the antique stone retaining walls with the stuff; he covered over quarried stone paths with cement; he built these rectangular flower beds with it, raised cement planters and perpendicular walkways with a rolled-in texture of little Xs everywhere—for traction in the bunker?

"Getting rid of the cement means jackhammers," Gil said. He had no idea then just how many jackhammers we'd set abuzz in completing the complex restoration schemes our future held in store, eight long years of constant work. But we weren't ready for any of that just yet—still kidding ourselves. "No jackhammers," Gil said, a pleading gesture with his hands.

"Pity," Albertina said, grimacing, puzzled. She put out her cigarette and, sighing, gazed off to newly narrowed parameters.

I had met Albertina Castoldi at a party (our house came with a series of dinner invitations from the sort of Anglophone expatriates who've lived here since Shelley fell in love with Bagni di Lucca). Albertina's perfect British English makes her an ideal guest for these bilingual affairs (point of interest: it's more often the natives who refuse to speak Italian in this milieu, jumping at the chance to give their nanny-learned English a run). Albertina was entertaining a group of British and American ladies with her tales of exotic travels to the Chelsea Flower Show—one knows that Albertina is a gardener before knowing anything else about her. She's jolly and down to earth by nature and by choice, yet she's the daughter of the late Princess Santa Borghese Ercolani of Rome. She never alludes to her noble origins (though they couldn't be more evident); she's modern. When I asked her how she was related to Princess Marcella Borghese, the cosmetics magnate of "Montecatini Mud," she answered, "Marcella? Does she really call herself a princess? She's the wife of a cousin of mine who's not at all the prince. Isn't that funny? But you know, the nobility in Italy was abolished by referendum after the war. If you want to call yourself a princess at this point, you can; there's no law against it. Princess Marcella! Imagine! Well, good for her!"

Albertina lived (she's since moved) in one of the great estates of Lucca, Villa Parensi, designed by Bartolomeo Ammannati. Its Renaissance walled garden was a plant collector's showcase. The assembled curios were not arranged or grouped in any curated way; they were simply there for Albertina's pleasure and for that of other educated eyes—a frangipani tree? In Lucca?

A dry breeze whispered in the camphor, and it rained its russet leaves. We ate my penne all' arrabbiata, my frittata di zucchini, my pomodoro gratinato al forno—Albertina praised my "*cucina Californiana.*"

The midday sun was almost too much. "Shall we go in?" Gil asked.

"No, no," Albertina said. "I'm here to work. Let's start with a garden overhaul."

"Now?"

"Well, why not now?" she said, up on her feet. "*Forza!* Where's Ugo? We need a hand. We need a chain saw! Too many plants and bushes and trees all on top of each other everywhere."

"You noticed," I said.

We made our way through the cement-edged flower beds (with their cement-hard compacted soil) to a wooden door in the wall that leads to Ugo's garden.

"Ugo," I called, opening it.

"O," Ugo shouted. What lungs!

We entered his dream-like Ektachrome wonderland of spring bloom, our own black-and-white, sharply focused so-called garden happily left behind.

"Why the hell don't you just move over here," Albertina said in English, looking sadly back towards whence she came.

Pale sea-blue solanum climbed the stone lemon-house walls like a rising ocean wave in tropical light. There were floods of blue scillas, pink hyacinths, sun-yellow daffodils. There was a sprawling white banksia rose—it was as if a down pillow had hit the fan.

Below one of the *lemonaia* windows was Ugo's iris collection. Albertina rushed to the brilliant, flowering, spiky beds of it. "Isn't that 'Dusky Dancer'?" She cupped a near-black bloom in her hands.

"*Ma*," Ugo shrugged.

"Oh, I adore Dusky Dancer," she said. "Hate the name, of course. Love the flower. Such ridiculous names these breeders contrive! There's one called Whoop'em Up? Can you imagine? Would you ever knowingly plant Whoop'em Up? Best to stick with the species, isn't it? That way you don't have to answer, breathlessly, 'Out Yonder,' when people say, 'What's that iris there?' "

She moved along the border as if over a showcase in a pastry shop. "Oh," she said, "and *Iris pallida* 'Variegata.' This one's marvelous; even when the flowers are gone you have these charming two-toned leaves. Don't you love these leaves, Ugo?"

"*Sì sì*," Ugo said, "*belle*."

"Of course you do," she said. "I'm sure you're sensibly impartial—not like me, the grouch! For instance, that acid-yellow bearded one there"—she pointed—"you can have that *monster*." She switched to English. "What do you suppose it's called? Pee Hole in a Snow Bank?"

Ugo and Ottavia had just had lunch in this lap of Arcadian dreams, surrounded by their heaps of flowers. Their wooden country table, covered with a white gossamer cloth, was clear now but for a jelly jar of campanulas. Against the wall was a thick profusion of plants interrupted by the odd visual joke: a hoop-handled basket fashioned of variegated ivy covering an armature of bent twigs; a dried gourd goose nesting on a wooden egg in a bed of moss.

"They so embellish," Albertina said in English, "that it's sometimes quite a bore."

"Look at this poppy," Ugo said, leading us to the corner of the lemon house. It was a five-foot-tall *Papaver somniferum*, and it held a single white pleated bloom. It looked absolutely Burmese, a beauty cruel as death; I thought of its benightmared victims and wondered, How can it be?

"These are very rare in Italy," Albertina said.

"It came by itself," Ugo said. "I've never had this plant before. Who knows how it got here." He looked up at the sky. "It just appeared!"

"That's the beauty of these cottage gardens," Albertina said to Gil and me. "God blesses them."

"But God hasn't blessed this," she said, shaking her head in disgust. The four of us were out front, in our miserable domain of post-winter shock. "You know what this is?" she said. "This garden of yours?"

"No, what?"

"It's an old auntie garden."

I chuckled. "*Cioè?*"

"Auntie came to Sunday lunch with a sapling in a bag, and while she was waiting for the pasta to be cooked she planted it. See that mulberry there?"

"Yes?"

"Auntie."

Gil laughed.

"That loquat?"

"Auntie?" I said.

"*Ecco,*" Albertina said.

Ugo showed up with his chain saw. Albertina pointed to the loquat. "Ugo," she said, "who planted that tree there?"

"That tree there?" Ugo thought and thought. "I think it was that old aunt of Professor Sorbi, the doctor who once lived here."

It wasn't a particularly good loquat, as its roots were no doubt tangled up with those of the sweet gum, whose roots in turn were tightly interlaced with those of the cypress at its side. I'd first seen the loquat, *Eriobotrya japonica*, in California. It was one of those subtropical plants that happily reminded me that I wasn't in New England anymore, that I was in temperate San Francisco instead. But only once or twice had I ever tasted the loquat's acidic, tangy fruit, yellow-orange, firm and sweet. You end up eating several at a sitting; you don't stop until your plate's covered with a mountain of shiny black pits.

"*O Ugo, caro mio*," Albertina said. When she spoke to Ugo it was in his own vernacular—though she fell just short of the blasphemous *Dio cane* (dog God), she offered up lots of *porca miseria*. "*O Ugo*," she said, "*Quel nespolo lì . . .*"

"*Sì?*"

"*Aria!*"

Ugo looked at me for approval. I thought about the word *aria*, air. I guessed Albertina meant that she wanted to see air instead of a loquat tree. I felt perfidious, but I nodded, *sì*: death! I put my trust in Albertina; "I know everything," she'd promised.

Ugo drew forth the brand Excalibur—you deserve it, you mess of a garden you!—and with a flip of the starter cord we were in a cloud of diesel fumes. The chain saw's shrill cry shivered to the invisible stars. The smell took me back. I was on a motorboat on Lake Winnepesaukee, glassy and cold. When I returned to Italy and my unlikely current life in Massa Macinaia, the tree in question was felled: there it lay—no sympathy from any of us—on a bright strait of barren land like an old downed warrior. The stone wall beyond was awash with sunlight for the first time since Auntie's loquat spread its hairy-leaved limbs.

"Gosh, that looks better," Gil said. "I have to admit."

"Doesn't it," I said. After several years in foggy Marin County, California, an extra ray of sunlight was worth any number of loquat trees to me.

Albertina said, "What do you think, Ugo? Do you miss it?"

"*Ma*," Ugo said. "*Non mi ha mai detto niente.*"

I liked this way of putting it: It never spoke to me.

Albertina was gazing up at the cypress-liquidambar entanglement. "I don't suppose you'd let me take *that* out?" she said.

"What?" one of us said.

"That liquidambar is such a lovely thing. You don't see them everywhere, you know. But what a pity it has that *cypress* in it."

"*No!*" Gil said. The outrage! "I mean, I moved here for the cypresses! That would be like moving to Los Angeles and cutting down the palm trees."

Albertina produced a white handkerchief and waved it like the lone survivor of an ambush. "Never mind," she said, "OK, OK."

We walked on, Albertina's secateurs cutting only air in unconscious frustration. Wrens rustled in last autumn's fallen zizyphus pips, and the budding tree over their heads was the gallery of a spring recitative.

A distant stand of eucalyptus drew Albertina's eye. The two parent trees were thirty feet tall. When I'd pass beneath them and churn up their shed debris I'd think of Mill Valley, California, with its deep, ragged eucalyptus groves. Their leaves have a very peculiar smell: cat pee.

Along the front parapet were several self-seeded eucalyptus saplings, most about eight or ten feet tall.

"Surely you don't want *these*," Albertina said. "What nerve our botanist forefathers had, scattering the southern hemisphere's rubbish about the civilized world as they did!"

"I've never particularly liked eucalyptus," Gil said agreeably.

"Well," Albertina said, going a bit more British than usual as the horticulture critic in her rose with a distinct point of view, "the leaves of the young plants are already ugly *enough*. You see how they're round? But those leaves up there, those of the older plant? Those long, nasty tongue-like things! Did you ever see *The Exorcist*? I say *aria!*"

"To all of it?"

"You object?"

"Well," Gil said, "it's just that . . . What'll we have left?"

"Look at the bright side of the penny," Albertina said. "You won't have *those* left. Besides, it could be lucrative. Don't you know a local florist to sell the prunings to? One could do the most inventive arrangements with those foul-smelling little branches: a few gladioli, one spectacular strelitzia all blue in the face, and lots and lots of prickly ruscus everywhere. Divine for a golden anniversary!"

By the time she'd finished reasoning, in her way, Ugo had whipped his magic sword through the entire stand of eucalyptus, little ones and big ones alike. For a moment I thought that he was acting independently, out of the same eucalyptus dread that motivated Albertina, but then I realized that the only word of ours he'd understood was *aria*.

By mid-afternoon the front garden looked like a slashed rain forest waiting for the match. Two loquats were down, and the big old misplaced mulberry had been brought to its knobby knees. Great hunks of the mimosa Albertina talked us into removing (it was in the wrong place, and besides, there were plenty of others elsewhere) lay in log-length chunks, in a dusting of sawdust, like the fallen columns of Olympus.

Albertina stood at the far end of the garden and gazed back at the newly revealed site—that's what it was at this point, a site, stumpy and scuffed. She stood there in her Burberry knockoff hunting jacket and smiled with satisfaction. She wasn't born to sit on her duff, that Albertina.

"You're a hurricane," Gil said.

"Real gardens are made according to plans," Albertina said. "Plans are drawn on a clean sheet of paper. Courage is what you need, my friends. Sacrifice. Vision! Otherwise, you'll never have a garden at all; you'll just have plants." She was busily gathering a bunch of eucalyptus branches, bending one off here, clipping another one there.

I looked off at the devastation, squinting to reduce the scarred panorama to clear volumes within which some unimaginable garden would one day present itself, fully formed.

"That's it," Albertina said, "look hard, think hard." She arranged the eucalyptus bouquet in her hand as if it were a vase. "There's no end to what you could do here with conviction and a bit of daring."

"What are you doing with those foul-smelling eucalyptus twigs?" Gil asked.

"My entry hall," Albertina said. "You don't mind, do you?"

"What's this smoke?" Ugo said.

I'd thought I'd smelled smoke.

We spun our heads. A Vesuvian cloud rose up from the terrace in a single white champignon, and a great tongue of flame leaped through it with a clap.

Ugo dashed up the steps, and the rest of us, panicked, followed.

The compost heap was a bonfire. The wretched tool shed by its side was already engulfed. Ugo rushed off to get a hose, but by the time he got back even the shed's asbestos roof was aflame. The gold dust plant was no more.

Gil looked at me. "Those fireplace ashes," he said. "Were they live?"

"I guess they *were*," I said. It had never occurred to me to check—they'd been there for days.

Once the flames were doused and calm had returned to the afternoon, we stood in the ruins like a halted pack of stampeding elephants. But it was as if we'd discovered a whole new garden at this point; I'd always disliked the tool shed and whatever that sprawling bush was by its side—a spirea? Light filled the cleared scene of our rampage as the smoke died down and the last few pieces of the shed's roof beams fell to the ground like half-burned logs in a fireplace.

"What a beautiful wall back there," Ugo said. "I haven't seen it in years." He cleaned away the soot with his hose, and the huge ochre stones gleamed. It was definitely the best wall we had.

"Talk about *aria*," Albertina said, lighting a cigarette.

"Doesn't that look better?" Gil said. "You know, Paul, I think you did the right thing burning all this stuff down. Aren't you clever."

"*Sì sì,*" Ugo said, "*bravo, Paolo.*"

"Now then," Albertina said. "Let's all go and have a cup of tea in Ugo's lovely garden."

UGO'S BROTHER, LUCIANO, WAS ON THE ROOF. UGO
was squatting down at the fireplace in the bedroom. They were holding the ends of a length of rope. Tied to it, somewhere in the flue, was a beautiful bundle of acacia twigs whose cut tips were to scrape away thick deposits of soot. When Luciano pulled the rope from above, soot rained down on Ugo's hands, his face, his sweater, his knees. When Ugo tugged the rope, it was worse: hornets' nests and a long-dead bat.

Spring was here, but the nights were still chilly. Even with my Italian electric blanket (with an on-off switch, no temperature control) I'm cold in bed. I'm especially cold in the morning when my own crowing roosters and an oratorio of birds wake me.

Maybe I'd give the bedroom fireplace another try. Maybe Emanuela knew what she was talking about when she said that all it needed was a good sweeping out.

"Yes, yes," Ugo said, down on his haunches now, doing the nasty, unthinkable job so good-naturedly. It was as if his *padroni* asked too little of him. "What business!" he said. "Chimneys have to be swept. Look at all this stuff!"

Luciano came by most Sundays to give Ugo a hand with the jobs he couldn't do alone. He was shorter than Ugo and not as good-looking: a beak-like nose and bulging eyes. Though he tended to bow when speaking to Gil and me, he was slightly more casual with us than Ugo allowed himself to be—familiarity concealing his greater unease with the young foreigners and their odd ways.

"Do we have to pay him?" Gil asked. We were standing under the wisteria, which was just going into its first burst of lavender bloom. Luciano, on the roof, knelt at the chimney-churning rope.

"Midge said Ugo takes care of him," I said.

"How?"

"Who knows? A bottle of olive oil? Lunch?"

"Is he doing these favors for Ugo or for us?"

"Both."

"Then maybe we should give him something. Sweeping chimneys is no fun."

"A bottle of Jack Daniel's?" I suggested, knowing that Italians love a glass of bourbon after dinner.

For years Luciano had worked full-time on this farm. But shortly before the Olivers arrived he found a better-paying job. He works for the post office in Viareggio, the city in which he now lives with his wife, for whose hypochondria Ugo and Ottavia have no patience. Luciano loads packages onto vans, and has frequent nervous breakdowns—Ugo gave us this information as though we were entitled to it. Earlier today, when I asked Luciano, "*Come sta?*" he said, "I lack the ground under my feet." I repeated that line to myself a dozen times—*mi manca la terra sotto i piedi.* It was the syntax that surprised me, not the condition.

While Ugo and Luciano were cleaning the chimney, I sat in the living room on the Brunati sofa we'd just bought, our modern-day take on classic villa style. It was designed in the sixties and already had, to the better-informed eye, a doleful, dated look—it wouldn't be long before it thoroughly embarrassed us both. Perhaps this was why Emanuela, who accompanied us to the furniture store, had seemed to want to rescue us as money changed hands.

Just outside the living room window, smack in the middle of our newly stripped garden, was the only reasonable parking space around. Once it had been an *aia*, a wide cement pad where corn was sun-dried. It was just as full of strange cars this Sunday as it had been last weekend. Cars came and went. Doors slammed. Raised voices carried. I was quietly upset with myself for finding all this activity irritating, and so I searched for calming arguments to see me through the day: Well, it's only on weekends. Well, they have to have a life, don't they?

This morning Ottavia's brother from Pisa was here. His chubby eleven-year-old son had a knowing look in his eyes, which seemed to regard things only in a sidelong way. Ugo's sister was visiting with her husband and two children, a boy and a girl, close together in age. I went to the window and peered out as Ottavia's sister drove up with her husband. She left her car door gaping wide. She was carrying what appeared to be a cake, wrapped in white paper and tied with golden ribbon. She had an upwardly mobile carriage. There was a color scheme to her good Sunday clothes. She was a cut above and conscious of it. Her husband is a *geometra* (a kind of architect), and everyone knows they make lots of money.

Ottavia had an elaborate Sunday dinner going. I knew she was a fabulous cook, as she'd often give me subtle recipes requiring technical finesse. I recognized just now the meaty smell of *fagioli* simmering with sage leaves and garlic. I imagined them dressed with our own delicious olive oil and fresh-ground pepper. Salivating, I thought about the fact that I hadn't remembered to buy groceries for the weekend—on Sundays everything is closed. Perhaps it was the thought of my empty camp cooler of a refrigerator, my domestic ineptitude compared to Ottavia's, that made me impatient with all this neighboring confusion.

Gil came into the room to find me looking out through the rippled, flawed glass. "What's happening?" he asked.

"They're having a party."

"Is it a party or is it just people?"

"What's the difference?"

Another car pulled up. Our little Peugeot was blocked in; if we'd decided all of a sudden to go out, four drivers would have had to descend to move four cars.

Our study shared a wall with Ugo's bathroom. It was mumbling in Italian now—this family never runs out of news to tell, arguments to raise; even the bathroom sink can be the forum for a heated gathering. Today Ugo's toilet got flushed after every use. Baby cousins engaged each other with trilling shouts. Upstairs, in Ugo's daughter's room, there was a tapping of footsteps, but fortunately no music. Luciano was on the roof. Ugo was in the bedroom fireplace.

"It's not easy getting used to all this," I said. We'd been here almost two months, and I wasn't used to it yet.

In Point Reyes, our closest neighbors had been half a mile away. Only members of Virginia Veech's family had any reason to drive by our house. Rare were the mornings I'd wake to find Virginia grazing her horse in our adjacent field. Rarely did she pass, herding her quiet-footed goats with a manzanita goad. Nights, no lights burned anywhere in sight, though our view stretched clear to Elephant Mountain ten miles away; all was silence and stillness, a domain of rural tranquility I still remembered vividly—it *was* only yesterday.

"Boy, their family's big," Gil said. He picked up a magazine and turned pages.

I had an idea.

"We could get them to park around back," I said. There was a farm road that led to the *limonaia* which faced Ugo's garden. It would not be at all inconvenient for Ugo and his visitors to park in the lemon house yard and enter Ugo's part from above. I wondered, Why hadn't the Olivers ever thought of making that sensible change, introducing a single, straightforward new rule?

A car started up. A horn blew! It was like a wedding. Brakes squeaked. All of this right under our living room window.

"I can't stand it either," Gil said. "It's much more their place than ours."

"Let's have them park in back," I said insistently. "A garden shouldn't have cars in it."

"I think it gives them a sense of 'living in the villa.' "

"Huh?"

"I think they like that idea. They're all coming to visit Ugo who 'lives in the villa.' Asking them to park in back is like moving them down a class."

"Maybe you're right."

On Saturday nights, cars continued to come and go well after midnight. Even at one in the morning Ugo's guests broadcast their greetings and grateful farewells to the open distance for all the valley to hear.

"It's really something," Gil said as yet another car pulled up, this one with muffler trouble.

Ugo was in our entry hall. "Finished," he said, summoning us in this way.

"Let's tell him now," I said. "The new rule starts tomorrow."

"OK, you do the talking."

"Fine."

Ugo was in his stocking feet. He held his chimney-blackened hands like a surgeon, fingertips up.

"Ugo," I said, starting in. "There's something we'd like to talk to you about." Why was my heart beating so?

"Yes?" Ugo said, smiling. The soot on his face had dissolved in sweat and was dripping down his handsome, unshaven cheeks. The top of his balding head was dusted black. In the window behind him, Luciano was climbing down the ladder and would soon have the ground under his feet.

"Thank you, Ugo," I said.

"*Prego*," said Ugo, "*o*."

"Thank you for everything," I said.

Ugo laughed. "For nothing," he said. "*Niente*."

"COURAGE. SACRIFICE. VISION." THESE WERE THE words (Albertina's words) that visited my mind as I lay in bed, absolutely immobile, wondering when I'd ever regain sufficient strength to put to use her tried and proved garden principles.

We'd just spent the night at Saturnia, the ancient thermal bath center in the Maremma, just to the south of us. Though the old Grand Hotel Saturnia has since been bought and beautified, transformed into one of Europe's most luxurious spas, in those days it was a clinical destination of bare, antiseptic halls reminiscent of the wartime hospital wards in *For Whom the Bell Tolls*. The hotel's centerpiece is an enormous pool of Las Vegas proportions half surrounded by the monstrous, crescent-shaped hotel which hugs its shore the way Monte-Carlo does its azure port. The pool is filled with the sulfurous waters of a nearby hot spring, reeking and dark, fouled further with floating wads of sulphur—*stronzi*, we laughingly called them, little turds.

We were there with a doctor friend of ours and his wife, Franco and Donatella Martini. Living in the chilly damp of Lucca's *centro storico*, they couldn't get enough of these thawing baths. We floated together in the steaming brew for hours on end even though the signs, posted everywhere, warned guests not to exceed the advised limit of fifteen minutes. "Oh, don't worry about that" was the professional advice we got from our overruling friend Franco, our own health coordinator who never glanced at his water-repellent watch. There we lingered, up to our necks in the curative subterranean juices that attracted water takers from far and wide till we were thoroughly marinated.

The first sign that something was wrong: I could barely lift a forkful of my glutinous, boiled chicken dinner, the spa's idea of just the sort of healthy meal one needed after a day's treatments, whatever they might be—a violent sulphur power wash or a mud bath: an hour *en croute* like a beef Wellington.

When I got home the next afternoon, I went to bed, and so did Gil. There wasn't a gram of strength left in my limp, odorous body—the smell clings to your skin for days. I felt like the oldest patient who'd ever made the taxing journey to Saturnia's fountain of youth. Gil at least could muster the muscle to pick up the phone and call our doctor friend. "Franco, we're both at death's door. Any advice?"

"You must have overdone it," he said.

"Do you think?"

"It's lowered your blood pressure. Go to bed."

"We've done that, now what? Salt?"

"Don't worry. It'll pass."

Well, it did—three days later. Three days of killing fatigue and sent-over soup from Ottavia. Three days of endless thinking, and rethinking, about all the daily problems I had no chance of solving until I'd regained enough strength to raise an arm or a leg.

For instance, I thought about that short strip of driveway just inside the garden gates—our not particularly imposing pair of brick pillars topped with terra-cotta pinecone finials. Didn't that little strip of gravel driveway need something to dress it up? I raised the issue with Gil, barely able to open my mouth to speak. "The driveway," I said, "let's plant something. Something formal to give it a little . . . *je ne sais quoi*. What should it be?"

"Roses," Gil muttered assuredly.

More roses, I thought. Didn't we have enough *roses*, for God's sake?

"What about four balls of box," I suggested, showing, perhaps, the first spark of excitement I'd felt since Donatella called with, "Oh, what do you say we go down to Saturnia for the night?"

"Four balls, two on each side of the driveway, two pair, a certain amount of space between them?" I could see the finished planting so clearly in my imagination; it was the sort of roadside treatment you might have found at a great Lucchese villa, but if I'd come across this exact scheme in my local garden travels, I couldn't remember where.

In spite of a partially withheld resistance on Gil's part, I pushed ahead with my formal garden initiative as soon as I was back on my tingling, wobbly legs. I was certain he'd love it in the end; after all, I was only talking about four green balls here. When I asked Albertina where I should go to get these box balls of mine, she said, "Dino Monti's the man."

Monti Vivai, Dino Monti's nursery, is Lucca's largest and best-furnished garden center—and it's only fifteen minutes from my door.

It was with no small amount of trepidation that I entered, weakened as I was, Monti's courtyard on this warm spring morning that had awakened gardening passions among the valley's masses. Driven by the competitive zeal with which one buys silver trays, cups, and vases at Marchi Silversmiths in town, where you literally have to take a number to be served, they were buying geraniums. I felt a bit overcome. It could be hours before I'd find anyone to help me. And then what? I didn't know the names of plants in English, never mind Italian. And all these people!

Under a long greenhouse roof stood thousands of well-brought-up, perfectly shaped French geraniums of various pinks and reds popping excitedly out of their flimsy plastic pots. There was a vast selection of other summer flowering plants: petunias, verbenas, fuchsias, marigolds. Though gardening, with a few exceptions, isn't practiced on any serious level here in Lucca, absolutely everyone has a yard or a balcony redolent in summer with an embarrassment of blooms. And this is where they buy them each spring, showing up, as if it were required by law and not by mere custom, on exactly the same day at exactly the same time—unison is the Italian way: on *Ferragosto*, in August, the entire population goes on a two-week vacation and everything in the entire country is closed.

But it isn't only *mamma* (in her high heels, good suit, and lots of jewelry) who's here to buy her three French geraniums and half a flat of sweet alyssum. *Mamma* doesn't drive, and so she has to have *papà* along. Not only that, she's got her sister in tow for further approval, and the sister's daughter as well, with her young *fidanzato*. *Mamma* lingers and pokes and studies and thinks as her selection committee patiently follows. But being Lucchese, she has far more important things to consider than the color or shape of the very same plants she bought last year and the year before. The price! "*Quanto viene quel fiorellino lì?*" she asks Dino Monti's not terribly relaxed wife.

"*Due e cinque.*"

"Well, it seems to me that in the supermarket it was a thousand lire less."

"*O signora,* don't talk to me about the supermarket."

"*Sì sì,* and it was precisely this one, this very *fiorellino* here, a thousand lire less, at least."

"Well, *signora,*" a smile-free Signora Monti says, "you're welcome to go back to the supermarket. Their doors open automatically."

Mamma goes into a well-rehearsed sulk (sometimes it works, sometimes it doesn't). "*Ma non so, a me sembra un pochettino alto, il prezzo.*"

I strolled the courtyard, hoping that in a few minutes all the *mammas* of Lucca would make a beeline back to their kitchens. The larger plants and bushes were lined up, on display for impulse buyers, along a sunny wall; Monti hauls out shrubs with the best show of flowers, as his clients never buy anything that isn't in bloom. I recognized the bougainvillea, as I'd always admired them in my travels to the tropics. I'd been especially impressed by the bougainvillea in Antigua, Guatemala, where their purple petal-like bracts (they aren't blooms) spill over the ancient whitewashed walls, pointing their tips to the sun. Though they've adapted well to the Mediterranean—you see them doing nicely along the Lucchese coast, even if they do go a bit spindly in winter—they're actually from the subtropics of South America. I had all I could do to keep myself from buying one, but bougainvillea wasn't part of my modest day's plan. One thing at a time.

Hidden somewhere among these tubs of greenhouse-perfect

flowering shrubs was the object of my search. There was just one of them, but if they had one, it seemed to me, then they must have others. I dragged it out into the open and looked it over. It was a *Buxus rotundifolia* formed into a nice round ball. Yes, that was it! It never occurred to me for a moment to ask if they had such balls as these made out of *Buxus sempervirens,* the preferred species. I had no idea that real gardeners poo-poo the rotundifolia as an inferior second cousin of the far more desirable real thing. The rotundifolia is so under-esteemed, in fact, that it's not even listed in any of my four garden plant encyclopedias.

Though simple in concept and scope, box balls such as these are in fact topiary. The Romans used balls of green in their pleasure gardens as focal points and accents; these were the roots of my design whether I knew it at the time or not. But box had fallen out of favor during the Renaissance, when topiary was fashioned of almost any plant material *but* box. There was a reason for this: the smell. You think eucalyptus smells of cat pee! English gardeners of the sixteenth century felt that the evil and loathsome smell of box irreparably damaged the brain. If they'd somehow foreseen the many thousands of miles of box hedging that would one day cross and recross the British Isles, they'd have emigrated to Massachusetts and its box-killing, sweet-smelling chill.

With a great deal of effort (at this point, I was ready for bed again) I managed to have a salesman pull out three more such plants. As I'd hoped for, they were all alike, exactly the same size and shape, trimmed perhaps by a single hand with a single eye for roundness. There in the courtyard, I arranged them in pairs just as I'd plant them at home. I stood back and, squinting, considered the composition from various viewpoints. The salesman, in spite of the fact that I was sold on what I saw, started in with his Lucchese sales pitch, a relentless rant that informs you of the obvious in a round fugue. The Lucchese are famous merchants, while their age-old methods of moving merchandise are infamous. I've seen people buy coats three sizes too big for them because the persistent flattering salesman so insisted that voluminous bulk was in.

I loaded my goods into the rickety old Peugeot that Midge Oliver left us as part of our purchase and sales agreement and headed home, the smell of box filling the car as if a cat had sprayed on one of its wheels.

It had rained a bit in the night, and the site of my new formal planting was still damp. Ugo and his brother, Luciano, who'd stopped by for a friendly visit, helped me unload the car and place the balls of box where I wanted them. They had good advice as to how to plant them, foreseeing their slow but ample growth. Out came Ugo's spade, an ancient, highly sharpened blade at the end of a curving, hand-hewn handle, buffed by hard use to the warm gleam of a fine piece of furniture. In a matter of minutes the four holes were dug and filled with enticing manure from the vegetable garden—I wouldn't have known how to do any of this. In they went, my four spiffy balls, surrounded now by rain-catching rings of mud. Time would heal the wounds—that much I knew.

I heard a car. It was the first car to pass my new welcoming topiary honor guard. Well, it was Carol MacAndrew, our neighbor, doyenne of Lucca's expatriate set. But who was this elderly couple with her?

Gil emerged from the house, looking a little peaked. His eyes widened at the sight of my formal planting but no comment followed. There was other business at hand.

"*Carissimi*," Carol said, her arms extended. She was radiant, as if in anticipation of a lovely lunch. This visit, I'd soon learn, had been hastily arranged in my brief morning's absence. One of Carol's frequent "I've-got-some-people-I'd-like-you-to-meet" calls.

Carol introduced her friends, a certain Mr. and Mrs. Frost, who'd also been dear friends of the Olivers. The Frosts had owned a villa here, a rather important one, but had sold it and moved back to Sacramento five years ago. They were coming by to "see the garden," of all things. It was their first trip to Lucca since they'd moved away, and they were visiting all the sites and sights they'd loved and now sadly missed—she especially regretted their ill-advised move back to the States. They were both imposingly tall and white-haired, of Republican-looking stock in gray-blue tweeds. I was reminded of my Uncle Clifford and Aunt Jenny, pinions of the conspicuously Episcopalian side of my mother's family: that high-browed whiteness and those downturned smiles.

"We don't want to take up much of your time," Mrs. Frost said, all business, "but Midge Oliver asked us to stop by and see Mac's garden. She'd like a little report. You don't mind, do you?"

"Oh no," Gil said, his eyelids half closed.

I almost said, Well, I'll just go back to bed while you all have a look around; my Saturnia's kicking up.

Mrs. Frost went icy as her gaze swept across the front garden with its raw stumps poking up everywhere, but I attributed her pallor to age and not to the fact that in my convalescence I hadn't mown the lawn. When a lawn is not a particularly good lawn, that is, when it's mostly weeds and very little grass, it's all the more important that you keep it mown, providing the illusion of quality. I suppose our lawn looked especially scruffy that day, but I felt no need to apologize for it to drop-in visitors.

"Well, in Mac's day . . ." Mrs. Frost managed to say.

"Yes?" I said.

"Well . . . it's just that . . . Mac was a very keen gardener, you know. He had an eye. No, he had more that an eye. He had heart. His heart was a garden, and it was immaculate."

I thought of the immaculate heart of Mary.

Mr. Frost groveled in: "He was a groundskeeper, Mac was. Always in his overalls showing us the way."

I looked at the Frosts' good town shoes. "Would you like to walk around?" I asked, gesturing off to the wet, weedy lawn which was especially boggy by the parking area, where we've always had a drainage problem.

"Yes yes," said Carol in her water-resistant country shoes, a broad smile on her face; the garden is her domain.

"No no," said Mrs. Frost, frowning. She clutched her bag as if a band of gypsies were about to scoot out from behind one of the philadelphus bushes Albertina had spared in her visionary clean-up. She turned her head this way and that. "Rhynchospermum," she muttered. "*Olea fragrans.*"

Should I run for the smelling salts?

"Aren't you going to ask us in?" Carol said.

It had never occurred to me.

"I think we must be going," Mr. Frost said, taking his speechless, trembling wife by the arm.

"What's your hurry?" Gil said.

"We're leaving in the morning."

"Really," Mrs. Frost said, "I'm quite looking forward to it, after all. You know, one should never look . . . back."

Carol broke in, "But aren't you just delighted to see that this house has fallen into the hands of such nice people?" Neither Gil nor I had shaved in days. It was like *The Beverly Hillbillies.*

Mrs. Frost seemed to have heard only the word "fallen."

"Oh, but you have to take a look at what I've just done," I said, so proud of my decorative balls. I managed to march our visitors over to my planting site, keeping them to the dry gravel.

A long silence, five of us gazing down.

"What are we looking at?" Carol said.

"The balls," I said. "We just planted them. This morning."

"Marvelous," Carol said, ready to kiss us both goodbye.

"It looks great," Gil said. "It kind of . . . rounds things out. That what you had in mind, Paul?"

Mrs. Frost had stepped up onto the grass to smell one of our nameless red roses that proffered a single highly scented bloom. "Mac planted this beauty," she said, briefly enchanted.

"It tends to reflower," Gil complained.

She stood there with her nose extended, having completely ignored my glorious formal planting scheme so reminiscent of Versailles. When she pulled the bloom her way, its entire cup of petals fell loose and fluttered to the ground. "Oh dear," she said, recoiling. Her high heels had sunk into the boggy lawn, and her shoes were stuck. Back she went without them—"Woo woo," she screamed—falling right on top of one of my *Buxus rotundifolia,* where she now sat like a garden gnome upon a sagging mushroom. When the mayhem died down and we had her upright again, I looked at my poor squashed box ball, dimpled like a *gnocco,* and hoped that nobody noticed that I had far more concern for my newly recast plant than for Mrs. Frost's ruined shoes.

.   .   .

There's an addendum to this.

A month later a letter arrived from Midge Oliver—and I quote, "My dear Mrs. Frost wrote to inform me that your garden is in a 'critical state of abandon.' How I regret this discomfiting bit of news. Mightn't you ask our beloved Ugo to give you a hand with the gardening now and then; he really doesn't mind."

chapter three

FAUNA AND FLORA

"AND WHAT SHALL I DO ABOUT THE BIRD?" UGO
asked, excitedly. We'd just got back from a trip to Assisi. Our car
doors were still open. The motor tinged.

"*L'uccello?*" Gil said.

"Yes yes," said Ugo. "The bird. The man who works for Count
Tadini brought it in a box while you were gone. I put it in the outhouse, but it is a very big bird and the outhouse is very small, made for
one man at a time."

"A peacock!" Gil said in English, getting it. Tadini had made the
vague promise to give us a peacock out of his growing flock, but it was
one of those unlikely offers you never take seriously.

"I thought of putting him in with the chickens, but the roosters would surely peck him. Something has to be done. A decision has to be taken. What shall I do?"

Ottavia was standing beside him, one step back. She splayed her fingers and chopped the air with her hand. "If you only saw this bird," she said. "Enormous!"

"I think it is a species of peacock," Ugo said.

"No no," said Ottavia, wrinkling her chin. "It is not a species of peacock. Oh Gilberto, Oh Paolo, if you only saw how big—"

"Shut up," Ugo said. "*Stai zitta!*"

"Enormous!" Ottavia said, shouting. Her straight black skirt was creased at the pelvis. Without the makeup she wore to work you could see the fine colorless hairs that gilded her pretty cheeks. "Oh, how stupid my husband is," she said, her hands covering her face. "It's a species of turkey."

"No no," said Ugo. "It is a peacock. I saw one once in San Macario. Oh, Paolo, how it screams, this bird! It makes the same *versi* as the one I once saw there. This is a peacock, I know."

"It goes, *Ayyyah, ayyyah,*" Ottavia said, having fun with herself. "Oh, Gilberto, is that a peacock? You tell us. You understand things and will surely know."

"Yes," Gil said, nodding, "a peacock."

"Well, I am an idiot," Ottavia said. "Listen, don't ever ask me things. What a simple woman I am. You who travel the world, take airplanes!" She laughed and poked her husband in the ribs. "I'm an ignorant peasant!" she said.

"Count Tadini's garden is full of peacocks," Gil said, taking a step forward. "They're in the trees. They're all over the place."

"But it is a problem," Ugo said, "this poor bird cooped up in such a small space. We must move it to a proper cage."

"Let's see him," I said.

The four of us walked together around the abandoned farm-house, across the *limonaia* yard to the disused outhouse, whose usually wide-open door looked, to me, monstrously closed. Ugo lifted the latch and slipped into the tiny brick structure sideways. In a second he emerged holding the peacock by its wings.

"What a bird!" Ottavia said. "Look! Look!"

The tail feathers that make a peacock what it is were shredded to bits. Bright-colored feather eyes were dragging in the dirt. "What happened?" asked Gil.

"He arrived like that," Ugo said. "He was transported in a very small container."

"How should they be, the feathers?" asked Ottavia.

"What a pity," I said.

"Oh, don't worry," Ugo said, "they grow back."

"How soon?" asked Gil.

"*Bo*," said Ugo. He had no idea.

Suddenly the peacock broke free, taking awkwardly to the air. As Ugo dove for it, the peacock's bowels moved and Ugo got showered with loose green-black stool. It was all over his sweater and his plastic sandals. He laughed, kindly making light of it all.

"Oh, Ugo!" Gil said sympathetically.

"*Ma, fa niente*," Ottavia said. "He's used to that."

Count Giovanni Tadini, the man who gave us this unique gift, lives at the foot of the Pisan Mountains. In this arid, olive-dotted landscape Ruskin picnicked and Byron rode. If I climbed the hill to the south of my house and descended through the woods, I'd arrive at Giovanni's doorstep, a distance of only a few miles as the crow flies. But the

woods are thick, the grade steep, and so one travels there by car, half
an hour's drive, give or take.

His house, a sixteenth-century villa, belonged to one of the lesser
Medici. It's a grand structure of imposing proportions. Its rooms are
chock-a-block full of period paintings and antiques. Giovanni's a busy
collector. A connoisseur of noble genealogy and bon vivant, he speaks
perfect British English, giving himself away as Italian only when he says
"yesterday night."

When you enter his courtyard, a dozen or so white doves spiral
up with a whoosh. It's as if you've happened upon a sudden snow
squall, out of season and place. This effect alone can make a garden
brilliant, something no common bank of hydrangeas could ever hope
to achieve. Someone recently asked me what I thought to be the most
essential ingredient of the Italian garden. After a moment's reflection,
I answered, architecture. If you removed the stones from an Italian
garden, what remained would have so lost its quality of style and place
that it could be anywhere. There are no plants in Giovanni Tadini's
courtyard of stone and birds and falling water in a niche, yet it's just as
much an Italian garden as is the parterre at Villa Lante with its
sculpted, light-catching hedges: there's solid geometry in the volumes
of Villa Tadini, in the classically carved stairways and balustrades.

Passing through a wide gallery running directly through the center of his house, you arrive at the villa's high front terrace, a crumbling
expanse raked west into the Mediterranean's brilliant, often hazy glow.
Below lies a large walled garden, a true *hortus conclusus*.

The first time I stood there with Giovanni and looked down into
the thicket of his garden's neglect, he said, "But of course, it really
should be kept in quite another way." I don't think I could have begun
to imagine then what this walled garden of his ought to have looked

like, for I'd never given those lunettes by Giusto Utens the time of day, those fascinating bird's-eye views of the Pitti Palace and its gardens that show fruit groves and parterres in a utopian-ordered plan.

That morning of my first visit, Giovanni gestured to a neoclassical pavilion closer to the house and off to the side. "Over there you have my grandmother's conservatory," he said. "It is my grandmother's in that she was the last to use it. Throughout the winter when I was a child, she saw to it that the fires were diligently stoked. On Easter Sunday we would feast on our very own pineapple, a single piece of fruit each year." Remembering this story now, I think of *Portrait With a Pineapple*, by Hendrick Dankert, in which King Charles II stands on a country terrace, his Baroque garden off in the distance, holding up the first pineapple ever grown in England.

Just as I was about to risk "How marvelous!" I heard a cry. It was like that of a child in distress. "Help," it seemed to say. "Help." There was a rustle in the walled garden, and I turned my head to see a peacock gliding heavily, its wings extended beneath the dark canopy of maritime pine. Suddenly peacocks seemed to be everywhere—the fact that I'd not seen them right away pointed out the extremes of overgrowth on Tadini's jungle floor. All at once I was fascinated. I wondered, Is this neglect and ruin as intentional as the birds now made it seem? This garden was a fitting home for them, and they were its dazzling occupants who were every bit as engaging to the senses as most flowering plants.

I had a portable drawing board that I'd shipped from Point Reyes. Just then I finished my plan for the aviary. It was to be built on the site of the burnt-out garden shed. It wouldn't be as refined an aviary as the one modeled after a Victorian conservatory that stands in the corner of Tadini's walled garden. It would be made of chicken wire, framed by milled boards painted green. It would have a terra-cotta roof. It was a sensible design, not at all ambitious. "See," I said, showing my plan to Ugo, who would help me build it.

"No," Ugo said, scratching his head.

"Well, never mind," I said, "here is the list of things we need."

Ugo went to the hardware store and lumber yard and came back with a bundle of virgin-white American wood. I felt sad to see the stamped word WEYERHAUSER. Our forests, I thought regretfully.

"Cut here," I said, drawing a precise pencil line on one of the boards with a graphic designer's triangle.

Ugo sawed with soul. "Good God," he said, impressed with my planning skills—to anyone but Gil and me he would have said, blasphemously, *Dio cane*, dog God!

"We'll use these screws," I said, "not nails."

"*Dio bono!*" said Ugo.

"We'll join the corners like picture frames."

"Good God," he said. "We are building something of beauty here."

"*Ayyyah*," called the peacock, still imprisoned in the outhouse, anxious to move into his spacious, airy new home.

"Those cries!" Ugo said, and then he cringed.

For two days Ugo and I worked. Ugo's amazement with every touch of quality I lent to the job convinced me that the aviary was already overbuilt. "I'll come live here myself, *Dio bono*," Ugo said, far too many times.

At about noon on the second day Gil showed up on the construction site. Close behind was Ottavia, who held a bouquet of wild edible greens. It was as if they were violets and she a bridesmaid. It had drizzled for a while early that morning. Raindrops now fell in the pomegranate tree. The bright green lawn all around the new aviary was scuffed away to mud by the crew's work boots.

"I love these with lots of vinegar," Ottavia said about the greens, which are far too bitter for my palate. "I put garlic on them, oil and vinegar—our own—lots of it. Look at my stomach. It shows how much vinegar I eat. It makes you fat, and so does bread. My, how much bread I eat, Paolo! I can't resist. I eat half a kilo of bread with every meal." She pantomimed slicing a loaf that she held in the curve of her arm like a wrestler whose eyes she was about to gouge.

We'd stopped working; it was time to talk. "It is good, our vinegar," Ugo said. "It is genuine, not like the vinegar you buy in supermarkets."

"Oh, how I love it," Ottavia said.

"Certainly it is a beautiful thing," Ugo said, "our own produce. Our salad. Our tomatoes. Our peaches."

"Our rabbits," Ottavia said.

"*Ayyyah*," cried the peacock from a hazy distance.

"Our peacocks," I said.

"I'm hungry," Gil said.

"Hurry, hurry," Ugo said. "Quick to lunch and then back, for that peacock there is an angry beast!"

At the end of the day Ugo placed the gnarled trunk of an old dead olive tree in the center of the cage: a perch. To one of the upper branches he tied an enormous dried sunflower. "Ugo has a touch," Gil said. It was true.

That done, we moved the peacock in. Free at last, but not too free, he sat there on his olive branch picking out seeds: peck, chew, spit. The four of us looked in and watched, fascinated by his every strange and awkward move; it was a zoo.

"Certainly he's a beautiful beast," Ottavia said.

"But none too smart," said Ugo.

"How smart are you?" she said.

"Shame about his tail," said Gil, even though Tadini had told us on the phone that peacocks lose their tail feathers once a year and that fresh ones soon grow back.

"When can we let him roam free?" I asked.

"Three days," Ugo said. "He has to get used to his place here. When he's used to it we'll open the door. This will be his house and we will feed him here. At night he'll return to this place and sleep, up on that branch there. By day he'll grace the garden with his beauty. What an affair!"

Three days at a sumptuous buffet of lovely grains. They smelled so good I'd have eaten them myself for breakfast, with raisins and milk. Ziggy seemed adjusted now (a friend named him Ziggy, after Ziegfield and his follies). He cried only when he was supposed to, at dawn and dusk. By day he walked the floor, the broken, fallen feathers at his feet; by night he slept on his olive branch, all hunched in upon himself.

On the fourth morning I opened Ziggy's door. But he didn't seem to notice. I went away and left him there in peace. An hour or so later I went back to take a look. He was still inside. Open or closed, the concept of a door meant little to him. "Come on out," I said. "Take a stroll." But the peacock just stayed there on the terra-cotta floor, nervously pacing.

There's a glassed-in conservatory, built by Lionel Fielden, just off our kitchen. In the cooler months, this is where we eat lunch, looking out towards what would one day be Gil's rose garden. We were sitting over our plates of *spaghetti agli zucchini* when a little head appeared in the window looking in. A peacock's eyes are mounted laterally, and so he has to turn his head sideways to see straight. Ziggy tried his left eye and then his right, his little blue comb aflutter, his tiny head bobbing at the end of a long, glistening blue neck wrapped in a cerulean choker. Soon we realized that he wasn't seeing us at all; he was looking at his own reflection. Lonely bird.

He preferred the back garden, the shade, the safe enclosure of high walls. Whenever he chose to sit, he'd dig a good hole. Once he'd lain in it awhile, he'd give it up, never to sit there again. The mossy green carpet beneath the camphor was scuffed away in bird belly–shaped ruts. The paved walkway to the grotto was soon covered with his slimy droppings. If you didn't see them, you were apt to take a good spill, and it happened more than once to both Gil and me.

We'd hoped he'd like the front lawn, the wide expanse of green, weedy grass. Wouldn't that be decorative, we'd thought, a peacock on the lawn like at Isola Bella on Lago Maggiore.

It took the two of us to shoo Ziggy out front, so little interest did he have in exploring. But with much hard coaxing, clapping, herding, we finally got him off the terrace. With his blue, almost useless wings spread, he took a broad leap, softly gliding. He was so pretty, strutting out there on the grass in circles. He cried for help—he'll get over it, I thought; peacocks are just naturally quarrelsome. He looked up into the trees, the lowest branches out of his range. We left him there in Paradise, rosebuds to nibble on, a broad expanse of cool, dewy grass underfoot.

Ten minutes later, he was at the front door, admiring his own reflection in the door glass. "Shoo, shoo," I said. "The lawn! The lawn!"

We had lunch. He showed up at the conservatory window: his left eye, his right eye, back and forth. Nothing changed. He liked company, especially that of his own reflection. The front lawn wasn't for him, lonely and sad.

An hour later, he was in the entry hall—I'd left the back door open.

"You can't come in here," I said. "Out, *out!*"

He took to the air. His wings seemed to work. He was high on the newly whitewashed wall looking for something to land on, but there was nothing. Just wall. He made his way into the dining room through Lionel Fielden's open Rajastani arch. He flapped his wings, a thunderous wind and roar. His bowels moved. "Oh no!" Loose feces dribbled down the wall, and his claws scratched it left and right. Seconds later, he was back down on the floor, thank goodness. I shooed him to the hall towards the door, but doors had never meant much to Ziggy, peabrain. Up another wall he flew, his dirty feet scumbling the green-black slime with an expressionist's bravura and reach. The peacock was Hera's favorite bird, but I wasn't sure it was mine.

We invited Giovanni Tadini to dinner. Ziggy wasn't the most suitable gift we'd ever received, but even so. I was more than justifiably nervous; at Tadini's villa, silver plates engraved with his family crest are set before you by the white-gloved hands of liveried butlers.

Planning, I asked Gil, "What shall we serve?" As usual, Gil

responded, "Spaghetti and meatballs? Chicken-fried steak? Peanut butter and *jelly* sandwiches?" It's always seemed odd that Gil emphasizes the word *jelly* in that phrase and not the word *sandwich*, but with this dinner approaching, it almost angered me.

When I had asked Ottavia what she might prepare for a special evening, she had only the most common suggestions: tortelli with ragú, roast veal, and potatoes. I decided to do the cooking myself. I would not attempt anything Italian so as to invite unwelcome comparison. I would do Moroccan honeyed beef, a dish that I'd always ordered at Mamounia, in San Francisco, where you sat on the floor and ate with your fingers. Unfortunately, I didn't have a Moroccan cookbook. I'd have to improvise. "It can't be difficult," assured Gil, who wouldn't have known where to begin had it been up to him. Ottavia would be on hand, in any case, to assist me in the kitchen, though the thought of serving at table terrified her.

I invited the MacAndrews, Albertina and Alberto, Frances Reynardson, Victor Glasstone. I was anxious to prove to Emanuela that the modern stone dining table Gil and I had bought wasn't so impractical as she'd promised it would be.

All the cars arrived together, as if they'd met along the road somewhere to form an intimidating caravan.

"Everything will be fine," Gil assured.

Carol MacAndrew was the first to come through the door. She had kisses for her hosts, who were wearing the new semi-tailored, semi–ready-to-wear suits we'd bought at Principe in Florence. Carol's husband, Jim, wore a dark shirt with an open collar and the eccentrically styled sports coat that was his right as an artist. I decided I liked Jim a lot when at one of their dinner parties I said, "Very good wine," and Jim responded, "I'm no wine connoisseur. I'm from Chi-caaaaaaaago, if you know where that is."

In the entry hall Jim said, "You know, I've always *hated* this house, but with you in it, it looks better somehow."

I thought this over. What had we done other than whitewash the walls (several extra coats, thanks to Ziggy) and dye Lionel Fielden's curtains that lugubrious shade of green?

"Visiting here," said Francis Reynardson, "I think of Midge's raspberries. Oh, they were just *too* wonderful!"

"You haven't got r-r-r-id of them, I trust," trilled Nicholas Trev-ellian. His green woolen suit had bell-bottomed pants; on him they looked conservative.

"You do still have the raspberries?" asked worried Victor Glasstone.

"They're down there in the garden," Gil said, "but they're not ripe yet."

We drank spumante in the living room. Gil and I sat on either side of the fireplace in the red armchairs whose exaggerated neo-baroque style we were both beginning to loathe.

"Oh, Giovanni, Giovanni," everyone said to the count. He was the center of attention that night because he had just returned from a visit with the exiled King of Italy in Lisbon. I knew that Italy had once had a king, but I couldn't remember the exact details of why he left or where he went. "He's in great form nevertheless," Giovanni said. "Not a trace of despondency."

"And so tell me," Frances Reynardson said, addressing Gil. "I've been dying to ask you this. What, exactly, are you *doing* here?"

The room went silent. Hope was palpable. She wanted to hear that Gil was busy at work on an eagerly anticipated revisionist tome that would represent a fundamental paradigm shift in our understanding of the Renaissance.

"Am . . . waiting for the raspberries to ripen!" he said, his shoulders coming up.

"Oh," Frances said disappointedly. "I see."

The dining room had what was called a *passavivande*, a hole in the wall with sliding doors through which Lionel Fielden's cook once passed platters to the butler. Serving, I took the long route around to the kitchen. How embarrassing it would have been to hand dishes to Gil through that foolish hole in the wall.

"I see that Midge took her marvelous *scaldavivande* off to England with her," said the count.

"Her what?" I asked, serving leek vinaigrette à la Boston's St. Batolph Street Restaurant.

"That nifty trolly that kept her food warm," Albertina said.

"Oh, it was *too* wonderful," said Frances Reynardson.

"Ah, that," I said, glancing at the special English electrical outlet the Olivers had installed in the corner of the room. I remembered having seen that tasteless food warmer when I toured the house. The top of it was made of Corningware, and there was a homely pin-striped vegetable motif in the milky glass.

"The Italians have never understood the concept of warmed plates," said Frances, raising her own up off the table and peering under. Not only was it cold, but of an insignificant manufacture.

I'd seated her to my left, as I admired the understatement of her Irish wool shawl and the "stick" she carried, whose handle was a silver flaming torch.

Frances was talking to Victor Glasstone. "The controversy about Queen Victoria didn't excite the 'Lost Generation' in the least," she said. "Victoria died when they were still in *pannolini*, for heaven's sake."

"Pannolini?" I said. "The island? I'd like to go there in June. I saw an article about it. You pick up the ferry in Naples, don't you?"

"*Pannolini?*" Frances said. "*Pannolini* . . . are diapers."

I took a few empty plates to the kitchen. Ottavia, who was standing by the sink, was dressed like a hostess. "Would you please get the rest," I asked.

Blushing deep crimson, she couldn't control her grin of terror. "*Non posso, non posso!*" she screamed.

"Never mind, then," I said, responding to her apparent phobia with empathy.

"Oh, all right," she shouted, suddenly game.

The two of us went to the dining room together. Ottavia, keeling over in her high-heeled shoes, preceded me. I was worried for her.

She positioned herself at the head of the table, grabbed two plates and, like a percussionist, started scraping off leftovers with one of the guests' forks. All eyes were on her nervous, blushing grin. "*Datemi i piatti!*" she screamed at the top of her lungs, "Let's go, hand 'em up! *Andiamo!*"

I returned to the kitchen to put the finishing touches on my honeyed beef. I was at the stove when Ottavia came back with a stack of dishes. "What a beautiful perfume," she said, with the air of a forced compliment, about my sauce. I didn't know that one should never introduce foreign methods into the Tuscan kitchen, as I was about to do now. Local recipes, having undergone centuries of refinement, are more sacred to these people than religion.

Ottavia set down the plates, then watched suspiciously as I opened a jar of honey and poured its entire contents freely into the steaming pot of braised beef chunks. You could have heard her gasp throughout the house. "*O Dio!*" she screamed with horror, her hands on her blanched face. "*O no!*"

Over dessert, I raised my glass. "Thank you for the peacock, Giovanni," I said.

"Oh, my pleasure," said the count.

"What a difference he's made to our garden," Gil said. "People say, 'You have the most beautiful things. The most beautiful cypresses, the most beautiful grotto, the most beautiful birds!' "

"Then I must give you another one," Giovanni said, beaming. "I must find your handsome cock a hen! And straightaway!"

I hoped no one saw my raised eyes—was that a Ziggy stain I saw coming right through those three coats of touch-up whitewash?

"That's settled, then!" Giovanni said. "Your Ziggy shall have a wife!"

Smiles of delight all around.

"Oh, thank you, Giovanni," I said, "Thank you so much."

"NEVER," FRANCES REYNARDSON SAID, "NEVER plant red salvia!"

It was a hot summer day and I was giving a luncheon party. I'd worked hard to bring some order and color to the rear garden, and now I was anxious to show off the presentable—so it seemed to me—fruits of my late spring preparations. What I'd done wasn't gardening, it was a purge. Away with the cement-edged flower beds' weedy perennial dross! I dug up everything and heaped it out of sight somewhere off near the shepherd's house—if the Olivers had chosen these fluffy pink blooms, whatever they were, then they couldn't possibly have been right for Italy or me—*far* too English, definitely.

Frances Reynardson made her way under the wisteria arbor to

the grotto, where I'd laid a table in the cool, musty shadows. Halfway there, her head turned gently to the left and a can't-be-helped smile appeared on her lips. Her silk Madras shawl fell away from one shoulder as she raised her ebony walking stick and halted in her tracks. "Never," she said with a little laugh. "*Never* plant red salvia!"

I gazed, with that, at my greenhouse-forced blooms of red salvia bedded out in meandering rows, as if I'd never seen them before, as if I hadn't selected them myself from the competing flats of petunias, begonias, dwarf dahlias, and the like.

But what's so perfectly despicable about red salvia? I wondered as Frances, over lunch, shared with me an alternative recipe to my *patate dauphinoise*: "Try it with stock instead of milk."

I hadn't as yet read Vita Sackville-West on the subject: "*Salvia splendens* should be forbidden by law." Nor had I consulted Christopher Lloyd: "That dangerous plant, beloved of parks and public gardens, starts off with a flower endowed by nature with a uniformly blatant scarlet colouring throughout both corolla and calyx, while the foliage is coarse and characterless. Having reduced the plant's natural stature to a low, compact blob of condensed blossom, man then proceeds to mass it in the bedding schemes with which we are only too familiar." (Isn't that exactly what I'd done, poor me?)

Not surprisingly, Frances was dead right about salvia, as it's commonly called. As were many of our new friends in this unique community of mostly older expatriates who seemed to have lived dozens of rich lives before finding their niches here in the Lucchese hills, Frances Reynardson was a woman of style. She was a Parke-Davis. She'd been married to a Scottish baron and had lived in a castle on the river Tweed. She had a collection of Italian old master drawings and paintings, and hers was one of the prettiest converted farmhouses in the valley. Once our guests had left, I should have got to the offending red salvia forthwith, even before the luncheon dishes, but I didn't. I waited until mid-summer to dig up those vulgar blooms, by then festering in the hot Lucchese sun—I might have known nothing about gardens in those days, but I did have my pride.

I had no idea that such a thing as a socially imposed hierarchy existed in the world of plants. I'd always imagined them to be equal in the eyes of the creator: red, blue, short, tall, leggy, bushy. I learned, with this bit of unsolicited advice from a luncheon guest, that gardens are not to be taken casually, that gardens can tell you as much about people as the clothes they wear, as the food they serve, as the books they read. I would not be so misrepresented! It was time to do something, anything. But what?

Nearby are some of the most admired gardens in Italy: Villa Reale, Villa Torrigiani, Villa Bernardini. But such monumental landworks as these couldn't possibly have been the ones I'd refer to when imagining the improvements I'd make here at my humble hunting lodge in Massa Macinaia. It was the more personal gardens of my friends I'd logically emulate, hands-on gardens created by people I knew, people with direct experience, with advice to give, the very people who'd one day approve or disapprove of what I did when my gardening season arrived and its blooms were my own doing—or undoing.

By the time I'd met her, Frances Reynardson was a bit too old and unwell to bend to the weeds as she showed me around her garden, but she could still gesture avidly with her stick for the yard man, striking the right balance of helplessness and authority. Her garden wasn't at all worth a detour, but it was intelligent in its choice of suitable, simple materials, in its unself-conscious homeliness. There was a shallow terrace of hand-cut stones off her dining room, wild marjoram and thyme coursing in the cracks. There was the occasional curiously scented pelargonium (rare ones are something of a status symbol here) in a crumbling terra-cotta pot. There were a few genuine marble statues posing with airs in the lavender or stachys beds, where the more gardened garden suddenly ended and everything went wild. Frances knew the Latin names of genera and species, but she'd never have had more plants than she needed; she preferred pets of the four-legged variety.

Her kitchen was hopelessly topsy-turvy and her silver flatware was tarnished, but Frances's much-loved bank of rambling roses behind her sun-bleached pink house was clean of weeds and richly mulched. What *were* those roses of hers? I wonder now. It's been ages since I've visited that garden in Pieve Santo Stefano, with its view of the Serchio river and Lucca's misty plain—Frances passed away in 1989. Showing me around, Frances must have explained, and with eloquence, why those roses of hers were so special, naming their names in the same very good French she'd later use in telling me about the first-growth Bordeaux she'd laid down herself in the 1950s, the wines she'd one day open for me when the right occasion presented itself—sadly, that day never came. Is it too romantic of me to imagine that she'd have grown such lost varieties as "Beauté Inconstant," or "Comte de Paris," roses that graced the more celebrated smaller gardens of Italy at the turn of the century? I'm sure her antique roses are by now long gone, the new owners having cut them down and tossed them out with as much regret as you'd have mutilating an expired credit card; I'm sure of this because I too have thrown away, in impatience and ignorance, more than a few great treasures left over from earlier tutelages here.

But Frances Reynardson wasn't a *true* gardener. She was a mood-struck dabbler compared to Nigel Sundius-Hill and his wife, Lady Helen—now, they were the real thing.

If the garden could ever be in one's blood, then it was in Helen's. She was the daughter of the Marquess of Londonderry, who together with Helen's mother, Edith, created, in the 1920s, one of Ireland's most spectacular gardens, Mount Stewart, in County Down. Helen, by the time she and Nigel settled in Lucca in 1980, was in her seventies, while her eccentric and droll husband was barely forty—a strikingly unusual couple, about whom there was never a shortage of surprising things to say.

They came here "to make a garden," Helen told me when I first visited them at their restored farmhouse, "Cuckoo," in Compignano, where Paolina Bonaparte once lived, then later, Sarah Churchill. I think this was the first time I'd heard of this motive for buying a house somewhere and moving there, and I was intrigued that people of such background as Helen's, of such style and sophistication as Nigel's, allowed the activity of gardening to plot the course their lives would take.

Compignano sits on a hilltop high over Lake Massaciuccoli, Torre del Lago, and the sea. One can grow almost anything in that mild, maritime climate. Bougainvillea blooms almost year round. The lemon trees are in the ground, not in pots as they are at my house, pots you wheel off to the *limonaia* at the first threat of frost. Nigel and Helen were especially fond of Mediterranean plants; they had great, sweeping masses of santolina in full yellow bloom, their curious, distinctive scent at once alluring and nauseating. Dropping in on Nigel and Helen, I'd find them in heated argument about whether or not cool and hot yellows could stand side by side in the same border.

If Nigel talked like a field notebook, it had something to do
with the fact that he'd owned a nursery not far from Mount Stewart,
where his and Helen's romance, founded on common interests, began.
They bought a van their first year together and took a botanical drive
to India, crossing the Khyber Pass, before settling down to their colonial lifestyle here in Tuscany. Their world was one of black-tie dinners
with roast beef and Yorkshire pudding, of afternoon tea, of sword
dancing on New Year's Eve. Neither of them bothered to learn a word
of Italian—though Nigel, in a bar, could manage, "Haig and Haig,
ah, *con ghiaccio.*"

Lady Helen and I got along well. I was good at pretending to
understand her incomprehensibly aristocratic, closed-mouth English.
The Celt in me (50 percent) came up like an orange flare when Nigel
put a record on—Helen and I, on more than one occasion, reeled into
the wee hours transported to our (very different) whirling origins.

Nigel's "life's work" at Compignano was Helen's Rose Walk.
Along a grassy lane, through an olive grove, he'd planted a twin bank
of ramblers, expertly pegging them down so that their blooms poured
in upon you as you made your way towards the sunset, as if it were a
destination Nigel himself had erected there instead of the usual
reproduction urn. Nigel offered me lots of advice and help early on.
When setting out to plant up pots our first spring here, I asked him if
I ought to buy bagged soil. "With sixty acres of land," he said, "it
seems rather silly to buy dirt, don't you think?" But Nigel's influence
was more general than specific: he inspired in me the *will* to garden.
He described the pleasure of gardening with a feeling he couldn't help
but impart, and that's the best gift any seasoned gardener could give
the novice.

Carol and Jim MacAndrew's garden offered inspiration as well.

The MacAndrews were among the first Americans to settle in Lucca, having done so back in the early sixties simply out of love for the place, a most unlikely motive at a time when the war was still fresh in everyone's mind. In creating his perfumed garden in the sun, with its seemingly made-to-order view of a perfect Lucchese country church, a medieval bell tower, the sharp accent of a lone cypress tree, Jim, who died some years ago, did his best to seek out the unusual—not an easy task here in the provinces, where nurseries tend to stock only the obvious. Jim's was the first *Teucrium fruticans* I'd ever consciously noticed. His dichondra lawn, which still survives in the care of his indefatigable wife, Carol, was daringly different. It was on the terrace at Poggiolino, the MacAndrews' house in San Lorenzo a Moriano, that I first heard such plant names as rhynchospermum and *Olea fragrans* [*sic*] batted lovingly about, names which, if I'd dared to utter them then, would have sounded like prayers on the lips of a heathen, names that are still repeated like a litany whenever the subject of gardens comes up at dinner parties here—and it *always* does.

Jim's garden was entirely white: white plumbago, white *Penstemon* "Snowstorm," white *Phlox* "Europa." I'd never asked myself until now why the *Campanula poscharskyana*—the delicate yet fearlessly sprawling perennial which, thanks to Jim, has found its way into so many Lucca gardens, mine included—why this native of the mountains of Croatia is affectionately called, by all of us here, "Jim's plant." *Campanula poscharskyana* is blue, not white! Perhaps Jim made an outcast of it the day he raked all his chips to the Sackville-West all-white color scheme. (I knew nothing of Sissinghurst when I first puzzled over the concept of a colorless garden, an approach I presumed to be uniquely MacAndrew.)

Though the garden at Poggiolino was based mostly on Jim's

artistic dreams (he was a talented amateur painter, Cocteau and Erté in equal parts), it was looked after just as keenly by Carol, her luminous silver hair hanging pageboy-style beneath a wide straw hat, the cuffs of her immaculate linen shirt efficiently folded back. Carol still picks Japanese beetles off Jim's white rugosa roses and drops them one by one into a mason jar of kerosene; "She's wicked," Jim would say.

Italians of an equivalent ilk (with the odd exception here and there) aren't so delighted as we Anglo-Americans are to put on their old clothes and bore their fingers into dirt. The first human-scaled Italian-owned gardens I visited in this region were in a depressing state of abandon. Gardening had always been thought to be something the gardeners did, not the lady or gentleman of the house, an idea that made reasonable sense perhaps in a climate of blinding sunshine, in a culture where gardens are traditionally green and geometric, the focus on broad strokes, not subtlety or texture, the personally coddled detail. Gardening was digging, hedge trimming, sweeping: hard work. While once there were self-renewing legions of willing and able groundskeepers about, by now the industrial boom has delivered them all from their ancestors' fate: the land. In fifteen years of my living in this house not once has a neighborhood lad rung my bell to ask if we needed a hand with the lawn, and yet there are waiting lists for starting laborers at the paper mills. All this explains, in part, why Giovanni Tadini's garden looks the way it does.

I suppose I'm too intrinsically American, too suburban and middle-class, to ever have the kind of garden that prides itself on overgrowth. The British seem to admire vegetative chaos as much as they love the alternative: awesome, clipped precision. And I too appreciate those gardens of advancing, created-equal self-seeders and weeds out of which spring the rare species, often miraculously, given the inhospitable climate or unlikely soil conditions. These are the gardens of collectors, of plantsmen, gardens full of narrative. There are a few good examples of them in these parts, and they're always tended, or anti-tended, by the most eccentric, and certainly most sophisticated, members of our gardening community.

The garden of Nicholas Trevellian is perhaps the first of these that comes to mind. Though it no longer exists as he made it, his house having been sold upon his death a few years ago, his garden still lives in all our memories.

Nicholas was an antiquarian from Bath who settled in Lucca in the sixties and tried to make a go of a B&B. Hygiene in his disintegrating villa high above the Val Freddana was of small concern to him, but it mattered a good deal to certain groups of British holiday makers who were sent there each summer by American Express; more than once did Nicholas's neighbors spot panic-stricken guests, half-dressed and clutching all their belongings, sprinting in horror to their hired van in the cover of night. But the house had endless appeal, enough so to have been published in *World of Interiors*. The *salone*, nineteenth-century in style, was decorated with fourteen oval mural portraits of the villa's founding family, and Nicholas knew the names of every member, their relation to the next, their individual dramas in full. I often wondered if he'd dreamt the whole history up in his mind, every fascinating, perfectly credible fact. But so what if he had? It made for a lively house tour.

Nicholas's garden was no cleaner than his amusingly appointed bathrooms, which conserved sloshing, chalky porcelain at the expense of common efficiency. At the top of the hill, with its rolling forest view, was a basin he audaciously dubbed "the swimming pool." If you dared to dunk your head while swimming there perhaps you'd have had as much as one inch of visibility, as there was no filtration system and there were no chemicals employed to achieve the all-natural soupy consistency—this too caused consternation in Nicholas's guests, who'd been dreaming back in England of an azure exaltation, a swatch of Mustique in the Tuscan hills.

I was amazed to eventually learn that Nicholas worked in his garden every day, all day long, all year round! It was full of impressive rare species, no doubt, but discovering them without his guiding help would have entailed an exhausting—even dangerous—scavenger hunt through the bush—there were sudden drop-offs to the valley everywhere.

One late November, Nicholas had a dinner party. It was unusual for him to entertain at that time of year; his annual lunch was usually held in late spring, when his garden was in just the kind of condition that pleased him most. But when, after dinner that night, he invited us, with ceremony, out into his chilly courtyard, I understood that this party had a garden function as well. In a south corner, in the glow of a complicated lighting system he'd rigged up just for the occasion, stood a fifteen-foot-tall candelabra dahlia, *Dahlia imperialis*, one of the great gifts of Mexico, its sprawling branches sporting huge lavender-pink blooms. It was almost extraterrestrial in the mist, its enormous shadow drawn crisply upon the powdery ochre facade. We, his several dinner guests, stood there in amazement, our arms folded, our shoulders raised, our breath of surprise palpable in the frigid night. He'd done what he'd been trying to do for years (prior to that, October frosts had always committed it to sudden dormancy), and the stunning result was almost enough to have made a gardener out of the least likely among us—me?

And Victor Glasstone's garden! Another uncultivated (seemingly) wonderland. It's full of little hand-hewn benches and stools where bearded Victorian gnomes smoke their pipes when your back is turned. Victor looks forward each spring to the bloom of marguerites, those invasive, low-growing daisies, in his narrow, meadow-like lawn. I, on the other hand, regularly decapitate mine with the mower, preferring a clean green expanse to one that's irregularly speckled white. "The marguerites are finished now," Victor's apt to say wistfully, as if to imply that his garden had completed its spectacular annual show. Victor's favorite gardening activity is walking along his woodland footpaths, a sickle in hand, hacking away at the brambles "*en passant*." A distinguished, now retired, architectural critic, Victor "loathes" the Italian garden, that prodigious conceit we all bow to unquestioningly: "All that dull order," he says, "the cold-heartedness—extraordinary deficiency!"

His unique house is a fragment of what had been, in the Middle Ages, a small castle, nowadays completely unrecognizable as such. The borders between inside and out aren't so clearly defined as they are in most houses with gardens, as Victor is likely to chop down an unwanted sweet bay bush and bring half of its massive spread into the kitchen, its branches, set in an English galvanized pail of water, reaching to the roof beams. And it's just as likely, in summer months, that his interior furnishings find their way outside, living room chairs arranged in an arc around a three-legged stool, as if Happy the dwarf were about to give a nature seminar to Victor's teatime guests.

The entire front garden is sheltered by a leaning, warped pergola that's thick with purple grapes in August. The atmosphere under its sagging canopy suggests a kind of Mediterranean country life that no longer exists, as we now prefer living on paved terraces you can hose down in the morning after breakfast. The old teak chaise longue under this creaking arbor, where Victor does his ambitious summer reading, seems so much a part of the soft ground beneath its feet that you wonder why it hasn't taken root and sprouted leaves. Victor grows *Iris unguicularis*, pennisetums, rudbeckias, and pink sedum where the sun rakes in, but most of his plants are shade-loving, like the ubiquitous, two-toned snapweed, *Impatiens balsamina*, something once found in all the old peasant cottage gardens here.

If gardens are meant to transport, then Victor's is a success on the highest level; I've learned important lessons there in Montemagno, finding myself all of a sudden with a smile of delight on my lips, an inexplicable flame of pleasure within, wondering about the nature of its igniting spark.

Lunch in the grotto went well enough, though it soon grew warm and close—the cooling water function, that trickle from the mouths of our five ancient stone masks, hadn't as yet been replumbed. Everyone found Gil's ricotta pie, an improved American version (stiffly whipped egg whites), humorous in its shimmering, high airiness. Just as well; the occasion needed comic relief: too much heady conversation for a hot July day, I thought. I was getting drowsy.

"Though I must say," Frances Reynardson concluded, "my heart has always belonged to Père Teilhard the 'poet.' He's just *too* illuminating."

"Indeed," said Nicholas, "but we mustn't forget, Teilhard *is*, above all, the scientist-priest."

"Oh, but of *course*," said Frances, getting up on her final sung word.

My guests rose in a body—thank goodness our expatriate

friends were so assimilated as to require afternoon naps. As they made their way towards the house, I glanced at my garden of thirsty red salvia plants, vermilion in the sun. Frances did the same, one last time. She turned to me with a half smile. Her eyes seemed to burn in the fiery shock of it all. "Never," she mouthed, winking. "*Never!*"

chapter four

BREAKING OLD GROUND

THE MID-EIGHTIES, PROSPEROUS TIMES. GIL AND I were taking advantage of a favorable exchange rate (50 percent off on everything you bought!) by making a few improvements to our *azienda*. Work on Ugo's *casa colonica* was just about finished. The new floors were laid and the windows were in place. In less than a month, Ugo and his family would move out of the villa into the newly restored stone ancillary building Ugo always called *la stalla*, the stable. Up until a hundred years ago this building was a farmhouse. Before that, in the twelfth century, it served as an observation tower. But in the Olivers' day, and in the days of Lionel Fielden who preceded them, the *vacche* lived there, a pair of cows.

When we first mentioned our plans to move Ugo into a house of his own, he said, "I refuse to go and live in *la stalla*." We tried softening him up by calling the stalla the *"casa colonica,"* its official designation as a dwelling place on the deed and recorded maps. But Ugo was not at all disposed to adopting the more correct, less pejorative term *farmhouse*. *"O, quella stalla lì!"* he said, oppressed by its musty volume there beside the lemon house. I understood that he couldn't quite envision a medieval building such as this restored to its former habitable state.

I went to great lengths to reassure him. "Look here," I said, pointing out the hinges on the *finestrini* where interior shutters had once hung. "Why would the cows have needed shutters?" One wall was black from chimney smoke where there had been a fireplace. "How did the cows build fires?" I asked, reasoning.

"O," Ugo said, *"quelle vacche lì!"* He pointed to the broad wooden door behind which the cows had once been confined to a lifetime of darkness and tainted air. He told of getting up before sunrise, before the cows started mooing, awakening the entire household. He would scurry down to the *stalla* with a bar of soap from his bathroom, and he would wash the udders well before milking them. Twice a day he did it. Three times a day when the cows had calves. "Oh, but how delicious, that milk there!" Ugo would pour fresh cream into a *fiasco*, then shake it in cold water, making butter. "My daughter grew up on that milk, so tasty, nothing like the pasteurized stuff from the supermarket. Thirty liters a day these two cows produced, and every afternoon the milk man would come to collect it. Oh, but I don't miss those beasts," Ugo said. *"Per niente!* Oh, the flies! No no! How fast I used to work to get it done. How I'd sweat! What a happy day it was for me when they finally took those cows away."

The day Gabriele and Augusto, the builders, first came to work, Gil told Ugo, "It will be beautiful, your house. Wait and see."

Ugo regarded Gil as if to humor a lunatic.

"A beautiful antique dwelling," Gil promised, "yet with all the modern comforts."

"*Sì sì,*" Ugo said, "till one day it falls in on me." He covered his head with his arms, his obstinacy with a smile.

"Boy," Gil said, "the things we put them through!"

He was reminded of when we bought an antique stone fireplace at the *mercatino* to replace the small, fake one in our living room. The builder, installing it, broke clear through the wall. For the next two weeks, supervising the work in progress, we looked right into Ugo's bedroom where the terrorist attack had occurred. It was like a faded, torn-edged photograph of a war-ravaged interior. Abrasive dust coated everything: Ugo's metal dresser of simulated wood, the religious prints on the walls, the double bed still clothed with sheets and blankets even though Ugo and Ottavia had long since moved upstairs till the wall was rebuilt and they could begin the nasty task of cleaning up. It was incredible to me that Ugo never allowed himself, not even for a moment, to appear inconvenienced.

But in truth, the quality of Ugo's life has improved in recent years. He bought a new four-year-old Lancia which still had the original packing plastic on its upholstered doors. Ugo had no telephone when we arrived. Even today he hollers unnaturally into the receiver as if his voice has to carry to where the call is coming from. Ugo adapts slowly to change, to new ways. But always, in the end, he can't conceal his happiness. "I live the life of a gentleman," he told the local miller after we bought him an Echo weed trimmer and he could put away, once and for all, the ancient scythe he'd always used under the olives.

.   .   .

Throughout construction on their new house, I visited Ugo and his family in their tiny kitchen. Their table was covered with a plastic cloth that mimicked printed cotton, always sticky to the touch. An umber-colored smudge on the wall hung like a place name behind Ugo's head, above his self-assigned seat, which faced an old television set. The stuffed woodcock perched on the refrigerator had a glassy, fiendish stare. The kitchen window was always closed—in winter to keep out cold, in summer to keep out flies—and so the walls were impregnated with accumulated cooking smells: *fritto, fagioli, spezzatino.*

"Me, I can't wait," Ottavia said about her new home. "When will we be living in it, Paolo?"

"In just a few weeks," I said.

"Are you sure?" Ottavia said. "*Così presto?*" It was always as if she were hearing these projections for the very first time.

"*Sì sì,*" I said. "What is there left to do?"

Ottavia never sat when her *padroni* were around. She fussed over phantom pots at the stove. She opened cabinets needlessly and closed them, ill at ease. She pointed to Ugo. "He hates change," she said. "Even this move of a few meters away upsets him. He holds it in, and this is bad. I, instead, holler when I'm angry. He suffers from stomach pains. He doesn't sleep."

"*Sì sì,*" Ugo said, his head down, his lips set in a pout. "I don't want to leave here. *Io, ci sto bene, Dio bono. Non voglio andare proprio!*"

I wondered what Ugo's unvoiced objections were at this point; nearly finished, the house was obviously beautiful. Perhaps it hurt his pride as a man, as the head of a household, to move at someone else's convenience and not by his own choice. It eroded what little self-esteem he had as someone who still "worked the land," as he called it.

"Oh, Paolo," Ottavia said. "You should have seen us last night! Listen to me a minute—*stia a sentì.*"

"*Ma che fai!*" Ugo said, embarrassed. "*Stai zitta!* Don't tell him that!"

"Tell me," I said.

"*No,*" Ugo said, laughing.

"*Sì, sì,*" I said.

"I was awakened in the night," Ottavia said, holding her laughter in. "The bed was shaking something awful. '*O Dio!*' I screamed. 'What's that?' I opened my eyes. The room was all dark. There's Ugo standing on the bed. 'Whee-ee-ee,' he goes, shaking me to bits. Shaking the whole room, the whole house. '*O Dio!*' I go. 'What is it?' 'Whee-ee-ee,' he goes, throwing his head back, like this, Paolo. You see this? '*Ma, Ugo,*' I go. 'Are you crazy?' 'No no,' he goes. 'I'm a horse!' " Ottavia laughed and laughed. We were all laughing, even Ugo at himself. Ottavia tells a story well: " 'Are you crazy?' I go. 'Whee-ee-ee . . .' he goes, 'No no, I'm a horse! Whee-ee-ee!' "

"That's great," I said, laughing hard. I loved the way Ottavia reined herself in gently when she whinnied.

"I told this story to the girls at work this morning," Ottavia said. "How they laughed! 'Whee-ee-ee!' he goes."

All at once Ugo's smile vanished. "And soon I'm living in the stable like an old nag," he said. "Good place for me."

WITH UGO SAFELY IN HIS NEW HOME, OUR ATTEN-
tion turned to the main house, sixteen more months of construction.

Builders are perfectly happy to stop whatever they're doing to take care of extra little jobs in the garden. The grid of cement in back where the red salvia had once staged its unpopular tragedy was finally gone; in its place lay a dull patch of crude, weedy grass: a clean slate.

I saw a picture in a book. A medieval cloister garden that had survived, pretty much in its original state, to the photographic age. Bordered by a loggia of stone columns and arches, this vestige of early Christian times was laid out in the shape of a cross. The picture was taken at the turn of the century, when such convents still housed the odd hooded monk; one of them was shown at work here among the aromatic and medicinal herbs these disciplined, highly cultured men once grew. It suddenly occurred to me, seeing this, that my rear garden adjacent to the loggia, with its arches and columns, resembled the yard of a cloister (even if the loggia didn't go all the way around); all that was missing was the cruciform planting.

Thinking further, and studying whatever reference materials I could find, I concluded that a kind of medieval garden was entirely appropriate for a Renaissance hunting lodge such as mine. It was the medieval garden, in fact, with its Islamic roots, that had inspired the more elaborate Italian gardens of the fifteenth and sixteenth centuries. An allegorical scheme derived from ancient myth, the cruciform plan speaks of the four sacred elements of earth, fire, air, and water; of the four river heads whose source was Eden; of the four quadrants of the universe out of whose center a spring bubbled forth—fertility, eternity, life. The pure quadripartite layout that we see in the interior courtyards of so many early Renaissance palaces—one of the best examples is at Palazzetto Venezia in Rome—was taken from the medieval cloister scheme almost unaltered.

I decided to do a working plan, in scale. With Gil's help I measured the space and drew it out on vellum. The empty garden room I had to work with wasn't quite square, we discovered, but that didn't matter. If you study the layouts of classic Italian gardens, you see that the angles are seldom really right.

Ideally, a fountain would have gone at the garden's center, but I had no such fountain. Old ones are obtainable from local antique dealers, but for tens of thousands of dollars. And plumbing it out to work would have cost thousands more, what with all the digging and man-hours. I decided to draw in a conical box bush at the center instead, surrounded by two concentric circles of dwarf box. The spring of life would indeed rise and ripple here in a shallow pool, but its font and waters would be green.

When I drew out my four quadrants, they looked a little dull to me, even with their angles cut away on the inside with curves. And so I decided to update my scheme by adding another layer to this basic cruciform. I put eight paths leading to the center instead of the traditional four. I wanted my garden to have more complexity, more dwarf hedging, more mini avenues, more design—offer more pleasure.

When my drawing was done, the results surprised me. Without really having intended to, I'd retraced the garden's historical progress across an age; I'd made my medieval cloister garden Renaissance.

I laid out the design in situ with stakes and string, then looked at it from all angles—the best view, unfortunately, was from my bathroom window. I bought the required hundreds of young dwarf box plants and with a little help from Ugo planted them in their rows. Doubtfully I left the prescribed amount of growing space between one and the next; how long would it take, I wondered, for these plants to become a hedge? Patience is the gardener's greatest virtue. I wasn't really a gardener. Not yet.

It was the first true garden I'd built here, and it survives, all grown in, these ten or twelve years later. But in its many incarnations it's traveled full circle, like a loyal squire alongside my own ever changing perception of this *hortus* (not quite) *conclusus*.

Once I'd planted out my eight hedge-enclosed beds, I faced the question of how to fill them. The dividing avenues, I decided, should not be laid with gravel, as they often were in Renaissance gardens. I'd carpet them in grass instead—a softer, warmer, less formal look. In sixteenth-century gardens the angular beds would have been planted very simply, with grass or else with some other green filler, such as

Ophiopogon japponicus. Within these geometric shapes there were potted lemons set upon stone bases: this was the Italian garden in its essential form, green on green with architectural accents of stone and terracotta. But I wanted something a bit more lively, richer. I wanted a garden that might have a useful by-product as well, an edible one. I wanted what the monks had: herbs.

If I'd been after historical accuracy in planting out my cloister-inspired herb garden, I'd have consulted the *Capitulare de Villis*, Charlemagne's horticultural decree of A.D. 812, in which he ordered the cultivation of more than seventy-three herbs in each and every town of the Crown lands. At the Cloisters in Fort Tryon Park in New York City, they've done extensive research into the history of monastic plants for the garden at Bonnefont Cloister; they've even managed to get their hands on the rare Blue Pod Capucijners, a field pea once grown by the Capuchin monks. But I would take it all much less seriously than that; I'd plant whatever herbs I could get my hands on, the ones my table wanted most.

I was much more interested in the culinary than the medicinal—I'd never contrived to imagine myself pounding a Taoist elixir in a stone mortar and self-prescribing the juices. I ended up planting the obvious: rosemary, mint, parsley, chives, coriander, chamomile, sage, marjoram, salad burnet, alpine strawberries, and three or four different species of thyme. I added among these the less delicious tansy, angelica, sweet woodruff, and bergamot.

I don't think I'd ever really followed the progress of a year's growth and decline of such herbaceous plants, and it was fascinating to see what tall flowerings they produced with which to welcome the tour groups of pollinating bees and gorgeous butterflies I'd never known existed here.

In the raised shelf against the garden's back wall we planted white Sea Foam roses, Gil's idea. Though he doesn't like modern, reflowering roses, he selected this one for its reputed vigorous cascade of blooms that just might conceal the cement-covered wall supporting them. Sea Foam was developed in the sixties in the States, a cross between White Dawn and Pinocchio, and its flowers hold a pretty blush tone. Against the south-facing wall I arbor-trained a ceanothus of a mysterious unlabeled species (when I asked Dino Monti if he had Trewithin Blue, he said, "Oh yes," pulled out the one ceanothus he had, and tied a hastily scratched "Trewithin Blue" label to it—I assure myself that he meant well). I planted *Solanum alba*, with its delicate, persistent white flowers, and the climbing rose Marie Viaud, with its clusters of tiny, single mauve-colored blooms. At its feet stands the long-spurred white columbine, *Aquilegia longissima.*

In high summer the herb garden peaked. I wasn't prepared for its feathery, meadow-like wildness; it looked no different from any ordinary section of unmown field along the roadsides here. Mixed herbs gave the garden an English, cottage look that didn't seem quite right in Tuscany. Nor had I expected the plants' disappointingly quick decline, the subsequent onslaught of competing weeds that had to be pulled out almost daily—the herbs themselves were already weedy enough at this point without the real thing wreaking further havoc in their midst. I suppose the old monks, in cultivating their one assigned cloister yard each, might have happily contended with these demands and difficulties, but I had other things to do in life, other gardens to keep.

After a couple of seasons the alpine strawberries, gathered from the wood, were soon overrunning everything. I took it that the garden was telling me what it truly wanted to be: a wild strawberry parterre. Not a bad idea, I thought; why not go with the natural flow?

I pulled out the mixed bouquet of herbs and propagated strawberries in their place: an easy task, as they spread with the vigor of weeds. This new mono-planting lent an order and clarity to the still ill-defined geometry faintly traced out by the young box plants that grew so very slowly. I now had green against green. It all looked suddenly right. Like an American cup of espresso, it was almost Italian.

The strawberries thrived and filled every bed, but not with equal resolve, I'm afraid. Out of eight strawberry triangles there were always at least two recalcitrant ones, some kind of inner struggle going on. Curiously, it was never the same two beds that fell through the net; they took turns going derelict.

Alpine strawberries do a funny thing, I'd eventually discover: they "run out." They reproduce themselves by offset plants which appear at the ends of long, wiry runners. If these new plantlings find themselves in a spot of rich, friable soil, they'll put down their roots, drop their umbilicus, and happily grow. But if they perch upon a tangle of older runners (which in a few seasons are thick as a jute carpet) they give up the ghost. Soon the mother plant dies her natural death, leaving no survivors. Opportunistic weeds take full advantage of the void. Once the most insidious of them get established, there's only one solution to the problem: dig up everything and start from scratch with fresh, weed-free soil.

This is exactly what I did for years and years. My newer beds would send up their virgin yellow-green leaves, then a wealth of the delicious tiny berries whose flavors of violets and rose petals outperform the cultivated strawberry hands down. But my older plants, weaving their self-strangling web, would quickly succumb. Every winter I'd promise myself that this year the eight strawberry puffs would rise together like a batch of muffins in the oven, and the whole garden would look as ordered as it had on paper. But no; that long-sought-for spring of utter harmonic formality never came.

I saw a picture in a magazine. A fashion ad shot in an Italian garden that resembled, in some ways, my strawberry parterre. But instead of strawberries filling the angular box-edged beds, there was grass. Clean, clipped, orderly grass. Grass inside the beds, grass outside. Suddenly, after all my experience with the herbs and the strawberries, grass no longer looked so bleakly uninspired. In fact, wasn't the garden pictured here, with its simple clarity, a feast for the eyes?

This year (ten years later?) I bit the bullet. I dug up all the strawberries, replacing the most oxalis-contaminated soil, and planted grass. With all the rain of the past few weeks, it's doing brilliantly.

In the spring I'll add terra-cotta pots, positioning them symmetrically upon stone bases at the eight right angles flanking the center path of each side. Instead of having lemons in the pots, as one typically does, I'll have orange trees. My newly revised garden will look presentable all year round, the grass always neatly cut, the forms always obvious and concise, its origins and implications fully Italian. Herbs I have in abundance elsewhere; I'll buy the strawberries. Why hadn't I done this in the first place?

What a show I'd get from my bathroom window.

REFERENCES TO THE *VENDEMMIA*, THE GRAPE HAR-
vest, are first heard in the spring as the vines soften and their warmed
sap rises. *Alla vendemmia . . . Dopo la vendemmia . . . per la vendemmia . . . tempo
di vendemmia . . .* Said, the word is imbued with the all-importance people here give the harvest itself, a *festa*, a day of pleasurable work and
celebration, one of the most important milestones in the progress of
a year.

I set the clock for 5:30 A.M., as we'd agreed to start picking at
six-thirty. It was the harvest of our white grapes, and they're said to
yield more fruit flavors when brought to the *cantina* still cool as night.
This isn't the way of old-timers but of modern-day winemakers,
innovative Californians and Australians. Still, Ugo, in his fear of

change, didn't seem at all put out by the idea of getting up at the crack of dawn to pick. Last night he drove the tractor, with its flatbed trailer loaded down with twenty-five empty red plastic *bigoncie*, to the verge of the vineyard so that there would be that much less preparation to do in the dark. He thinks nothing, after all, of getting up in the night to haul his singing caged thrush to the hills, where he sits awaiting non-existent flocks of them in a hunting blind as luxuriously appointed as many living rooms.

There are four of us vintagers today: Ugo, Gil, Alessio, and me. Even numbers are desired as it's best to pick in pairs, one on either side of a line of vines.

Traditionally, one invites friends and extended family to take part in the harvest. *Papà* organizes the equipment and directs the work; *mamma* makes *zuppa della frantoiana*, great yellow ceramic bowls full of the stuff. Various versions of "the miller lady's soup" can be found all over Tuscany. In Florence, for instance, it's called *ribollita*, but it's much the same thing as the ancient Lucchese dish. The recipe: fry finely chopped onion, celery, carrots, and thyme in lots of olive oil. Add black cabbage and swiss chard. When the greens are soft, add tomato concentrate and broth made from pureed white beans. Toss in a few whole cooked white beans, then pour the mix into a bowl over broken pieces of yesterday's Tuscan bread. Let it cool down well before you eat it, each serving individually garnished with olive oil and freshly ground pepper. It's a soup that every cook makes differently, and so I've tasted hundreds of examples of it over the years. One of the very best I've ever had is served at Il Vignaccio in Santa Lucia above Camaiore. A modest ladleful is all you need, as it's rich and complex in flavors; more than a ladleful is a meal in itself.

Our first harvests here we invited everyone we knew to help.

When I think of all the sciatica relapses, the wasp stings, the sliced fingertips, the clumps of mud tracked through the house, the pickers who did it dutifully, without complaint (my mother), those who had so much fun that half the harvest ended up on the ground (the giddy young), those who only wanted the *zuppa* and spent the afternoon by the pool (too much wine at lunch), I know I'm right to have turned the vendemmia into a proper day's work—albeit a unique and enjoyable one. It's the way we approach our whole winemaking effort at this point. We emulate the efforts of the best; why not?

A month ago, for instance, I did a *diradamento*. (When it comes to winemaking, I think in Italian. Perhaps *diradamento* in English is "green harvest," or "July harvest." Or is it simply "thinning"?) I'll explain.

A vine can sometimes make far more bunches of grapes than it is capable of bringing to reasonable ripeness. If a vintage suffers from overproduction, then the wine will be diluted, acidic, thin in structure, weak in fruit flavor. Grape bunches that develop far away from the stock, in a second flowering, tend to stay green no matter how long or ideal the growing season. But in their desperate struggle to ripen they deprive the better grapes of nutrients. Though Ugo does the lion's share of work in our vineyard (the spraying, the plowing, the tieing), it's my job to complete the season's efforts with an educated thinning, a practice he thoroughly disapproves of: "Oh, I don't know, Paolo, all that waste there." How sad he always looks gazing at the severed grape bunches lying in the clay earth at my feet.

"It breaks my heart too," I always tell him, "but I know it's for the best."

He's not so sure.

In the old days here, nothing ever went to waste. Local farmers sought quantity over quality—Ugo claims that he and his extended family require twelve damigiane of wine to get them through a year, nine hundred bottles! He exaggerates nostalgically; no one drinks that much wine anymore.

It's generally agreed that my modernizing tyranny has vastly improved our wine, yet Ugo still feels that the old ways are superior. He cherishes the methods he learned from his father, who learned them from his, who learned them from the ancients: methods we've long since given up on. He laments, for instance, the *governo*: a small quantity of ripe grapes are dried in a cool, airy place, crushed a month or so after the harvest, then added, in full, fresh fermentation, to the barrels of already fermented wine. "What a lovely *frizzantino* quality the governo gives," he claims every year at what ought to be governo time. "My father always said, 'There's nothing like a governo to give the wine such goodness.'" Our skilled young enologist, Massimo Motroni, disagrees, aside. "It doesn't do a thing," he whispers. Even though the pendulum inevitably swings and we return sometimes to abandoned practices (there are those in Burgundy who've gone back to crushing with their bare feet), I doubt that we'll ever revive the *governo*.

Wine was made long before anyone had the skills to take written note of it. As with the pleasure garden, its historical roots are in the East, in Mesopotamia, but by 6000 B.C. wine had reached Egypt and Phoenicia. Four thousand years later the Greeks brought viticulture to Italy, where it seemed to find its true home; soon, in fact, they'd call this peninsula Oenotria, land of the wine.

When we first arrived here, Ugo made his wine much the way the ancients did. The Romans used wooden barrels of various sizes and shapes for harvesting, fermentation, storage. The wine was aged in wide-bottomed glass bottles shaped very much like those we've phased out of our cantina, as nowadays they imply a second-rate quality—jug wine. Roman wines tasted, perhaps, very much like my neighbors' wines do today—almost everyone in this "*Conca*" tends at least a couple of rows of vines. These simple country *vinelli* vary enormously in quality. Some, in their filthiness, can send a never ending series of gagging spasms throughout your entire system, while others can charm you with their light effervescence.

Most of us foreigners take up residence in Tuscany with romantic misconceptions about honest wines made by peasants using picturesque methods, tried and true—what could be better? The hand-cranked oak crushers, the open fermentation tanks, the rush-covered demijohns, the unlabeled bottles and *fiaschi* sealed with a few drops of liquid paraffin you later suck out with a glass tubular instrument that seems, in its archetypal design, old as winemaking itself. When the wine we produce is our own (made by our local help, of course) we tend not to notice its defects. "This is our own wine, by the way," we boast, raising our cloudy brown beakers, the rancid cellar smells already permeating. We have no idea about hygiene in the cantina; we've never stuck our noses into those blackened chestnut barrels, which almost always reek of vinegar, mold, insidious mutating bacteria. "Our wine isn't very good this year," we tell our friends, "but you're going to have to drink it anyway." They taste it. It isn't very good, they agree. But is it really any worse than last year's? they wonder.

I'm always surprised when I see today's travel writers recommending the house wine in European country restaurants. Some of these experts even go as far as to say that the house wine in Italian trattorias is *always* better than anything you'll find in labeled bottles. Perhaps they've fallen for the famous fib: Oh, this excellent house wine of ours is made by a little farmer down the road, no additives, no chemicals—*vino genuino*. Even a modest trattoria needs three or four demijohns of wine a week to keep their clients in drink. Very few little farmers down the road could possibly keep up with that kind of demand and still remain little farmers down the road. In general, "house wines" are made by huge business-focused producers who, having bought grapes, no matter how poor in quality, from anyone who's willing to sell them, proceed to vinify using every tricky industrial intervention imaginable to bring the wine up to a sellable consistency and quality. Though it's delivered to the restaurant in charmingly unmarked demijohns, in a rickety old truck, the wine is strictly plonk cleverly disguised in folksy garb. My spirits sink when my misinformed dining companions insist, "*Vino della casa!*" then look at me, awaiting my familiar snobbish objections, which I'm once again embarrassed into withholding so as not to hear, "There he goes again, Mr. Chateau Effete."

Our vineyard occupies a plot of land that's called "Rio di Massa" on the county estate maps. Planted in our early years here, it replaced the old vineyard further up towards the house that the Olivers planted ten years before we arrived. The old vineyard's Sangiovese grapes (the basis of most Tuscan reds, Chianti included) rarely ripened on a west-facing terrace that didn't see the sun until ten o'clock in the morning. Only twice in its life did that vineyard produce a wine one could serve without a healthy measure of compunction. Ugo's working methods in the cantina have always been clean and careful, and so our wine, even in the worst of years, never had unpleasant smells; but just two good vintages out of fifteen? Those were bad showings, it seemed to me. I reasoned, If we're going to bother making wine at all, then let's make a drinkable one. I tore the old vineyard out and planted, on this better, sunnier site below, a thousand grapevines (they all fit into the trunk of my car) of varieties that promised to do well here, on root stalks appropriate for our soil, which had been fully analyzed and evaluated.

Because our sub-climate is cooler than the better-known wine-producing areas of this valley, I planted French grapes: cabernet sauvignon, merlot, and cabernet franc. For white, I planted chardonnay and pinot blanc. Avoiding the native Sangiovese and white Trebbiano grapes that require a long, hot growing season, I would inevitably make international-style wines. This idea couldn't be more out of fashion to purists who mourn the sad disappearance of regional nuance, but I preferred to succeed, however modestly, with those grapes than to fail dismally making "typical" wines that couldn't possibly come out well in the foothills of the Compitese. If I lived across the valley, in the D.O.C. of *Vino delle Colline Lucchesi*, I'd be traditionalist to the letter, but for better or for worse, I simply don't.

When the bulldozers dug in, preparing the site of our new vineyard, the quality of the soil surprised us all. The job of site preparation is this: you remove the top four or five feet of soil and put it aside. You remove the next four feet and put that aside. The top soil gets put back in first, and the poorer soil goes on top. In this way the young grapes, looking for nutrients, send their tap roots straight down through the freshly loosened ground, establishing themselves more quickly. As the excavations ensued, more and more stones appeared: stones of all sizes in a thick minestrone of gravel and red clay. We were at the banks of a torrent, Rio di Massa, and our soil was as rocky as that of the Gironde in Bordeaux, where the red grapes I'd chosen make some of the best wines in the world.

In Roman times this area below Lucca, bordered on the south by the Monti Pisani, was alluvial and lacustrine. It was the route of a serpentine tributary of the river Auser, which today no longer exists. Interlaced with streams and brooks, the area is cool, fertile, lush. The Romans, in making their way northward into Gaul, planted their vines by the riverside. It was a matter of circumstance and convenience, as the rivers were their highways along which merchandise such as wine could be easily transported. We can't be sure that the Romans made wine on this very plot of ground that is now mine, but historical agricultural records show that wine was made in Massa Macinaia as early as the Middle Ages. Pilgrims, en route to and from the Via Francigena to the north, found lodging here, hot meals, wine for the road. The door of a sixteenth-century *bottega* along Via di Sottomonte down the road is framed out with stone upon which is carved the shape of a wine bottle and a glass, further proof that the wine of this area was commercialized as early as then.

Ugo has always been convinced that there's something about the soil here that gives our fruit outstanding flavor. It's true, for instance, that our peaches yield a wealth of tastes seldom found in commercially grown produce. Attribute this goodness to *terroir*, as the French call it, the blessings of the earth—not just any earth, but this particular earth.

Our production is minuscule, sixty cases of red, fifty cases of white; so little that it's sold out before we bottle it, mostly to those few restaurants we like best. I named our red wine Tempietto after our beloved grotto, whose reddish facade was inspired by Greek temples. The white is called Sorbus, the Latin name for the mountain ash tree. In the 1920s this villa was owned by a certain Dr. Sorbi. Local people still call it Villa Sorbi, and not Villa Massei, the earlier, historical name we've exhumed, preferring the sound of it. Though there are several mountain ashes on this land, our white wine is in fact named after the Sorbi family—a kind of posthumous dedication, a gentle bow to the villa's recent past about which we know so little.

Mornings in late summer, no one stirs. Wearing shorts, a T-shirt, and my Swiss hiking boots, I make my way past the kitchen garden to the vineyard. It's only eighteen degrees centigrade, but I know that by the time I've worked awhile, it'll be hot. The sky is overcast, but no rain is predicted. In my right hand I carry a pair of lightweight needle-nosed grape shears made by Sandwick of Sweden.

Everyone's on time. I heard Alessio's motorbike as I finished breakfast. Just eighteen, he's a student at the agricultural high school in Pescia. He began working for us in the garden several months ago as part of his academic field obligations. We had only the slimmest hopes of finding anyone when Gil first contacted the school offering this far-fetched "stage" arrangement. Alessio's a rarity: an Italian teenager who likes to work. In his entire circle of friends, in fact, he's the only one who does. They call him names because of it, he told me, preferring not to say what these names were. Throughout this summer he tended the garden pretty much on his own, as I become even less of a gardener when the sun is high. He's young, but he's learning. He loves the vendemmia. He's not so keen on tieing vines, but picking grapes appeals enormously.

The grapes this year are in a perfect state of health, no mold, no rot. The skins of the chardonnay are golden; handling them, your hands grow quickly sticky from the sugars. By the time the sun comes up, wasps will compete for the sweet juices, a good sign—foxes have already taken the odd nibble in the night.

I insist on placing a picking basket directly under the grapes as I harvest. Shaped like an English gardener's "trug," it's cut low and wide.

The modern versions of it we use are made of plastic, far less esthetic than the old wicker ones but more efficient. No matter how carefully you handle the individual bunches as you cut them away from the wood, at least a few grapes tend to fall to the ground. Inexperienced pickers leave the vineyard littered with severed grapes from one end to the other; it might not seem like much of a loss plant for plant, but by the time an entire row is picked so carelessly, a lot of potential wine has gone to waste.

Once my picking basket is full, I dump its contents into a *bigoncia*. When we first arrived here Ugo still used wooden *bigonce*, just as the Romans did. Now we have plastic ones, ugly but far lighter and easier to carry. A *bigoncia* stands three feet high. At its top it's about fourteen inches wide, but it narrows a bit at the base. Their design is ancient. Peasants—a human conveyer belt of them—once walked through the vineyards at vendemmia time with bigonce strapped to their backs like rucksacks. Pickers unloaded their grapes into the bigonce as the bearers passed, then went on with their work without losing momentum and precious time. Bigger barrels, carried on an ox-drawn cart, stood by. When these were full, they were brought to the cellars, where the grapes were eventually crushed by foot. Our modern method is to station the plastic bigonce here and there about the vineyard as we work, filling them in place. Once they're full we put them on the tractor's cart, then haul them to the electric crusher in the cantina.

Picking in pairs, we chat. It's a great social opportunity, a time of storytelling, full of easy banter and quips. We eavesdrop on the conversations of other nearby pairs of pickers, and we shout our unexpected retorts to them unseen beyond the grape leaf curtains.

Ugo, on these momentous days, takes to reminiscing, of course. Every year he tells the same story of Midge and Mac Oliver picking grapes in the rain. "*O, quell'anno lì,*" he says, "how it rained, but hard, I mean hard! I said to Oliver, I said, now we must stop or the harvest will be ruined. Water in the wine in proportions decided by God and not by us drinkers? This is not good, no no. Oh, but the *signora* insisted we go on. '*Andiamo avanti, finiamo tutto!*' Oh, that year there!"

I laugh every time I hear Ugo's old stories. "So how did the wine turn out?" I ask, knowing the answer.

"*O, Paolo,*" he says, frowning tragically. "*Quel vino lì! Ma era una cosa da buttar via. Una tragedia. Acqua, tutta acqua!*"

No sooner do these words pass his lips than rain begins to fall. Huge, slow-falling drops are hitting the grape leaves with brutal dull thuds. I look up at the darkening sky. I remember seeing photographs of the Burgundy harvest of 1975 when they were all out there picking in yellow raincoats.

"Stop the harvest!" I shout, only half-jokingly.

Ugo's smile appears through the canopy of grapes. "No, Paolo," he says, chuckling.

We go on picking. The rain comes down hard, harder. "Hurry." Ugo shouts. "Gather the bigonce and load the tractor." We rush and work, covering the full bigonce with empty ones. "We'll take it in," Ugo says. "It's not quite a full cart, but in with it!" At the vendemmia I do exactly as he says. Experience is everything; he has far more than I.

A few minutes later we're in the cantina. Alessio, who travels by motorbike, is wearing his ever ready rain jacket. Gil, Ugo, and I are damp, if not wet.

"Is the harvest ruined?" Gil asks.

"No no," Ugo says. "A glass of water we're talking about. Nothing. Not even a glass. Look here, the grapes are dry."

It's true.

Alessio and Ugo unload the bigonce into the noisy crusher the Olivers bought in the sixties. A wide, ribbed tube brings the soupy results, crushed and stemmed, to a stainless steel fermentation tank where the juices will stay in contact with the skins until tomorrow morning, when we'll press. It's the first time we've tried this skin-contact method, which promises to give us more pronounced fruit flavors. In previous years we've separated the skins from the liquid at crushing.

I look outside through the arched cantina doorway. Rain is falling hard to the green lawn and hedges, which have been irrigated nightly all summer—we're an oasis. The crusher wails, rattling. Grape smells fill the air. Riga the cat protests at the window—she hates cantina work for some reason. An interrupted harvest is a nightmare: one batch of grapes fermenting to one schedule, another at a different one. Big wineries are used to crushing over an extended period of days, weeks even. We're not. In all my years here to date the rain has never fallen on our vendemmia.

I taste the fresh juices—richly fruited, concentrated, full-bodied even at this point. I drink a whole glass of it.

The rain stops. The crusher stops. "Can we go on?" I ask.

"*Sì sì*," says Ugo. "*Non era niente.* You'll see; the grapes are still dry under the leaves, which protect them like little eaves."

Back at the vineyard I see that he is right. While the leaves are gently dripping, the grapes are as dry as they were at six-thirty this morning. We have to pick more carefully now—don't shake the leaves or the raindrops will fall into the picking baskets, diluting everything.

Ottavia appears. "Oh, Ugo," she says, a little annoyance in her tone. "Where is my sieve?"

"In the *limonaia*," he says, "in that brown box there."

"*O Dio*," she says, frustrated. She was busily preparing our customary lunch until this bothersome snag appeared—the vineyard's a long walk from her kitchen. "Oh, how I hate it when I can't find things," she says. "My sieve in the limonaia, who has ever heard of such a thing? I've looked everywhere, taken apart my whole house. Up and down, here and there I've looked. Why do you play these ugly tricks on me, Ugo?" Laughing from the pickers all around. A laugh from Ottavia, another from Ugo. "My sieve in the limonaia," she says. "What, are we all crazy?"

The morning is stop-and-go. The thoughtful rain has timed itself to our completed cartloads; just as we reach the cantina, down it comes. But lucky for us, it doesn't rain for long, and it never falls so hard that the grapes get wet. By late morning, in fact, the clouds have passed. The sun peeks out, but we urge it back under cover. With these cooling showers the grapes are chilly to the touch, just what you want.

By one-thirty the last bunch of grapes has been crushed. The harvest completed, we turn on our clever makeshift cooling system. White grapes are ideally fermented at 18 to 20 degrees centi-grade. Big wineries have refrigerated tanks, temperature-controlled. A similar system for our small cantina would cost about five thousand dol-lars, more than we care to spend on such a thing. Instead we bought a deep freeze and filled it full of plastic containers of water. Outside the cantina door there's a stone watering trough with a tap above it. The water at this tap is pumped up from the passing stream, and it's already naturally cold. What we've done is this: we've coiled up a long length of hose in the trough, then filled the trough with water cooled down to nine degrees by four or five of these large containers of ice. The hose leads to the top of the fermentation tank, where there's a perforated loop. The emitted water over the vat envelops it in a chilling veil as the water constantly runs. Twice a day we put in fresh ice. At the hottest point in its fermentation the must is at an ideal 19 degrees. Imagine, all this state-of-the-art technology for a modest investment of $300.

Ottavia calls us to lunch. We cross the sun-brightened entry court, where water trickles from the stone dolphin's lips in its niche of aquatic plants. Riga the cat cheers up, purring at the sight of us.

Ottavia has set her kitchen table with their best tablecloth and stemmed glasses. Their approach to entertaining has radically changed now that they're in their new house. While Ugo continues to insist that he made the forced move across the garden *"malvolentieri,"* he can't con-ceal the joys resulting from their advancement to middle-class. A month after moving in, they went shopping. A new bedroom suite, a new kitchen table, and to grace it with, new flatware, stemmed glasses, new white porcelain that looks somewhat like our *Antico Ginori*, the dinner service Ottavia so admires. Soon they were giving dinner parties. One evening I walked through the garden at dusk to spot Ottavia in her kitchen window lighting candles in tall crystal candle holders. Moments later, a late-model Mercedes pulled up to the limonaia. The next day Ottavia told me who it was: one of the bosses from the thread factory where she had been working for more than thirty years. "He's the nice one," she said, "a *bravo signore*. It's the first time I've dared to have him."

Breaking with tradition today, she serves us *pasta e fagioli*.

"Does your mother cook this well?" I ask Alessio, giving Ottavia the indirect compliment. She's very self-effacing in the kitchen. Whenever we dine with them there, she insists that she's ruined every dish we're served. In truth, she's an excellent cook for whom no amount of extra preparation is too much of a bother. Her pasta e fagioli is brilliant comfort food.

"This dish is a new one on me," Alessio says. "Ottavia, this is *very* good, truly. This is a *novità*."

Ottavia's fond of Alessio.

We eat the pasta e fagioli. We eat the vegetarian stuffed zucchini flowers Ottavia prepared for Gil and me, as neither of us eats meat anymore. I wonder why I'm feeling so sleepy until I remember that I got up at five-thirty.

"And by the way," Ottavia says, slapping her husband on the arm and smiling by half. "My sieve. It wasn't in that damn brown box of yours in the limonaia."

"Oh no?" Ugo says.

"No," she says.

"Where was it, then?"

"Never mind," she says. "Never mind where the devil it was, for heaven's sakes. But it wasn't in that damn brown box of yours, good God." She looks at me, a long-suffering smile, a laugh she can't contain. "I married a lunatic," she says. "*Dio bono! Ma ché, siamo matti?*"

chapter five

A HARD PRUNE

THERE'S A STORY THAT GOES HERE. THOUGH IT
isn't about my garden per se, it's the story of my garden's birth:

Nigel arrived. He was here to "view" our villa. The leather briefcase
he carried was bulging at its ripped seams with the brochures he'd produced describing the choice properties he'd listed and sold to his
mostly British clients. He hadn't set foot in this house since he and
Helen came to dinner more than a year ago with two gentlemen
friends of ours. The next morning Nigel phoned to say, "No no, you
see, you must never invite one woman alone in a group of men. No
no, you see, they need someone to go to the powder room with. You
must never, ever do that." This social gaffe seemed to mark the end of

our friendship until Helen invited Gil and me to Easter dinner. "She seems to like you chaps," Nigel commented in his ironic British way. "For the life of me, I can't understand why."

"What a relief to see you've redecorated," Nigel said. He was referring to the hideous pink carpet we used to have under the dining room table. "I was so afraid you'd have done it all up in some vulgar Hollywood perversion of what an Italian villa might be." Sometimes I'm mildly offended when Nigel, with his better English style, declares so tirelessly his cultural superiority to the American primitives.

"Yes, yes," Nigel acclaimed, strolling through room after finished, fulfilled room, praising everything he saw: the freshly completed tromp l'oeil molding with its egg and dart motif in tones of white on white, the brand-new handmade terra-cotta floor that looked as if it had always been there. His sincerity was made especially clear when he said that this was "*the* prettiest house" he'd ever been asked to offer and that its "infrastructure is the finest in the Lucchesia." But Gil, for one, didn't care to feel flattered just now, to be honored in such a way for his achievement. "This is my *home*," he whispered regretfully, already sensing the distance between himself and his beloved villa, which would soon go tumbling off into space at the end of a severed life line. "*My* home," he said in a weary voice heard only by me.

It was the nineties. Like a guest with expensive tastes, the eighties had come and gone, and we were left with all the bills. Not only had our independent sources of income suddenly fallen off, but our dreams of supplementing them with the farm's revenues had by now completely vanished. No matter how much fertilizing and pruning we did in our olive groves, the trees never seemed to yield any more fruit than previous years. The good wine we made we bottled and sold, but necessary reinvestment in the *cantina* ate up what little profits we'd managed to earn. Months passed and things got only worse; no hope of improvement in sight, only the gloom of accumulated debt. We weren't broke, by any means, but we were sitting housebound on nearly all the capital we had—not an intelligent way of life, it seemed to me. There had to be a better way.

I suppose I was the one who first made the unpopular suggestion that we sell the villa and move on. Perhaps we should go back to the States, I felt; there, at least, we could legally work. I invented whatever persuasive argument I could find to convince Gil that it was the right thing to do. It was a hard proposition for both of us, a decision we made together. Selling the house seemed like our only way out of a financial bind that grew tighter with every day that passed, and so that's why we called in Nigel Sundius-Hill.

It was the day the Greeks were scheduled to view the house. They'd been looking for a villa in the Lucchesia for two and a half years. Nigel was sure they'd find Villa Massei to their liking. "This sort of farm is just what Captain L. wants," Nigel said the other day, over his usual glass of whiskey with a lot of water and very little ice. "He wants to drive a tractor. No no, you see, you mustn't get the wrong impression. He thinks of himself as a regular Greek. He may have billions, but no no no." When I passed this information on to Ugo, his response was, "Perhaps we could plow a wide path through the woods to give him a course. It would be beautiful. Round and round he could go on that tractor there as much as he wants." Ugo, apparently, liked the idea of a billionaire *padrone* who would spice up his life with foolish extravagance, perhaps an outlandish raise in pay as well.

They arrived in a motorcade of four cars, all long and darkly reflecting. Carrying winged antennae like standards, they crept slowly, ominously, up the driveway, as if toward a battle or a burial. Ugo and his family were pasted to their kitchen window, watching with amazement. It was late September, 1993. It had started raining about two weeks earlier and had stopped only for an hour or two since. But the sky opened up now for the buyers' advance. All at once the front garden was flooded with sunlight; it brought out the revived greens of the lawn and made the roses straighten their stalks as if poised for a miraculous reflowering.

The visiting party was made up of Captain and Mrs. L., the captain's brother and his wife, two other couples who were part of the family in a more distant way, the local man who sold them their private sailing yacht, and his driver. "Greeks travel entourage," Nigel said, making arrangements for this visit.

Gathered in small groups, they lingered for a while out on the lawn, estimating the views to the valley and hills. All together they turned, following the captain's lead, to study the villa's colorful facade. Muttering a few guttural sounds, they seemed impressed.

"Only some of us will actually be coming in," Nigel said, climbing the steps with the aid of an aluminum crutch. He'd made a quick trip to London about a week ago and come back with a broken foot, saying he'd fallen while kicking up his heels at a wedding; I suspected he'd had a bit too much to drink. Nigel was followed by his own assistant, Susan, an Englishwoman who'd been living here certainly as long as he had.

Mrs. L. preceded her husband. She was in her thirties, I guessed. She wore black stretch slacks with stirrups that ran into her flat, sporty alligator shoes. Her enormous cashmere sweater expanded around her broad hips—Nigel said she tended to eat boxes and boxes of fine Swiss chocolates at a sitting. Her husband, who was a mere two-thirds her height and width, wore pressed denim pants and a light jacket. He was in his sixties and bald. His suntanned face was covered with freckles. They'd just returned from a cruise in the Red Sea on their twenty-million-dollar yacht—everything in their life seemed to have a conspicuous price tag attached.

I welcomed them at the front door. When Nigel introduced me Mrs. L. said, with a clear tone of disbelief, "I didn't understand. This is *your* house?"

"Yes," I said. Perhaps I didn't look wealthy enough.

Nigel started right in explaining the obvious. "This is the entry hall," he said. "This door leads to the loggia and rear garden."

While the L.'s viewed the inside of the house, the yacht magnate smoked a cigarette out by the grotto, where the stone masks grimaced like demons, spewing water to clear, dark pools. Gil and I fended off his exaggerated compliments. "Perhaps it is the most beautiful place in all of Lucca," he said conclusively.

"Thank you," I said.

"But you must watch out for these Greeks," he explained. He hardly lowered his voice as the L.'s filed past upstairs windows, glancing one by one into the cloister-style garden, which had finally begun to fill in. "They are a very irrational people," he said. "They know right away when they want something, and when they want something, they must have it. They are not like us Italians, who have to weigh all the factors pro and con and change our minds many times. They are impulsive, like children."

"Oh really," I said. I knew the L.'s had already decided; they loved the villa, and wanted it.

"I did not want to come here with the captain today," the yacht builder said, "but I am content to see such a beautiful place. The captain insisted I accompany them, and as I am in the process of negotiating with him on a new, still larger yacht, I would have been a fool to have said no."

"Maybe our price is too low," Gil told me when the man wandered off to touch the camphor tree.

In a while Gil and I found Nigel alone in the entry hall. "Susan is taking them through one more time," he said, "then they'll tour the grounds. I can't manage with this bloody foot. They love the house, of course. Listen, do you think I could have a secret beer?" The way he wore that crutch he looked like a pirate who'd taken our ship by force.

The L.'s spent more than an hour walking the garden and farmlands. When I caught sight of them way off in a distant field, where we'd wanted to establish a commercial raspberry patch, I was convinced that the L.'s were as serious as Nigel claimed.

The rest of the L. party made themselves comfortable in the wicker furniture of the loggia. They waited in clouds of smoke like passengers on a ferryboat with an all too familiar destination. I was relieved to hear voices out on the front lawn; I couldn't wait for them to go. I heard shuffling footsteps as they passed through the entry hall to join the captain and his wife, Nigel and Susan, for one last look at the front garden and its views.

When Gil and I went out to say goodbye, the captain and his wife climbed the stairs to meet us. "How shall we proceed?" the captain asked. He was holding an enormous unlit Havana cigar.

"Nigel here will handle everything," Gil said, hiding the sadness in his voice.

"We have fallen in love with your house," said Mrs. L. Her wide shoulders rose ecstatically, but her still face held no expression.

The captain flicked his cigar as if to knock off the head of ash that wasn't there. "You can have the money anywhere you want it in the world," he said, and then he smiled like Santa Claus.

That night I couldn't sleep. It wasn't until dawn's yellow light filled the bedroom windows that I drifted off and dreamt. Gil and I were in Africa, the deep, dark part—perhaps it was colonial Rhodesia, a long, long time ago. We were visiting an American couple who had enormous land holdings and a tumble-down wooden mansion that could have been in Mississippi. The man explained that he and his wife were selling the farm and moving to Portland, Oregon. "Enough is enough," he said, "the termites, the amoebae." They wanted a condominium now. He took us for a walk along his water meadows. The sky was convex, low as the roof of a tent made heavy with dew. The air felt trapped. Every living thing looked debilitated by the heat, which promised to be unending. In a while the three of us came to a village. The streets were unpaved. There was utter silence everywhere. There were groups of natives, in somber prints, gathered at intersections. The houses were painted in Tuscan colors, but the trees among them belonged to the subtropics. The master's servants, who'd been sent ahead, had laid a table with a white cloth along the riverbank. They were scooping vanilla ice cream out of a nickel canister. Gil said, "And you mean to tell me you're giving all of this up for Portland?"

"Mrs. L.," Nigel said, "has been staying on in Forte dei Marmi for a few days, eating herself into a stupor at Da Lorenzo. She would like to see the house once more before she goes back to London on Thursday. Her dear little unspeakably rich husband has advised her against it because he doesn't want to seem too eager, but she's coming round anyway, if that's all right with you."

Gil had gathered flowers. I'd arranged them in vases and placed them in visually dull angles of the living rooms. I'd flushed out the fountains in the grotto, Mrs. L.'s favorite thing. Water now rushed from the mouths of its sculpted masks like a single sung word of encouragement.

It was another freak dry moment in a period of endless thunder-showers. Mrs. L., no entourage in tow, got out of Nigel's broken down Fiat without having to throw an umbrella over her head. She was dressed in that same bulky three-thread cashmere sweater, those same black slacks that looked like sixties stretch ski pants.

I took her around. She already had detailed plans for the breakfast room, which I too found decoratively unexploited. "I'm going to stencil these walls," she said, as if the house were already hers. "I am very good at this kind of work. I did the bathroom on our yacht, and it came out very, very nicely." I remembered the photos Nigel once showed us of the L.'s sailboat, which was featured in an Italian yachting magazine. What made her think a folksy bath belonged in a futuristic yacht? I wondered.

We toured the garden. "This is an *Olea fragrans*," I said, pro-nouncing its erroneous name in the French manner as do our expatri-ate friends. "It blooms in October," I said, "little cream-colored flowers that have a strong perfume. You can smell it even in the kitchen, if the windows are open."

"Oh, I *love* plants with strong scents," Mrs. L. said. I was sur-prised that she could still enjoy, in spite of her billions, the simple pleasures available to anyone who bothered to go after them. From now on I'd speak to her in a lowered, more understanding voice.

She balked when I suggested it, but I told her that it would be unwise to put off meeting Ugo and his family, seeing the inside of their beautifully restored farmhouse.

It was lunchtime and they were all at home eating. I felt bad barging in on them like this, but of course Ugo insisted that it was no inconvenience. He made a big show of having his son, Fabio, turn off the television set, as though Fabio were the only one watching it. Mrs. L. offered Ugo her hand. I could see the reserve in his eyes. Ugo hated the thought of taking orders from a woman, especially, no doubt, one who outweighed him by a third. He positioned chairs by the fireplace and invited his guests to sit. He gestured to the *fiasco* of wine on the table, then glanced at a row of stemmed glasses, recent acquisitions, on a shelf in their newly acquired faux rustic credenza.

"May I show her the upstairs real quick?" I asked, glancing at their plates of *tortelli* with *ragú* and salivating secretly.

"*O Dio,*" Ottavia said, always worried about the condition of her spotless house, "*è un trasando.*"

We climbed the stairs. Mrs. L. glanced into Sandra's room. Her walls were no longer decorated, as they used to be, with posters of Italian teen idols, but with framed bird prints and hanging fringed silk scarves. Sandra had a fiancé now. She had a job, and her own brand-new Seat.

What first met the eye in Fabio's room was the Chinese paper kite Gil and I had bought for him in Xian last year. "A lovely child's room," Mrs. L. said.

In Ugo's and Ottavia's bedroom, Mrs. L. went straight to the window. It framed the ingratiating tableau of a terraced olive grove—one of the builders described the scene as worthy of Giotto, and that's how I'll always think of it. As her wide nose gently touched the glass, light filled her eyes and the room darkened. Why couldn't this stillness last forever? I wondered, thinking about Ugo and Ottavia. What does the future hold for them? I wished it was not in my hands. Why did it have to be in my hands?

"A lovely view," Mrs. L. said. She turned away from the window and the room brightened. Numbers clicked away, portentously, on the face of a digital clock by the bed.

Later, when she was gone, Gil asked me, "What other ideas did she have?" He'd turned on all the lights in the *salone*, as if guests were coming.

"She wants to make my study her dressing room," I said. "She said, 'Oh, we are so spoiled, we Greeks. We must have lots of cupboard space.' "

"Spoiled," Gil repeated, obviously thinking about how enormous the bedroom closets already were. "Is she some kind of an asshole or something?"

"No," I said, "not at all. She was sort of embarrassed to be telling me that. She's real shy, in fact."

"Well," Gil said sadly, "sounds like she'll be happy here."

"She'd like to make this her primary residence," I explained. "She's going to convince her husband to spend more and more time here each year."

"When you went into the breakfast room," Gil asked, "was Riga in there?"

"Yes," I said. "On her bed, on the chair."

"And did Mrs. L. go to her and pet her? Did she say anything to her, like, Oh, what a beautiful cat you are?"

"No."

"What did she do, then, just ignore her?"

"Right," I said regretfully. We'd been planning to leave Riga here where she was born (in the peonies), at home where she belonged.

Riga's in the window—in my mind, I saw this happening: back and forth she goes, on the outside sill, like a panther in a cage. Mrs. L.'s in the breakfast room. "There's that damn cat again," she says to the walls she's busily stenciling.

I tried different chairs as Gil asked me things. Just now I was in the green one, the one with the tufted "capitonnet" back and carved dolphin heads where your hands fall. This piece I would take with us, wherever we went.

"And what did she think of Ugo and Ottavia?" Gil asked.

" 'Oh,' she said, when we'd left their house, 'they're so nice. You have such lovely people working for you.' "

"She said it just like that?"

"Yes," I said, my own voice intimate, barely audible, "just like that. She's really very sweet. 'Oh,' she said, 'they're such nice, nice people. I'm so happy that's the case.' "

Gil went to one of the windows and adjusted the folds where a gilded rosette held the curtain open and in place. So much research and work, so much love, had gone into this house. Gil leaned his elbows on the windowsill, the way he does at the dinner table, looking out. He stood there, bent over and staring for the longest time, as if it were the feast of Santa Croce, as if the village congregation had come back again after not having bothered for the past several years, as if they were out there on the lawn, all of them, Franco the butcher, Jessica from the *bottega*, and Don Pera, the stirring orator, back from the grave, stepping, with a conscious holy look on his face, through the yellow carpet of banksia rose petals Gil had laid, as if the long path his life followed were forever strewn with them.

In a while, he turned and looked at me; I'd just given up my favorite chair for a more comfortable one.

"I'm so happy to see you crying," Gil said. "But what is it? What's come over you?"

"She'll be flying back to London this morning," Nigel said, speaking of Mrs. L., "where she will run into the open arms of her dear husband, Croesus, who will be meeting her at the airport. I just hope she doesn't miss him and fall on her face, that's all. I mean, it's just that she's so-oh big, and he so-oh little."

"When can we expect to see an offer?" Gil asked.

"Tomorrow," Nigel said. "Is that soon enough?"

The next day, after numerous telephone conversations with Nigel, Captain L. agreed to pay our slightly lowered asking price. But when the confirming fax came in at Villa Massei, something was wrong. The captain was suddenly willing to pay only one-third of the purchase price in dollars. He wanted to fix the balance in Italian lire, converting it to dollars at the time of the sale's completion three months later, doing so at the "forward rate." An international businessman, he knew the dollar could do nothing but go up in the coming quarter. This plan of action would have ended up costing us more than fifteen percent of the sales price.

"And what is this 'forward rate' stuff?" I asked Gil. "What's that supposed to be?"

Gil made a few phone calls to banks and learned that the forward rate was based on the difference between the interest rates of the two currencies exchanged. There was no doubt that the forward rate in this transaction would work in the captain's favor.

"He's tricking us," Gil said. "We'd lose big if we agree to this.

He's a shifty bastard. He's got a computer with all this stuff in it and we don't. He's killing us."

We sat down and did some calculations. What could we buy in New York, for instance, with so much less money than we'd thought we were getting? We'd be trading our beautiful home in Tuscany for nothing in return, it seemed—for a modest apartment in an unappealing neighborhood in transition.

"We can't accept this," Gil said. "If I have to give up my house, I want to be paid for it, and paid well. This offer's no good."

I went to my computer and wrote a counter offer in response to the captain's fax. We asked for the full amount to be paid in dollars, fixed against our lire asking price at its current exchange rate. A few hours later, the fax rang. We watched as the colonel's letterhead got printed and a negative response rolled out. The Captain wouldn't budge.

"It's off," Gil said, angry but resolute. "That's it. I've had it. I give up. Let's take a little trip. Interested in Greece?"

That evening, Nigel called. "Mrs. L. will be closing her legs for a few days," he said. Gil, wanting to pass on this comment, found me in the breakfast room studying the white walls as if I'd never seen them before.

"What are you looking at?" he asked, the way he always questions the object of my gaze, whatever it might be.

"I thought I'd stencil this room," I said. "What do you think of pale gray against the white, with a sky blue border all around?"

We were about to set out for Brindisi and the ferry to Greece, where we'd reconsider everything. I decided that we'd follow Oscar Wilde's itinerary across the Peloponnese. Perhaps we'd have pictures taken of ourselves in *fustanellas* and white stockings with red pom-poms, as Wilde and his friends did. I wanted to climb a mountain on the back of an ass to a little-known temple at its summit, where Gil and I would undergo a kind of redemption, where we'd be safe from distress and harm, where we'd be free eternally from the consequences of our mistakes.

The telephone rang. As always, Gil answered. The way he raised his brow, I understood that it was the captain on the line. Gil spoke to him calmly, softly, and not the way he would have spoken to a tricky bastard who'd been trying to kill us. "I see," he said. "Yes, of course," he said, nodding as if the captain could see him, "but I'll have to talk to Paul about it and get back to you."

When Gil hung up, the sadness of a few days ago threw a dark veil over his face. "He hadn't meant to upset us, he said. They love our house and will pay us what we want on our terms. He was very nice, very apologetic. He's sorry for the misunderstanding about the forward rate and all that. They'll pay the full price. I said I'd have to check with you first. What should we do?"

"Let's go out to lunch," I said, "think it over."

"OK," Gil said, "but I know what the decision will be."

"You do?" I asked. Why didn't I know myself?

"Those motives of ours for selling will never go away," Gil said. "We'll have to say yes, I'm afraid. We have no choice."

It was the day of the *compromesso*. The L.'s had flown down in their private jet. We were with our lawyer, Michelle, an American friend of ours who lives in Florence. I was surprised when the L.'s, accompanied by their two young sons and their Greek financial adviser, showed up for the meeting at their attorney's office wearing sports clothes.

"I misunderstood," Captain L. said, holding a fresh, unlit cigar. "I thought we were going to the house first." He looked at Gil and me. "Do you mind if we do that?" he asked. "Go to the house? I'm not interested in all these legal documents. This is what we have lawyers for. Let's let them do what they are hired to do."

Captain L. had to go to the bank first. Gil and I, along with Nigel's assistant, accompanied the L. family to Piazza San Michele. While the captain and his wife were in the bank, Gil lectured the children on the history of Lucca. "And do you know who completed the work on these walls?" he asked Alan, the older boy, who was a student at Eton.

"I suppose I *should* know," he said.

"Well, it was Elisa Bonaparte," Gil said, confusing his information. "Napoleon's sister?"

"Oh yes, of course," Alan said.

"And do you see the columns on the facade of that church?" Gil asked. "Do you know why each one is different?"

"No, I don't," Alan admitted.

"Well, they asked for samples from the best studios in the area, and then, instead of commissioning one studio to do all the columns in one style as they'd originally planned, they just put up the samples. Get it?"

"I never knew *that*," said Nigel's assistant, a shade of disbelief in her voice. Gil loves to stretch the truth if it gets people to pay attention. History is really fiction, he always says.

We took two cars to go to the house. I rode with the captain, who drove very badly for a former fighter pilot. "I apologize for the way I am dressed," he said, glancing down at his perfectly pressed twill pants. I was pleased to see how small the captain's feet were in a pair of moccasins with deep rubber treads, a style that better suits teenage boys. "I am dressed for the farm," the captain said, sneaking a sidelong look at the conservative dark suit I wore once every six months to certain *alto borghese* dinner parties that invariably bored me to death.

We pulled into the driveway. Little Ray, in the backseat, said, "Who's house is this?" He was ten years old. He spoke a very elegant English.

"This is *my* house," I said. I turned to find Ray's face in mine. He was a handsome boy with wide blue eyes and full, flushed lips.

"It's *yours?*" Ray asked. I wished I knew why he seemed so surprised.

"It belongs to me," I said, "but soon it will belong to you."

"Shush," said the captain as he brought us to a stop. When Ray jumped out of the car his father said, "He doesn't know yet that we are buying this. You see, he talks too much at school." He formed a little alligator mouth with his hand and set it chattering.

In a moment the captain, his wife, and children were off to roam the land. Gil and I waited with Nigel and Susan in the entry hall. Once in a while I went to the window and spotted the L.'s way off in the distance holding hands, walking through the grasses that were too wet for Ugo to cut. In the silence of their remove they were the generic family of four, without race or nationality, without billions. That's what this place has always needed, I thought, suddenly having to fight back the sadness I felt; this is a house for a family, not for us, not for two people alone.

Nigel went out for a smoke and left the loggia door open. The white, hand-woven curtains waved like bedsheets on the line, gently turning. Dry, coral-shaped cypress leaves found their way in and under foot. "It's like a funeral," Gil remarked. All these figures in dark suits standing in the rainy-day shadows of loss, hands stuffed in their pants pockets holding back their raincoats, mourners all, gazing at the floor, at the lost bits of cypress, like coral, skittering over the *cotto* in the draft. I longed for this day to end, for the distorting lens of pain to be removed from my eyes.

Mrs. L. was the first one back. "Do you know what Ray said?" she asked, smiling. She was amused by her young son, the creative one, the one who was more like her. "He said, 'These people must be very wealthy to have so much land. Tell me, what are they doing?' " I laughed with her because I understood that I should. But I didn't really get the joke, if that's what it was supposed to be, a joke.

Ray came into the entry hall following Riga. She was not used to small boys and was frightened.

"Is that your cat?" Mrs. L. asked sternly.

"Yes," Gil said. "We've thought about taking her to New York with us, but really, it wouldn't be fair; she doesn't belong in a city apartment. I asked my parents in Massachusetts to take her, but they said they couldn't. We thought we'd leave her with the farmer and his family, but I can't guarantee she won't come around here looking for us when we're gone."

As I held my breath, a heartbeat came on too soon. I could tell she hated cats.

"I don't mind the farmer having it," Mrs. L. said, as if to concede some minor point in the rounds of negotiations that seemed to be in progress on every front. "Ray loves animals. He is not like Alan, who only wants to work inside and doesn't care about nature. Ray loves to pick the flowers and to look at the bushes, but Alan only studies. He is interested in business and in money. He loves that, money and studying money. It is why I think this place will be good for him. He

is not so sure about country life, you see. I brought him here to convince him that he needs to relax once in a while. I want him to learn
how to do things, to go to the garden and pick the vegetables and
fruits."

The captain and Alan came in and made themselves comfortable
in the smaller living room. Everyone gazed silently into the cold
hearth of the huge stone fireplace we had bought at the antique market when we made the very first improvements to the house.

"This is a nice room," said the captain. He seemed to take pleasure in small spaces; perhaps this was why he was so at home flying. He
was sitting in a big down-stuffed chair, and his feet didn't quite reach
the floor. "Did you clean your shoes before coming in?" he asked
Alan, who was wearing a plaid Ralph Lauren shirt and a Swatch
Chrono. Alan glanced timidly at the dirt-clogged soles of his Timber-
lands, then shrugged.

Nigel, on his best behavior, looked like the L.'s polite third son.

"And do you have music?" Mrs. L. asked. She took off her plastic headband to give her long, thick hair a moment's free rein.

"We mostly listen to music in the car," said Gil, withholding
information about its ten-speaker CD system. Italians don't believe in
background music. Gil and I, Europeanized, prefer quiet in the home
when people get together for conversation or dinner.

"I have music in London," said Mrs. L. "The unit is in my bedroom, but I have speakers all over the house. You can adjust the volume
and the program by remote control wherever you happen to be, simply
by pushing a button." As she looked up into the high corners of the
room, I heard the jackhammers pounding. I saw plaster dust falling,
then heard Whitney Houston. "We Greeks are so spoiled," she
reminded us, as if Greece ranked with Sweden in overall quality of life.

They wanted to tour the inside of the house once more. At the bottom of the curving staircase in its pure white stairwell, Mrs. L. said, "And here I would like to paint each riser a different pastel color. I saw that in Sardinia once, and I think it would be lovely. You must come back and see the place when I'm done."

Oh God, I said to myself. Sardinia in Lucca! "What a good idea," I said, suddenly feeling abused.

We would never come back here once the house was theirs.

"She has so many good ideas, my wife," the captain said. "People are always coming to her with their questions. What do I do with this room? What can I do here and there, how am I handling this?"

His wife blushed at the truth and climbed the stairs.

The captain invited everyone to lunch at Buca di Sant' Antonio. Gil and I took Mrs. L. and Alan to town in our car. Ray, Nigel, and his assistant rode with the captain in his rented Peugeot. As I started the engine, Alan said something to his mother in Greek.

"What's that?" Gil asked.

"He says, 'Oh, I suppose it might be nice to come here once a year and relax for a week or two.' " Mrs. L. snickered, getting a kick out of her fifteen-year-old man, proud to have made him what he was.

At the restaurant, Alan and Ray tickled each other when their father's head was turned. I wondered what it must be like for a little kid to have such an old father. Ray was wearing the Mickey Mouse sweatshirt his mother had just bought for him at Disney World in Paris. "Oh yes, and how was that?" I asked about their trip.

"The queues were terrible," Mrs. L. said. "We waited two hours for the Magic Mountain."

I wondered why she didn't buy their way to the head of the line somehow. Aren't there first-class tickets to the Magic Kingdom?

"The hotels are international style," she said. "I mean, the baths are very fine and they give you the dressing gowns, of course. But the service is typically American, I'm afraid."

Ray was restless, up on his feet. "Mother," he said, "I want to go to school in Italy. I hate my school. I hate it. I hate it."

"Why do you hate it?" Gil asked. He liked little Ray, and Ray could feel it.

"Because it's in London," Ray said.

"And you don't like London?"

"No," said Ray. "London is in England, and I hate England. I hate it. I hate it. All it ever does is rain. Rain, rain, and nothing but rain. Oh, and you mustn't go outside, our Filipinos tell me, you'll get wet and catch cold. But they're the best cooks in the world, our Filipinos."

"Is that so?" Gil said.

"I want to live in Italy. I hate England. England is evil!" Ray began to dance around behind my chair. "England is the devil," he said. "The devil!"

Gil and Mrs. L. were discussing local restaurants. "And do you like Vipore?" she asked.

"Not particularly," said Gil. "We made the mistake of inviting the owner to visit us once, and now that he knows where we live he charges us more."

"That's the one thing I hate," Mrs. L. said angrily. "If something is expensive and I want it, then I am willing to pay the price. But if I have to pay more because I am who I am, it makes me furious. It makes me crazy."

Overhearing this, I wondered if there was a hidden message here.

The L.'s three Italian attorneys arrived with Michelle, our lawyer, and Mr. A., the captain's financial adviser.

Before sitting down to lunch with the other negotiators in a far corner of the dining room, Michelle asked to have a word with us. "This guy A.'s nuts," she said. I'd never seen Michelle at work before. She was cautiously wide-eyed and stern. "There are fifteen points on the *compromesso* they've drafted, and we're still negotiating point three. It's like they're buying Rockefeller Center or something. Do you know what he's hung up on? He's worried that you might take their down payment and then go and do another compromesso with somebody else, taking another down payment from them. They feel they have no security under the Italian system. He's driving me nuts. I don't know when we'll be done with this." I could see the columns of figures broadening on Michelle's bill.

It was four o'clock. The only people left in the restaurant were the ones involved in this real estate deal. The empty tables were reset for dinner. The waiters were standing around with nothing to do, looking silently ill-humored and weary. Negotiations were still in progress at the attorneys' table even as they ate their *mascarpone*. Across the dining room, Captain L. yawned at the clean tip of his unlit cigar. Nigel was pie-eyed and still sipping wine. His assistant was patience incarnate. Gil was leaning on the bar talking on the phone to our bank in Boston.

"Ray doesn't like to study," Mrs. L. told me. "He is not like Alan, who is so interested in books, in money, so serious like that."

"He's a numbskull," said Alan.

"No, I'm not," said Ray, "you are."

"That's enough, now," said the captain.

Ray was up on his feet again. He was holding onto the back of my chair, stretching and doing deep knee bends. "Do you know what a bonk is?" he asked me.

"Ahm," I said, "I'm not sure."

"It's what Alan does to me all the time. He goes, 'Empty, bonk!' " Ray rapped his little knuckle once on top of my head, and it hurt.

"That's enough, now," said the captain.

"It's because you refuse to learn to read and write," said Alan, the fifteen-year-old adult.

"I'll learn to read," said Ray, jouncing me in my chair. "I'll surprise you with what I'll do. I'll write and I'll write, and there will be books and books of all I've written, books and books, and when I die they'll take all my books and they'll throw them into my coffin and they'll bury the whole lot of us, me and my books, my thousands of books, and then I suppose you'll all be proud of me, won't you?"

Mrs. L. turned to me and smiled as if to apologize.

Gil and I were at home. The L.'s had gone back to their hotel in Forte dei Marmi. The plan was that we would all get together for dinner at Da Lorenzo, where we would quickly sign the *compromesso*, which would surely be completed by then. But it was already nine o'clock. Mr. A., Michelle, and the captain's attorneys were still negotiating.

Michelle ended up spending the night at our house. Gil made a bed for her and found her an unused toothbrush. She retired, exhausted, as soon as she got in. Gil and I read the draft of the compromesso in its current, supposedly finished form, then slipped it under Michelle's door with our written comments. She'd review it all before breakfast and her eight-thirty meeting with the L.'s representatives.

When Michelle emerged in the morning she said, "You can't

sign this document. I'm sorry, it's just no good." Everyone agreed, by telephone, that Michelle could redraft what they'd prepared yesterday and present it to Mr. A. and the others after lunch. Poor Michelle. She was wearing yesterday's clothes. Her husband and child, in Florence, missed her. We felt bad asking her to face, all alone, those four tough men. But at the same time, it felt right to be represented by a demure, though fiercely clever woman with enviable resources of power.

It rained all afternoon. The drainage ditches swelled and roared with muddied runoff from the hills. The telephone rang every hour, and it was Michelle voicing her frustrations. "Mrs. L. wants to have unlimited visits before the closing of the sale, A. says. She wants to bring her decorator down from London and get him started. I told them she could have five visits provided you were at home and in agreement to scheduling, but A. said, 'She should have fifty visits if she wants. She should have a hundred visits.' Now he's going over the things we drafted yesterday. He's disagreeing with the points he wrote himself. I'm losing patience. I can't believe this."

"Hang in there, Michelle," I said. "We think you're doing a brilliant job." I almost told her we loved her, but I thought better of it. Perhaps I'd tell her that some other time when I'd had a couple of drinks.

Gil and I passed the day idly, ineffectually thinking about the business at hand. I looked out windows, watching the grass grow. I wondered what in the world the L.'s could possibly be up to in Forte dei Marmi in the rain. "Let's face it," Gil said, "what they're really trying to do is to get us down in the price. They're chipping away at our patience until we just can't stand it anymore and end up having to say yes to everything."

It was ten o'clock at night when Michelle, shaky and hoarse, called to say, "I'm thinking of walking out. They're trying to take advantage of you. Here's the latest contingency. A. wants to have an engineer look the property over the day before the close of the sale. If anything is wrong he wants you to make it right at your expense or else refund the deposit and free L. of all obligations. You can't do this! I won't let you sign a compromesso with a hitch like that in it. This is no compromesso at all. It's a sham." There was loud, heated discussion in the background. "Hold on a second," Michelle said, and then she screamed at them in Italian. I could tell by her voice that she'd been screaming all afternoon. "You tell 'em, Michelle," I said, rooting for the underdog, for the ripped-off and the abused, for women and for the marginal, for people like us. The captain was as slimy as we'd thought he was.

Michelle was back on the phone. "It's hopeless," she said. "What should I do? You tell me."

Gil took the phone. "We're coming to get you," he said. "Fuck 'em, pardon my French." He knew how much Michelle and her husband disliked bad language, but he was upset and he didn't care.

"That's what I say," said Michelle. "Fuck 'em!"

"I'm going to scream and yell when I get in there," I said. "They can't do this to us. Who the fuck do they think they are? They think their billions can buy them anything and everything, but they're wrong. They're ruined by their riches. They're so rich they can't even buy the house they're in love with. I'm not going to hold back when I walk in there. I'm going to tell that A. just what I think of him and his boss, that's what I'm going to do. I want you to be prepared for this, Gil." The windshield wipers beat with the same fury that moved my voice.

"Now, hang on, Paul," Gil said. "I think we should try to be calm a minute, OK?"

"I can't be calm. I'm furious."

"Try to relax."

"Gil, I—"

"Look, could you do it just for me? You can't go in there shouting; it's not going to accomplish anything. I think we should just walk calmly into the conference room and say, 'OK, now, listen, Mr. A., *what is the problem? Why can't we seem to put a simple contract together?*' Being hotheaded about it isn't going to work in our interest, Paul, all right? Trust me. Let's do it my way."

Dripping wet, we were admitted into a hall whose palatial murals had suffered a heavy-handed restoration. The secretaries had that blanched, overtime look on their faces. One of them escorted us to the conference room as if to a morgue where there was a corpse to identify.

I said to myself, Be calm, as I confronted them, all seated there in a blueing light like hostages in a hijacked jet who had not been allowed to move for forty-eight hours. Nigel was at the head of the table, hoping against hope to get a check so he could buy a new pair of shoes (his expressed motive). Susan was beside him, with her fixed half smile. The three Italian attorneys were dreaming of fagioli and grilled steak. Mr. A., with those occasional white hairs that coiled out of his face in odd unshaven places, was politely on his feet. Then there was Michelle, dear Michelle, holding the fort single-handedly, like Davy Crockett at the Alamo, I thought.

"Now, you listen here," Gil shouted, a finger in the air. He was louder than I could ever be, even at the height of my anger. "We've had enough of your so-called negotiations, and we're not going to take it lying down! We don't need the money and we won't stand for this abuse! The deal is off!"

Mr A. was holding a single piece of paper in his hands. He glanced at it in silence, as if it were the script to his response.

"This is our home," Gil said, less hurriedly now, full of feeling. "This is our home and we love it. It's not just another toy to us the way it would be to your clients, Mr. A., a little thing to play with a couple of weekends a year when we're bored and feeling cooped up in our city lives. This is our home. We've put a lot of love into it. We've hung every door, we've laid down every stone. . . ."

It was as if the room were filled with music, a movement labeled andante—music that stirred different, quiet passions in everyone. The negotiations were over. This was no longer a business meeting. I looked at Michelle. Behind her serious glasses there were tears of pride brimming in her eyes. It was one of those real-life dramas that must make her work meaningful. The documents had been set aside. All that remained were human beings in the course of a struggle to make sense of each other. I remembered Michelle's once having said, "I've never thought of myself as a particularly beautiful woman." Perhaps she'd never held up the mirror in moments like these.

"Come on, Michelle," Gil said, his arm around her, "we're going home."

Hearing this, I saw home in our windshield. I saw it in the glow of our headlights, beyond wipers that worked together with our common will to bring this life, as we'd loved living it, back into focus, holding it there in perfect clarity.

WE TURNED OFF THE HEAT (THAT IN ITSELF WAS A big savings) and went to New York. We'd stay there for six months to sort out our financial affairs and develop creative belt-tightening schemes to get us safely down the bumpy road ahead. A friend of ours had taken a job in Singapore for a year, and he offered us his apartment. When Captain L. left messages on our answering machine—well-practiced apologies and overtures to further negotiations—we did not return his calls. The house in Massa Macinaia was ours and would stay ours and this brought joy, but the injuries sustained in recent months needed their healing time.

Soon we had a city life of distractions, a full calendar. It felt as though we'd never left the States, that we'd been living in New York forever, that Italy and everything we'd made of it was a long way off. We saw friends new and old. We learned how to use the latest expressions. We adopted a New York mode of dress. We caught up on the newest films and plays and operas and talked about them in loud, smoky restaurants with our artistic dining companions whose first-hand knowledge of American culture was, in fascinating contrast to ours, forever ongoing, unbroken.

Mornings I wrote. Gil volunteered six days a week at Safe Space, a shelter in Times Square for homeless kids. He was an "advocate." He'd talk to them, gain their confidence, find out their needs—eyeglasses, shoes, a dentist. The surrounding city held a curious dark energy for me, and I loved the freshness of its daunting jumble; it was a clear break from all that beauty I'd been living with in Lucca, the classic purity of another era, unreal perhaps, but wonderful. It was a reminder, a sobering one, that those other worlds, so different from my limited, privileged one, were connected to me nevertheless, mine as well as anyone's to consider and mind.

It was a long, snowy winter of gutter slush and freezing rain and temperatures that sent you rushing into the nearest corner Korean convenience store. When bright signs of spring proved false, I was ready to go home. There our fields would be carpeted with crocuses, our cherry trees abuzz with hungry birds, and they would still be *our* fields, *our* cherries. Perhaps we never fully value the things we love until we put them on the scale, in trade. There was nothing I wanted more now than home.

It took me forever to find Riga. She was on the farm track above the shepherd's house hunting in the box hedge. She wore a thick winter coat, black and shiny, and her stomach was round and full. She stopped in fright and stared at me, unsure. Had I changed that much in six months? Did I look all that different in black? In a moment she recognized me; she came my way purring and crying all at once, grand emotions for a cat.

The entry hall was full of mail, bursting boxes of it. I saw the evidence of our absence everywhere, in every misplaced chair, in the curtains gone askew, in the sofa cushions too perfectly puffed— Ottavia had cared well for these rooms while we were gone. The house felt enormous compared to our New York apartment. The ceilings were breathtakingly high, the quiet countryside vast and unspoiled— those little intrusions of ugliness one only notices in time seemed to have vanished like shallow-rooted memories. All was perfection, serene and gorgeously true. All but the garden, that is. It took only moments to move the furniture back into place, to readjust the curtain folds, to pound out the sofa cushions, moments to fill the kitchen with comforting food smells, baskets of fresh vegetables and blood oranges from Sicily. All of this was easy.

But the garden? That was another matter.

April rains began to fall in their ceaseless-seeming way. "*Siamo all'acqua*," the Lucchesi say. The grasses grew, weeds advanced and multiplied, bushes broadened in new leaf, all tangled up in themselves. I'd go to the window and look out and wonder, What do I do?

I'd bought a book in New York, a photographic look at gardens of all sorts, Italian, English, French, big, small, city, country. It was the first garden book of its kind I'd ever bought, as picture books had never been my thing. It brought home to me the idea that I'd cared very little about gardens in the past; it was a world I'd taken only brief peeks at as if through a half-open door, a world I'd never truly entered. I knew almost nothing about plants, their origins, their requirements, their uses in a scheme.

This book intrigued me with its portraits of gardens and the people who made them. With a fire going those rainy afternoons, I sat and studied its text and illustrations. Before long, a garden idea would come to mind and I'd soon be elsewhere with it, in my own imagined garden space, its volumes and colors made of my newly informed invention. I'd go to the window and look out to the garden I hadn't seen in months, and I'd gaze and think, then I'd sit and study more and dream and plan. I was beginning to understand, after all we'd just experienced, what exactly a garden was; I was standing at the threshold of an unexplored universe, and I felt the way I must have as a child when I first took a crayon to paper and moved it with my mind's master plan.

When at last the rain stopped, I went out. Where to begin and how? I had no skills, no experience; I had only the will.

I went to the garden room in the *cantina* and got a hoe and a rake with which to clear the gravel driveway of all the unsightly weeds that had so blurred its edges while we were gone. I worked very quickly and hard, inventing methods, trying, failing, succeeding. As the hours passed, almost unnoticed to me, I thought about those pictures I'd seen in the book, the gardens of Roderick Cameron or those of the Viscomte de Noailles. I manipulated these recalled images in my mind, drawing out of them new dreamed-up garden views of my own speculation.

It was nothing short of momentous that afternoon in April, when I stood in the cleaned-up courtyard after a day's work to admire the very good job I'd done of redrawing its edges of lawn with string and stakes and an edge-cutting tool. My back ached, but I couldn't have felt better. This plot of ground was a garden, and I was its keeper who'd made a vow.

Ottavia leaned out her kitchen window, a pot holder in her hand. Smells of frying *involtini* circulated in the downdraft. She seemed to somehow know that things were not the same. Smiling, she gestured to the work I'd done and said, "*Ha tutto un altro aspetto così.* What a difference you've made! I'm so glad you're home."

chapter six

RENAISSANCE

THERE ARE RED BLOOMS IN MY ENTRY HALL WIN-
dow at Christmas time. The tree they belong to blocks out the light, its leathery dark leaves nodding in a glaze of rain. It's like the Christmas tree I don't have to remake each year; it decks, on its own evergreen bows, its own red yuletide ornaments. It's a very old tree (one hundred and fifty years according to one expert who measured the width of its trunk), and it flowers profusely five months of the year, December through April. It's a *Camellia japonica*—which cultivar is anyone's guess— and it couldn't be happier where it stands, its roots shaded by a high, curving box hedge, its budded branches stretching in the late afternoon sun.

On the opposite side of the front stairs there's another camellia, this one planted more recently, perhaps in the fifties—it'll be a century before it fills the window over its head the way the other one does. Its candy-cane blooms, variegated red and white, are far more scarce than those of its neighbor, which I pick copiously each winter for a green blown glass vase that seems to have been made just for them. My two camellias are among this garden's greatest treasures, and I'm indebted to whoever planted them there. Yet in spite of these extraordinary components, this front garden of ours just didn't come together for me now that I'd been so blessed with a new way of seeing. It was incoherent, like a room whose furniture had just been delivered by the movers. Making a garden that was never planned seem as if it was—the self-commissioned task at hand—isn't easy.

There was the problem of the lawn, for instance. So vague—where did it end, and where did it begin? By studying formal gardens and their structure I came to understand that a lawn needs clearly defined edges; only in a woodland garden (or a very naturalistic one) should it be allowed to fade off into wildness. For years I'd been mowing ragged circles around the cypress trunks, the sprawling yucca, the several bushes and small trees that hug the long, low parapet on the valley side. In classic Italian estates the villa sits on a base of clean, unadorned ground, all planting confined to more distant, formal or informal gardens off to the sides and in back. If the house is on a hillside, as mine is, then the level front terrace, covered with gravel or grass, is bordered on the valley side with a stone balustrade. Unfortunately, I had no such balustrade; I had only an ugly, menacing little wall.

The wall is fashioned of an unfortunate melange of materials: field stones, old bricks, new bricks, modern cinder blocks. Entire sections of it, thanks to Lionel Fielden, are made of poured concrete whose nasty ingredients inhibit the potentially saving grace of a mossy patina. In all, it's anything but pretty. As long as this wall exists, I reasoned, my garden, no matter how well I'd remake it, would suffer in its unflattering context, like a painting in an ugly frame.

And to make matters worse, the ground at the wall's feet isn't level. To compensate, the wall is stepped at two random points. From the side gate where you enter the garden you're conscious of a significant uphill sweep as you look off across the terrace—the wall is shoulder height where you stand, but barely calf height at the far end. Though there are many garden situations in which a slope works beautifully, this broad front terrace of mine isn't one of them. Our house has patrician airs, but the front garden, sloping from side to side, and with a stepped wall to boot, makes them seem just a tad unmerited. The terrace wants, with all its heart, to be nobly flat; that's the saddest thing. Wasn't there something I could do to help realize its bourgeois dream?

Bulldozing was out of the question; these were the garden's contours and I would have to live with them, just as I'd have to live with the little ugly wall that would have cost tens of thousands to rebuild. But why couldn't I trick the eye into believing that the terrace was level? Why couldn't I plant bushes and shrubs along the whole length of wall so that its level, twice-stepped top, which calls attention to the sloping ground at its feet, would no longer be in view? Not a bad idea; I'd run it by Gil.

"A hedge is what I'd like to see," Gil said, rejecting my proposal, "not just bushes and shrubs. That's the sort of thing you see in any garden anywhere. This is Italy. The garden should be about where it is. Let's have hedges."

I had to look deep into my daydreams for a practical solution to this twist of an order (he was right, after all); Gil, leaving it to me, had already vanished, off to the next item on his busy schedule.

Running a hedge along this monstrous wall was no easy task. A hedge is very unattractive when it's randomly interrupted by a tree trunk or a big shrub in its path, and my cypresses and pittosporum gum drops weren't going anywhere; it's even more unattractive if it makes half circles around obstacles in its way. And this hedge of ours would have to be awfully high to conceal the ugly parapet; walking along you'd inevitably look down behind it and there it would be, in all its repugnance.

Days passed before a reasonable solution finally occurred to me. I could run the hedge at a distance of four or five feet away from the wall and the trees that hug it. I could plant my proposed bushes and shrubs behind it, adding to those that were already there. The result; my lawn would have a hedged border, straight and unbroken, backdropped with a varied collection of shrubs that would both conceal the ugly parapet and offer plant interest. I could see the completed scheme in my mind's eye; it was all so logical, so simple, so right.

That night I hunted for confirming images, historical examples of this kind of border, in my growing stack of garden reference books. Garden research had become my evening's pastime by now, a welcome change from reading narrative literature and the depth of concentration it demands of a weary mind at the end of a long day's work. After dinner I sit by the fire in the smaller, cozier of my two living rooms, the piles of garden books covering every surface. There's a Schubert piano piece playing in the next room, music for a garden stroll. The olive wood fire in front of me hisses and tumbles, and I'm off into the garden makers' visions of paradise, the masterpieces of those artists who've found nature the ultimate medium.

I came across an eighteenth-century engraving of the fountain garden at Villa Aldobrandini in Frascati, one of the great gardens of the Italian Renaissance. This narrow garden room, with its central cascading water feature, is bordered on both sides by box hedges behind which blowsy mixed bushes and shrubs rise up as if to say, "The garden ends here where the natural world begins." This was all the endorsement my plan needed. My scheme had classic origins and this engraving was proof. With this reaffirming discovery I'd now proceed.

With string and stakes I laid out my scheme. Gil and I squinted and stood back, trying every angle.

"Why does it look so boring?" Gil asked.

"Well, I haven't planted it yet," I said. "It's just strings."

"But . . . don't we need statues or something? Urns on columns? I don't know; this just doesn't look Italian enough to me."

Italian enough?

A bit of further research on my part suggested that Gil was right again. The most interesting hedge borders in Italian gardens mimic Greco-Roman architecture and are punctuated with faux structural features, masses of vegetable masonry, angular, and solidly "erected" by the hand of man with a visionary, ordering scheme. To further convince, real stone features might occur here and there along these walls of clipped evergreens: armless lady caryatids, or "terms" (tapering pedestals out of whose tops human heads seemlessly sprout), or columns with urns on top where the hedge turns corners or ends or begins. Just a straight, unadorned hedge isn't all that interesting. Wasn't there something I could do to make it more—what? Baroque?

I needed input here.

Not the sort of input that pictures provide—I needed three dimensions. It was time for a field trip. Perhaps the Pfanner garden in Lucca had something to tell me.

THE SAUCER MAGNOLIAS WERE IN BLOOM IN CORSO
Garibaldi, the filled-in medieval moat. I walked along Via Vittorio
Veneto to Piazza San Michele. Until the eleventh century fluted
chunks of toppled colonnades must have lain here in the brambles, a
playground for cats—this is the site of the ancient Roman forum. In
the *campanile* the quarter hour struck a tonal code the Lucchesi understand, a familial dialectal phrase. I was reminded of those first few
nights I had spent in Lucca in November 1979. The guest room I
occupied in Leonardo's attic apartment had a single high, shuttered
window. I couldn't have been more than fifteen feet away from the
tower's rack of bells, the noisy medieval mechanism that rang them.
And yet I remembered welcoming the disturbance; it assured me

throughout the night that this extraordinary trip wasn't a dream after all.

In Via Santa Lucia, by the apse of San Michele, the flower seller threw her baritone voice to passersby. *"Duemila, mazzi belli! Duemila al mazzo!"* Two thousand lire, beautiful bunches. In this spring season they were poppy-flowered anemones, eye-catching hot pinks and pale purples. When her calls woke me those November mornings here, she was selling gladioli, which I'd buy and place in an antique brass vase in Leonardo's living room.

I dodged handsomely dressed women on bicycles who rang their tiny handlebar bells, *zing zing*, a detached, genteel shooing. A bar waiter passed, delivering breakfast, coffee, and pastries on a silvery tray to a neighboring shopkeeper. Children brought warm *focaccia* to their lips in Via Calderia, a narrow street flanked by plain-faced palaces with contrastingly opulent interiors—like Renaissance Florentines cloaked in black capes, the Lucchesi have never worn their wealth on the surface.

It had been years since I last visited the garden at Palazzo Pfanner. But at nine-thirty this morning the enormous turquoise *portone* at number 33 Via degli Angeli was closed. I scanned the simple brass *plaquette* of doorbells. Raimondi Pfanner, Virdis Pfanner, two P. Pfanners, and one A. Pfanner—names incised with niello permanence in a timeless cursive script. The only regularly pushed bell belonged to Bruscuglia Baisi (all the others were tarnished). Perhaps this was the concierge. I entertained the thought of ringing for entrance but didn't want to make a nuisance of myself.

The Pfanners, a Swiss family from Lake Constance, bought this palace in 1860. They were merchants in the beer trade. It was the local Moriconi who commissioned its construction, in 1667, but they'd go broke in their extravagance, sell everything, and move to Poland, migrant fortune seekers. Another Lucchese family, the Controni, completed the house with an enlarged, still more grandiose plan. The garden they built is the only one of any note that survives in this historically wealthy city, which once included many such *angolini verdi*.

I decided to walk up onto the city wall, where there's a view, though limited, down into the garden. Perhaps by the time I came back the great doors would be open as they promised to be, daily; the Pfanners welcomed all for a modest fee.

In front of the palace next door, high school students gathered for a break between classes at the Liceo Classico N. Machiavelli. They wore jeans, captioned sweatshirts, and friendship bracelets, but there was history in their faces, in their high-bridged noses, in the depth of their eyes: Roman, Celtic-Ligurian, Etruscan. In a group of three, one boy, blond as a Lombard, invaders of the sixth century, glanced at me and said to his friend, "We really should be speaking English." Was I part of a new invasion?

I turned left into Via Cesere Battisti, the sharp echo of well-shod feet against cold paving stones the only sound heard here. Piazza del Collegio offered, ironically, no access to the school, but there was a narrow walk to the ramparts at Baluardo San Frediano. The path I followed was paved in gray river stones the size of pears, harvested from the Serchio. They were cut in half lengthwise and laid in mortar, rough side up, offering a secure step in wet weather. The walkway was edged in quarried stone strips from Matraia. In this city of skilled artisans and craftsmen, such finishing touches are everywhere, even under foot.

There's a belvedere up on the wall facing the Pfanner garden below. Two young linden trees are staked straight in the clay ground, promising shade for future generations. I stood between them now and gazed down into the distant, light-filled garden with its long-shadowed statuary, its audible water jet in a central pool.

A garden doesn't fully reveal its secrets until you're there within it, but the Pfanner palace itself could be studied well from here. The great porticoed staircase, with its high arches and broad terrace landings, faces the garden like the tiered gallery of a Baroque theater. The building's volumes and schemes, seventeenth-century reinterpretations of late Florentine Mannerism, attest to the family's social standing and good taste. French doors on the *piano nobile*, the main floor, open to waist-high stone balustrades. All the windows and arches are framed with moldings in fine classical relief of *pietra serena*, the ubiquitous gray stone of Tuscany.

The future King Fredrick IV of Denmark and Norway found this house palatial enough to live here in 1692 as crown prince. Lucca was the backdrop of his courtship of aristocrat Maria Maddalena Trenta, the details of which are imagined in Börge Janssen's novel, *The Girl from Lucca*.

Suddenly I was surrounded by a group of schoolchildren. The elated, piercing tones (gutsy voices), a bouquet of peculiar young smells. This was the *gita* season, when class groups make outings in huge, plushly upholstered buses with white antimacassars. A young teacher read from a guidebook and gestured toward the garden's lemon house, where there was a toppled balustrade, a statue of a lion, a twisted-necked marble eagle checking out the newly arrived disturbance behind its back. Within the garden itself two young women crossed a gravel path. Signs of life. I made my way down the way I had come up.

The *portone* was open and I entered.

To the right was a carved stone tub, cordoned off. It was decorated with a crumbling oval-shaped relief. Had I not known from guidebooks that this sarcophagus was from the third century A.D. I'd have thought its medallion depicted an eighteenth-century high-busted noblewoman, a seductive fan to her chin—Crown Prince Fredrick's paramour?

I climbed the imposing staircase to view the garden from above. On the wide banister a white marble putto rides a lion-pawed eagle whose body emerges from a triton, a conical seashell. The loggia's walls and ceiling are richly decorated in false perspective. Above Alessandro Pfanner's apartment door an ethereal Fame blows a brass horn. In another ceiling panel two plump putti admire their reflections in gilded hand mirrors.

In 1996 Hollywood descended upon Lucca for the filming of *The Portrait of a Lady*, Nicole Kidman as Isabel Archer. Palazzo Pfanner became the home of English expatriate Gilbert Osmond, played by John Malkovitch. Henry James had housed his esthete/cad upon "an olive-muffled hill" near Porta Romana in Florence. With its grand Ammannati proportions, Palazzo Pfanner bears little resemblance to Osmond's "incommunicative" weather-worn house of irregularly sized windows, but in the film's final version we're shown so little of the palace that these reinterpretations don't matter. Director Jane Campion's portrait of Italy is uncharacteristically dark, a disenchanted April. Only the keenest Lucchese eye could recognize the Pfanner garden, Victorianized as it is in the blue shadows of huge brought-in pots of flowering hydrangeas—scenic designers working overtime to justify their fees.

The view from this high terrace shows the garden's concept of inclusion: garden, nearby campanile, city walls, hilly countryside; all of a piece, all characters in a single drama true as life, veiled now in a thin mist that tumbled softly in on a seasonal shifting breeze.

I entered the garden through a cast-iron gate, a turn of the century security fence. It was topped with spear heads and miniature urns, strangely empty. There were four *Cycas revoluta* in antique lemon pots; one of them was five feet tall, and so ancient. I love the dark feathery *Cycas*; neither palm nor fern, it looks like both. It's a primitive cone-bearing plant, in fact, a sort of conifer, and it evokes the nineteenth century, when temperate Europe went mad for the tropicals.

I was welcomed by a pair of marble statues of a "not too vulgar chisel," according to eighteenth-century garden writer Cristoforo Martelli Leonardi. Hera, goddess of conjugal love, holds a broken torch, a peacock by her side. Peacocks once roamed free here, but this is the last of them, frozen in stone, the pet of Jupiter's bride. On my left, an old, bearded Zeus holds an eagle. But for the sounds of the central basin's jetting water, the caws of gliding crows, the polite cries of classics students at the *liceo* next door, the god of storms now stood in calm.

I tried to imagine this sort of statue standing in my garden's hedge. How would it look in the context of a house that's infinitely more modest than this celebrated palace? Where do you go to find works of art like these? The Pfanners seemed to have tons of statues, but they obviously weren't selling them off. A reception line of twelve of them leads to a central octagonal pool. The four elements preside: Vulcan, Mercury, Dionysus, Oceanus. Between the statues are potted lemons and new standard roses; one still wore its identifying tag: G. FIORE.

The basin drains via a carved stone sluice to three concentric half-circle pools lined with lava rock. Its raised border is planted out in a scheme of reds: red salvia, red geraniums, red standard roses, red canna.

Red was perhaps the gardenesque motif here when Felice Pfanner, in 1848, opened his beer garden. His café is said to have evoked Paris, the outdoor *Moulin de la Galette* painted by Renoir. Beneath the porticoed staircase, marble-topped tables were once stacked thick with glass mugs of beer brewed right on the premises. Local gentlemen tipped back their boaters and sipped through the froth, their ladies clutching parasols. Felice Pfanner was shameless. Winters, he froze the central basin with chemical additives so that he could ice skate as he'd done on Lake Constance when he was a child.

No coins in the fountain. I was the only visitor now, the two ladies having left. The rising mist thinned, forming low white spindly clouds; their shadows scanned the grassy quadrangle by the disused brewery buildings, where towering bamboo set its tips to the breeze. Cats scuffled under an old crepe myrtle. The only plant of any interest here is an eight-foot-tall *Buxus harlandii,* the long-leaved box that brings to mind a plangent Korea or Japan.

A formal garden's abandon is most evident at its edges: where gravel meets grass, grass meets soil, soil meets plantings. This garden's seams were splitting with the unraveled threads of neglect. The spindly plants attested to the fact that no true gardener had touched the place in years—surely not with his hands, much less with his mind or heart. The antique lemon pots are numbered in whitewash, but their positions were random now, their varied sizes of no concern when places are assigned each spring. The same sickly French geraniums, stored in the *limonaia* in winter, find their way back out each April to wrought iron etagere, their dusty potting soil ever poorer. The topiary are misshapen blobs. All lines are broken; muddled statements go misunderstood. This garden is an echo, a sunned memory of grand emotions no longer felt, but it's a real and evocative one—we must tread very respectfully in such worlds.

But what did the Pfanner garden have to teach me, the budding garden maker, what lessons did it impart? This visit threw very little light on the palimpsest of my garden proposal at home. But I did learn this: a garden lives by virtue of the gardener's presence. When that presence is felt, the visitor emerges in a state of exaltation, the gardener's love somehow assumed. When it's not, he's sadly aware of its absence. More important than filling my garden with objects, statuary and urns, fountains or topiary, I'd fill it with the presence of my commitment.

My mind was on lunch. The clock tower at San Frediano chimed twelve. I counted the tollings and looked at my watch; one of us was off.

Back up on the wall, I crossed the half-circle base of a decapitated Roman defense tower. Before me and behind me stretched Passeggiata delle Mura, a Gothic nave of plane trees—city ramparts turned public park for a belle époque of peace. If I'd continued along this route for forty-five minutes I'd have been back where I was now, having seen the city from all sides. Nottolini, architect to the Lucchese Bourbon court, was garden designer here. In 1818 he planted limes and mulberries and long double rows of sycamores by order of Duchess Maria Luisa. Some of the trees are dying now—of disease, of old age, or both. Huge low stumps, weathered gray, mark where the worst cases occurred. Newly planted replacements stand promisingly between them.

A young woman appeared following a dog. It walked with a showy swagger, its tail coiled. The woman watched the ground just ahead of her, a profoundly remote smile on her face; it was as if she were reliving a recent joy, fortune, or success. She was cradling an opera score in her arms, the printed word VERDI visible at the top. She sang a single note, then softly cleared her throat. Running through the scale in my mind, I concluded that her note was a G, and that she was adrift in the reverie of the unsung score that framed it. "What kind of a dog is that?" I asked.

"*Un incrocio,*" she said. "*Husky e chow-chow.*"

"Its tongue is black." I said.

"*Sì sì,*" she confirmed, flattered.

This section of wall I walked was the most ancient bit of all, thirteenth-century. Some of the stones, travertine blocks laid in plumb, date back to Roman times.

I passed the old city prison: walls of detention within walls of defense. Chet Baker resided here for a hitch on drug charges back in the sixties. People still talk about his red Ferrari that sat out gathering dust on a nearby street until his release. The houses in this quarter have balconies and terraces the same height as the ramparts. Potted plants, propagated from exchanged cuttings, were lined up in rows, watered by dripping laundry.

At Baluardo di Santa Croce a gardener took a midday nap on a park bench, his municipal orange overalls rolled up as a pillow. The woman with the chow sat at a picnic table and opened her music. On the clumpy grass by the circular brick battlements an American couple dutifully ate their *salumeria* (delicatessen) lunch, washing it down with mineral water sipped from a plastic bottle. Giulio in Pelleria was more my style: not a restaurant, an institution.

Most diners were single businessmen for whom a long central table offered plenty of room for each. One by one they laid down their cigarette packs, their sunglasses, their car keys: Merit, Armani, Alfa Romeo, status symbols all, consciously chosen. They crossed their legs away from each other. They unfolded their newspapers neatly, the pink *Gazzeta dello Sport*, the least expensive fashion accessory in Italy.

The owner seated me at a separate table even though I was alone. Foreign visitors are treated like dignitaries here—we'll sing Giulio's praises upon our return to that huge potential market of ours, won't we? His cordial welcoming is so practiced it reads like utter sincerity. He opened his arms as if to embrace me. He was chewing a Toscano, the twisted little black cigar that's manufactured here within the city walls. In the old days in Boston (this according to Gil's father) Italian Americans smoked cigars that looked like these. They were called "stogies." If you say the word Toscano several times fast it comes out stogie in the end.

Wine bottles, local labels, are lined up for display on shelves, but the inferior wine everyone drinks comes in *fiaschi* wrapped in straw; you pay for what you consume. The walls are hung with lithographs and drawings by Possenti, a living Lucchese painter who's been dining out on his inventory for years. The artist is self-portraitized in his every work. To my left, he's in bed with a ring-necked duck, an invasion of mixed fowl through the window over his washstand.

An elderly woman took the table to my right. Her pearls were dark, dated by their length: long as a flapper's. Her hair was gray, luminous, in place. Instantly she was served a plate of *panzanella*, a dish easily made at home: yesterday's Tuscan bread, onion, tomato, basil, olive oil. She took out a silver pill box and picked through it, carefully portioning her dose. Her fingers trembled; her hooded eyelids fluttered. I imagined that this was her ritual one meal a day; that she lived alone; that in the evenings she suppered on *caffèlatte* and a sweet *cornetto*.

I thought about the fact that I'd had my very first meal in Lucca at this restaurant, in 1979. Our guides led us through a maze of foggy gray streets into the still murkier darkness of a typical evening here. I felt unforgivably foreign having just come from Milan, where I'd been underdressed but otherwise in my element. I ordered squid in *zimino*: squid, Swiss chard, garlic, and tomato concentrate, sautéd quickly over a hot flame. It was so rich in complex strong flavors that I couldn't finish it. The middle-aged couples around us seemed, for the freshness of their guilty looks, to be cheating on their husbands and wives. They smoked and made vulgar sucking noises with their jagged yellow teeth. I'd just got off a train and it was late and I was jet-lagged. I went away hungry, unintentionally drunk, finding fault. A year later we tried it again. On a bright morning in late summer. I had the *maccheroni tortellati*: heaven.

The owner now sat down with a client at a table next to mine. He extended his legs in his café chair, bearing his round stomach in pride. His sweatshirt read, ORIGINAL FLYING WEAR REGISTERED MARK. He admitted to his friend that he'd been smoking for fifty years.

His wife brought me bread in a Chinese-made basket. Her hair was bleached lemon yellow to the roots. I knew enough to refuse the menu; it's only for tourists. The regulars listen to verbal suggestions, seemingly personalized. "I have fresh *porcini* mushrooms with *polenta*," she said. She has the sweet, plump smile of motherly warmth; if this hard life as a restaurateur has involved any sacrifice on her part, she'd never let on.

I started with a plate of *farro* in a broth of *fagioli*. *Farro* in English is "spelt," but it tastes and looks like barley. This is an antique recipe, a Lucchese specialty. You make a broth of white beans, pass it through a sieve, then add a puree of sauteed garlic, onion, celery, carrot, and tomato. The spelt is cooked apart and added to the finished broth; it makes a thick, richly flavorful soup to be eaten tepid, never hot. Here at Giulio it's served in a shallow bowl. A single ladleful is all you need, garnished with a dribble of the newest olive oil, a dusting of fresh-ground pepper over the top. It's important not to mix the oil in, or you'll lose the occasional impact of that burst of pure olive flavor.

The owner was telling his friend that male painters have more success than females do; they get better prices. The restaurateur's a collector, it seemed. I looked again at his gallery of Possentis, imagining them removed. "These days," he said, "painters are bums; they're a mess. In the old days, they killed themselves working and were poor. Now they do nothing and they're rich."

At the center table, one man smoked, did a crossword puzzle in the paper, and ate a plate of horse meat tartar, all at the same time.

The owner's wife appeared by my side. She wore the little lacy white apron of a café waitress tied tightly around her waist.

"Is that horse meat American?" I asked, pointing.

"I don't know," she said. "Why?"

"I'd once read that most of the horse meat eaten in Europe is American, shipped out of Boston, in fact."

"I don't know anything of this," she said, "but it's very very good, our tartar."

"Is it an antique dish, like farro?"

"Oh no," she said. "Not at all. Twenty years ago, the local football team used to dine here every day at lunch. They asked my mother if she would serve them horse meat because it makes you strong. My mother got them the horse meat and they were very thankful. They ate it grilled at first, like beef steaks. But then one day one of them said, 'Signora, why don't you serve it to us raw, ground up, like steak tartar?' We all tried it and it was delicious. It was so, so good, truly. You know, at first the idea gave me chills just to think of it, but then one day I tried it. Wonderful!"

"What's in it?"

"Garlic, olive oil, lemon, and fresh basil. And then we invented the *salsa verde* to go with it. We put parsley, onion, pickled cucumber and capers, and just a little mayonnaise. What a success we've had. Look around you. So many eating it."

A man at the center table picked his teeth with his knife. The old lady finished her panzanella and drained her glass of the same red wine I was drinking, a Chianti, according to the label.

My mushrooms and polenta arrived. On its white, wide-rimmed plate this could have been the work of a sophisticated chef who contrived total simplicity. The polenta was creamy and smooth and sat up like a soufflé in a gleaming rim of the mushroom's saucy juices: olive oil, pureed tomato, and garlic.

In 1990 this restaurant moved from its previous location, the rustic ground floor of a worker's house around the corner, to Piazza San Donato. This new space is three times as big as the old, and so the luncheon waiting lines of before have vanished. Unfortunately, they hired the wrong architect to remodel the sixteenth-century building they now occupy. He gave them an architect's statement, school of Gae Aulenti: a Quai d'Orsay of a trattoria, slick fittings of green marble and enameled steel in a pastel postmodern palette. All the furniture was moved straight over from the old locale, however: the country café chairs, the antique bread-making stand, the green-and-white-checked tablecloths, the Possentis. The end product is like Gropius's housing development in Dessau-Törten: its eventual occupants never completed the Bauhaus dream; soon they unpacked their old ways, spread doilies, and hung lace curtains. But the food here has remained the same, traditional and tasty. I barely notice the architecture anymore, these flavors so transport.

"Enjoying the mushrooms?" asked the owner's wife.

"They're wonderful," I said.

"You're American," she said, "or are you English?"

"American," I confirmed yet again. I knew she'd never remember.

"And you didn't order chicken?"

"Chicken?"

"All Americans order chicken."

"Oh?" I said.

"At night in the summer, all the Americans are here and they all want chicken. You know, for us chicken is something you never eat. You eat chicken only in a poor, poor house when the hen is too old to lay eggs. But you Americans, you eat it every day. How it makes me laugh! I can go through fifty chickens in a night. Can you imagine? Nothing but chickens for you!"

PERHAPS IT WAS LIONEL FIELDEN WHO CONTRIVED the stone benches that once stood precariously propped up against my famous runty wall in front. They were made of bits and pieces of the old sixteenth-century stone balustrade that until the turn of the century adorned our front twin flights of steps in classic Lucchese symmetry. Sections of the wide handrail were trimmed to form bench seats with curved ends which were then set upon two legs made of the dismantled stone railing. You couldn't sit on them; they were the suggestion of "bench," not the thing itself. I removed them years ago—too dangerous to the unsuspecting.

But it's nice to have a place to sit in the garden, isn't it? Couldn't I rebuild these benches somehow? One of the things that caused them to fail was the fact that they were standing in the dirt. Supposing I built individual rectangular bases for them, giving them solid ground on which to stand? Supposing I assembled the pieces better than Lionel Fielden had done, in new mortar, using a level?

I can't remember what inspired my turning these two benches into little, light-hearted salon vignettes, but after dozens of sketched studies, endlessly revised, this is what I did. I placed them within my hedge at an equal distance from the central *viale*; as the hedge runs around these fieldstone terraces, enclosing them on three sides, it mimics the look of a green upholstered sofa with overstuffed backs and arms. This isn't an original idea—originality, for originality's sake, is the last effect I'd care to seek. I'm after nostalgia, déjà vu. I want the visitor to have the sense, entering my garden, that he's come to a passage of forgotten experience, that he's seen it all somewhere before. I want the visitor to be reassured, not challenged.

But even though I now had sculpture in my hedge—i.e., solid form—there was still something missing, some additional element whose absence here stopped my garden just short of the evocative authenticity I sought. What was it?

Pots. A Tuscan garden just isn't Tuscan without pots. Lots of pots, outsized pots, terra-cotta pots everywhere, of every imaginable shape—pairs of them, groups of them, processions of them. At the moment I had only two, both filled with old lemons that once belonged to the Olivers. These lemon trees, their thorny limbs carefully tied with supple willow stems, were brilliant, thanks to Ugo's care. But two pots weren't nearly enough. I needed more.

There are so many types of pots in the world that it's rare to find a garden, anywhere, without at least one or two. First, they're convenient, as you can move them about as the occasion demands. And when you can't decide where to put that superfluous plant you've just reck-lessly acquired, you can always pot it up for the time being until inspi-ration intervenes.

Far too often the gardener settles for plastic pots, as plastic is by now so much a part of our lives that we've come to think of it as a raw material. Even the great arbiters of style and taste can yield to atmos-pheric pressure, falling prey to plastic's convenience. David Hicks was almost proud of his arrangement of eight plastic pots of artichokes in his otherwise flawless garden in the Cotswolds. I understand that terra-cotta pots in cold climates can crumble and disintegrate, and that in most parts of the world they're unavailable anyway. But what about copper, or tin, or wood? Anything but plastic. I'm quite spoiled in the pot department, as I live in one of the world's great terra-cotta cultures. Even machine-made terra-cotta pots don't do it for me; like tooled steel, they're too perfect. And they never take a patina. There's a not-so-old wives' tale: if your pot looks too industrial, paint it with manure water or buttermilk, and in a month it'll look as though it's been around forever. Not true. I tried it.

When restoring the main house several years ago I visited the various terra-cotta producers in Chianti, the industry's *centro storico*, looking for handmade floor tiles. As with machine-made pots, indus-trial terra-cotta tiles from any one producer are all the same, as the raw earth is mixed with emulsions in controlled proportions, in enor-mous quantities. They look very dull installed—uniformly flat, pre-buffed and hard. It was absolutely fundamental that the floor tiles we put in our antique house be handmade in the old way. I found the most beautiful *cotto* at the tiny factory of Andreini in Impruneta. Each one of their tiles, about eight inches square, was subtly different in tone from the next. The range of colors: golden sunset, pomegranate skin, smoked salmon. The tiles were all pitted and irregular, ever so slightly ground down at their edges, and their natural glow seemed to be emitted from the heat of the wood kiln fire trapped within. Installed here in my house, they look antique; it takes a very keen eye to know that they're not from the sixteenth century.

But Andreini also made pots, as I recalled, just the kind of pots I had in mind for the newly revised front garden.

What a wonderful excuse for an outing to the heart of Tuscany, lunch at Il Quercio in Panzano, where you sit on wobbly rough-hewn benches within the frigid stone walls of an old stable as the brilliantly prepared Etruscan-inspired dishes steam away in front of you.

Signor Andreini is among the last of the Old World cotto artisans. One could tour his small factory in a matter of minutes, but guided by him it could take half a day. He loved to show it off, proudly describing the appointments and procedures unchanged since ancient times: the pile of gray pulverized clay from the dig in back, the wall-sized oven which had to be rebuilt for every firing, the open space where the tiles were molded, one by one, on the sand-covered floor, the mud spread out by hand in wooden frames. On the underside of his finished tiles you could see the tracks of dragged fingers. "It's very hard work," Andreini once said. "It's very rough on the hands. No one wants to do it anymore."

"Couldn't they use latex gloves?" I asked.

He laughed.

His tiles were extraordinary, yes. But nothing Andreini produced matched for beauty the lemon pots I remembered seeing when I'd ordered the villa's countless square meters of new floor. They were like big gingerbread cookies; you wanted to break off a piece and eat it. Four feet tall and just as wide at the top, they're the color of dried pink rose petals. They're festooned and adorned with garlands and rosettes, but their overall design couldn't be simpler—classic Greco-Roman. They're utter perfection in their vague lopsidedness, a touching reminder of human frailty that adds depth to their complex beauty.

"These are the last such pots we'll produce," Andreini said sadly the day of our pot-shopping trip.

"Why is that?" I asked.

"In part because we're closing—"

"Closing?" Gil was shocked. He was very fond of old Andreini; we'd spent many pleasant hours with him down there at the *forno*.

"At the end of July," he said. "I'm getting old now. I can't go on. My son is an engineer, you know. He lives in Siena. He's not interested in this business, but of course I don't blame him. There's no one to run the place anymore, much less work here as a laborer."

"I'm sorry to hear that," I said. Seeing the tears at the corners of his eyes, I thought perhaps I should have kept silent.

"These are the last of our pots," he said. "The artisan who made them passed away in December, and his skills went to the grave with him."

"They're magnificent," I said.

It's not very often that I desire something so much that I just have to have it. But these pots! The sap of acquisition flowed within, and I was bursting with the kind of smiles that double prices.

"There were seventeen of them made in the last firing," Andreini said. "Carlo di Galles bought twelve, and now there are just five left."

It always takes me a second to mentally translate "Carlo di Galles" into Charles, Prince of Wales. Once I'd done that, I recalled that Prince Charles had passed through here last summer, and that he'd even eaten at Il Quercio, where we were now headed for lunch. Charles loves Tuscany. Diana, in an interview published just after her death, suggested that Charles might be better suited for the life of an esthete in a Tuscan villa than to being king.

I imagined four of these extraordinary pots in front of our house. I saw them standing on *sottoconche* of stone, of course, with plants in them. What plants? I had no idea just then, but it didn't matter; in this special case, the plants were secondary.

"I'll take four," I said without even consulting Gil. They were enormously expensive, but worth every penny, it seemed to me.

"No, all five," Gil said.

What would we do with the fifth? I wondered.

"*Benissimo,*" Andreini said, smiling, "take them all." He seemed pleased that these last jewels of his factory's crown would end up in our care; he loved the way our floor had turned out.

We went into his house to close the deal, a nineteenth-century *casa padronale* standing in the shadows of towering windmill palms, the shaggy *Trachycarpus fortunei*. It was cold inside and the shutters were closed. Food smells circulated with the maid, mama-style in her apron and carpet slippers. Signora Andreini appeared. The *forno* was her ancestral business and this was her family home. In fact, her husband's name wasn't Andreini at all, it was something else. "But never mind," he once said, "call me Andreini anyway. Everyone does." She remembered us, welcoming us into her study, where she did the factory's bookkeeping in a gallery of family photographs that documented the early years here when the raw material was brought down from the dig in mule carts, and even the laborers seemed to wear white shirts and ties.

"They've bought the last of the pots," Andreini said in a tone of acceptance and approval.

"*A, bene,*" his wife said, taking her seat at the dark old desk and pulling out her receipt book.

"I'll give them to you for a million lire each," he said. That was two hundred thousand lire less than his previously quoted price. It was generous of him; we'd have paid the bigger amount and he knew it.

As I wrote the check he showed me a framed autographed picture of Prince Charles. "He gave me this," he said. "He loved my pots. They're at Highgrove now, in his garden. He has a very good garden, I understand."

"So I've heard," I said.

He fumbled through a file at the corner of his desk and found Charles's bill payment, the cover letter with the word HIGHGROVE engraved at the top. "Look at the figure," he said. "Carlo paid a million two hundred thousand each. See. I'm giving you a special discount. Old friends mean more to me than any prince."

A few days later the pots were delivered all wrapped in straw like Chianti bottles. They were even more beautiful in our own familiar light than I'd remembered. They were so brittle-looking they might have been ancient, yet they were clean and sturdy as only new pots can be. They reminded me of the brand-new, hand-hewn ox carts I'd seen in Pagan, Burma; they were history, made for a journey back in time, yet they were as white as freshly whittled sticks.

I decided to line up four pots just in front of the house along the edge of the lawn, one at each end, the remaining two near the central steps—the fifth now stands in the loggia. I must have had French chateaux in mind with their laconic gardening touch of yew cones rising out of gravel aprons in symmetrical respect to the house's front entrance, for it was yews I chose to plant in my pots and not the more typically Tuscan lemons, box, or sweet bay.

The yew, *Taxus baccata*, isn't often planted here, as it prefers a humid climate. But Lucca isn't like the southern part of this region with its drying winds and killing heat, and so it seemed I could get away with it. And my yew plants would have only half a day's sun, as they'd stand in the shadow of the house until noon. I'd keep them well watered by hand; if they made it, fine; if not, *pazienza*.

It wasn't easy to find four matching cones of yew three feet tall, but Dino Monti came through. They were a bit malformed, though, whiskery and hunched. I thought about the yew cones at the garden of the Luxemburg in Paris that I admired for their perfect geometric shapes, which only a very professional gardener can manage to produce. I lay awake nights trying to figure out how it is done. These are the trade secrets that self-protecting gardeners (who can be as obtuse as master chefs) never reveal in the books they write. Not even Nathaniel Lloyd gives himself away in his unique little book *Garden Craftsmanship in Yew and Box*. The book includes a photo of a garden in Angers, France, where several box cones are lined up in unreal precision along the edge of a gravel path, but nowhere in the practical text does LLoyd explain how this uniformity is achieved.

In my daydreaming hours I invented my own method.

It would have been smart to have had an ironmonger make me the desired form out of lightweight rods, but ironmongers around here are so busy and arrogant that I'd have waited a year for the rig. Instead I sent a bamboo pole vertically down along the plant's trunk until it was securely grounded. That done, I tied a piece of twine at the bush's crown. At the bottom end of this length of twine I tied a weight that dangled over the pot's brim. The resulting taut string formed a straight line that ran from the crown of the bush to the edge of the pot. With that as my guide, I trimmed, pushing the string along as I worked. The great results surprised even me. And the nice thing about yew is that you don't have to go through this procedure every time you trim, as the plant, for the most part, keeps the crisp form you gave it, sending out its new growth in such a way that you can easily see it for what it is and clip it off.

It was even more difficult to find four *sottoconche*, the blocks of stone upon which such pots typically stand. In general, these pot bases are two feet square and ten inches high, and they're carved out on top with a shallow well and drainage canal. An Andreini pot can't be put down on a lawn without one of these underneath it; it just doesn't look right. And the stones have to be old, or better yet, antique. A newly cut stone, even hand carved, is too perfect, too gray, and it takes decades for a patina to form. Miraculously, I found the four stones I needed; but being antique they cost even more than the pots themselves. Ouch. Never mind; the guest house was booked for the entire summer at a high rent. I bought them. And there they now stand in a row: yew cones, pots, stones, four of them all alike, a great touch of elegance, not too extravagant for a country house of unassuming lines such as mine.

chapter seven

THE EDUCATION OF

A GARDENER

I MUST HAVE LEARNED THE NAMES OF A HUNDRED plants a month in my garden's formative days. Many of these remained names and only names to me, as my reference library contained no illustrations of, for instance, *Verbascum bombyciferum*, a mullein mentioned in passing by Christopher Lloyd in *The Well-Tempered Garden*. As much as I loved the way the word *bombyciferum* sounded, I still felt inadequate—I didn't deserve to be counted among Lloyd's readership if my experience couldn't instantly supply my mind with the visual image of every plant he named.

But I was studying in earnest. Now that it had the formal structure I desired, my newly revised front garden needed plants. It was up to me to decide what they'd be and where they'd go.

Along the south-facing stone wall by the gate I'd planted, more than a year ago, five La Folette roses. It was a lucky purchase, as I hadn't consulted with our more respected garden writers as to whether La Folette was in or out of favor these days—there are so many bold prejudices about. I faced high risk in planting the wide perennial border I proposed at this rambler's feet. Wouldn't it have been just like me to drop in the excremental Chilean glory flower, *Eccremocarpus scaber*, or worse? I felt that I needed a mentor at this point, preferably one with plants to sell. Not someone who'd go so far as to choose plants for me and tell me where to put them. Just someone to talk to.

A friend had informed me that there was a very interesting specialist nursery near Volterra that was owned and run by two Australians. Venzano it was called. Perhaps I'd go and have a look.

As its name implies, Volterra (rising earth, more or less) sits on a promontory high above its hilly surroundings; the approaching traveler's view of it today has changed only slightly since the Middle Ages. Where other important Tuscan hill towns have spread like rhizomes, this one has kept its ancient dimensions. Just beyond its partially preserved Etruscan walls the austere countryside stretches to the horizon in land swells that rise and fall like the not too distant sea.

It was January: halcyon days, often cloudless, green and mild. In many ways it's my favorite season here. I drove down past Bientina and Pontedera through a wide expanse of plowed fields, the odd hill village cropping up, clusters of stone houses with a church, perched on higher ground. The narrow roads were quiet in this off season of half-empty transatlantic flights and all that skiing up north to divert the German advance.

A few kilometers east of Volterra I made a right turn towards Mazzolla, an enclave of transplanted Sardinian farmers. Their sheep, in long white winter coats, kept to the hilltops; their sheepdogs, just as white, roamed the rough track to Capannone.

At what seemed like the end of the road stood a massive old compound of stone buildings, partially restored. Once an Augustinian monastery, today it's the property of horticulturists Don Leevers and Lindsay Megarrity.

The Venzano catalog explains that the nursery is developing in tandem with the making of its surrounding gardens. While in England it's common to find a garden furnished with plants that you can buy on your way out, it's virtually unheard of here in Italy.

Don was in Australia visiting his grandmother, and so Lindsay, minding the fort, welcomed me with a copy of their splendid catalog. A lean, sandy-haired man in his early forties, he was wearing jeans and a warm sweater, a red-and-white bandanna tied loosely around his neck. He has pale blue eyes, the sunny complexion of someone who lives outdoors. He's soft spoken, not a trace of an Australian accent; he was educated in an English public school. For one or both of the above reasons I'm often saying, "Huh?"

The nursery was closed until mid-February, but Lindsay didn't seem to mind my out-of-season visit by appointment. He took me to the Green Room first, a small square space completely walled in with sweet bay. You enter and exit via green archways. In its four interior corners lie square, box-lined beds, the dirt within now winter clean. The box smell is especially strong in a still, enclosed space—interestingly, Venzano specializes in aromatic plants. One should pause for contemplation in this garden anteroom; there isn't much of an earthly nature to gaze at. It's a palate cleanser, like a *sorbetto* in the middle of a meal. Here in Purgatory you leave the past world behind as you prepare yourself for the rarefied heaven to come.

The Dianthus Room features an extraordinary collection of carnations. The carnation evokes much more for me than senior proms and white sports coats with fern-backed pinks pinned to their lapels; I grew up a few steps away from the Trull family's carnation nursery, Mill Hill Garden Center in North Tewksbury, Massachusetts. They raised the tall, florist's variety, used mostly for funeral bouquets. I'll never forget the olfactory assault as I walked into their heated greenhouses, the glass roofs all whitewashed over. I played there winters in the diffuse light of a warmer season. In an inner yard they kept a pair of sheep to keep the grass chewed down; I once jumped in with them and got my belly butted savagely. I associate the smell of carnations not with funerals, but with a pain in my stomach—I never imagined that those cute, fluffy things could be so mean.

Venzano, with its dry, temperate climate and sunny exposure, is perfect for carnations. Their garden showroom has a long central flower bed with a brick plinth in the middle, a single round stone on top; assembled of found building materials, it's an essay in Zen simplicity. All around grow gray-green carnation tufts, grass-like in full sun, matted against the restraining tufa bricks. There are twenty-five "classic carnations" listed in Venzano's all-Italian-language catalog: "*garofanini classici.*" Most of these are described as "*profumatissimo.*" Of the five reflowering carnations listed, two of them are Venzano-created cultivars: "Arabella Lennox-Boyd" and "Damasco."

"Is this a Judas tree?" I asked. A young leafless sapling, its curious twisted seed pods gave away its identity.

"That's right," Lindsay said, tugging at a branch.

I'd just read one cranky garden writer on the subject of *Cercis sili-*

quastrum, the tree upon which Judas allegedly hanged himself. The author apologizes for the "fiendish" purply rose-colored blooms "screaming" over his garden wall. "Needless to say," he wrote, "that Judas tree isn't mine; it's my neighbor's." These comments gave me pause, as I have two Judas trees, an old mother along the driveway and her sweet young daughter which I squired off and planted behind my hedged front border, where she was now poised to make an absolute fool of me. Shit!

But this welcome encounter with a young cercis in a good—perhaps even tasteful—garden cheered me up.

"I'm glad to see you don't pooh-pooh the Judas tree," I said.

"Ah yes," Lindsay said. "But this is the white one, of course, *siliquastrum 'alba.'* "

"Huh?"

"It's *white*."

"I see," I said disappointedly.

On either side of a descending short flight of steps are single rosemary bushes expertly clipped into cones. "Israeli Commercial" is the cultivar, used in Israel for the production of rosemary essence. At the top of another stairway stand two "Cisampo" rosemarys shaped into perfect cubes. Lots of ideas here to process. Venzano lists twenty-six cultivars of rosemary in its catalog, the final entry being "Venzano Prostate."

"I'm too young for that just yet," I said.

"Oh yes," Lindsay said. "We're poor proofreaders here."

On a lower terrace, featuring still more carnations, was a *Teucrium azureum* in full deep blue flower. I'd mistaken it for the more familiar *Teucrium fruticans*, the bush germander, but Lindsay pointed out its subtle differences of color, size, and growing habit. That's what this garden is about: delicate distinctions.

Lots of things were in flower on this January day: roses, narcissus, *Iris unguicularis, rosmarinus* "Pointe du Raz" and "Gethsemane." There was even one pale blue crocus blooming brazenly out of season. An Italian might have said, *"Fa tenerezza"*—it warms the heart (rough translation). "I'm going to dig that up and paint it," Lindsay said, explaining that he does botanical watercolors—the catalog's graceful cover illustration is Lindsay's work, the winter blue *Iris unguicularis* with *Ipheion uniflorum* shown in vivid, true-to-life detail.

The gardens continue, up and down, along a series of high terraces with timeless views of bare, rolling pastures. To the west rise the Fortezza's walls of *panchina* (the matrix of alabaster). This forbidding castle—begun by Walter de Brienne, Duke of Athens, in the fourteenth century, and completed by Lorenzo the Magnificent—has lived most of its life as a prison. These further gardens we walked are a showcase for an impressive collection of phlomises and lavenders. There's the forever flowering *Lavandula dentata*. There's the lavender cultivar "Venzano," a hybrid of the tomentose, wide-leaved lanata. There are twenty varieties of origanum, fifty or so cultivars of thyme, thirty or more pelargoniums, and dozens and dozens of cistuses, jasmins, and salvias.

"I guess there's enough here for me to make a garden with," I said.

"Well, we have a lot of rare plants," Lindsay said. "But of course, you don't want to make a garden out of only these. The best gardens are made of common things for the most part. Mine are the plants you include for interest."

I was delighted with that good advice, as my garden, half made, had a very common start in life, thanks to the Sorbis's old auntie.

Lindsay invited me in for a cup of tea. In the yard, under a high, rose-covered pergola a live, chubby cat sat in a patch of sun next to its twin in terra-cotta. In the distance a wild boar hunter called and a series of shots rang out. There was a fire going in the convent's huge unfinished kitchen, an upholstered chair next to it, a stack of books, almost all garden titles. Everywhere lay garden magazines, garden catalogs, seed catalogs, plant encyclopedias. On a shelf beside the fireplace stood three miniature terra-cotta flower pots, half as tall as the aspirin bottle next to them. It occurred to me that my own sitting room at home was fast becoming this. My dinner guests, who once so curiously rummaged through my stacked trove of literary biographies, arcane novels, and poetic memoirs, now pick up Gertrude Jekyll's *A Gardener's Testament*, frown, then toss it back into the horticultural drink like an undersized fish.

"I'll be a regular customer," I said, compiling a list of plants I'd pick up in the early spring.

I had no idea that I'd just stepped onto a treadmill of acquisition. What was going on with me? I wanted one of every plant they had.

Now, years later, how does my "La Folette" border shape up?

At one end there's a pretty clump of the Chinese *Ceratostigma plumbaginoïdes*. Its spike-like clusters of deep blue flowers appear in late summer when you've forgotten all about them—*fanno tenerezza*. They butt up against the Cuban lily, *Scilla peruviana*, a bulbous perennial I found in the south of France; in early summer it throws up its conical racemes of star-shaped blue flowers—I *am* partial to blue. Against the wall behind it, in fact, is the *Ceanothus arboreus*, "Trewithin Blue," with its big terminal panicles in spring. It's not the one I brought all the way from London with me on a plane, as that one died in the August sun. I found this one at the La Landriana flower show outside of Rome—needless to say, it came down south with the stand contents of a Dorset nursery. At its feet lies a spiky sweep of the *Eryngium agavifolium*, whose greenish white flowers break up the single color scheme. *Phlomis* "Edward Bowles," a Venzano offering, adds a blast of sulphur yellow to the border's corner in spring, but for the rest of the year it's a quiet clump of gray, curious for its heart-shaped furry leaves that the slugs seem to love even more than I do. Multitoned (orange to yellow) *Helenium* "Autumn Sunshine" rises up out of a horizon of rolling blue *Nepeta* "Six Hills Giant," while farther along, *Nepeta sibirica* and *Veronica incana* complicate the palette. *Lychnis chalcedonica*, the Maltese cross, has scarlet flowers that heat things up for *Achillea* "Cloth of Gold" and the pink *Papavero vivace* "Princess Louise." The red-yellow show calms down to a mild sweep of *Gaura lindheimeri*, whose pale buds open at dawn into white blooms darkening out to pink. I'm allowed more blue now, aren't I? *Agastache foeniculum* was a gift from a friend's garden in Tofori. The blue penstemons I raised myself. *Catananche caerulea*, a native of these parts, leans out over *Cerinthe major purpurascens*, another plant I grew from seed. I went mad for cerinthe when I first saw it at Sissinghurst; what makes it so extraordinary is its deep purple-blue flowers, which are almost the same color as the tender leaves cupped around them—a gorgeous plant from Greece, very much at home here not very far from the sea. With an acanthus clump things come to a broad-leafed end, up against the hedge where a delicate mound of *Hosta* "Moonlight" brings down the curtain.

That's the way it was last year: a mixed-color border—a place at the table for all and sundry. None of this was planned, obviously. I very much admire garden colorists Nori and Sandra Pope of Hadspen (I can't help but call it "Headspin") in Somerset, who contrast subtle hues, composing; their borders are in constant planned harmony, brilliant with every change of light and season. I doubt that I'll ever make it to that high level of horticulture, especially here in Italy, where the summer sun takes its toll on herbaceous plants. My borders will never achieve such resonance, not even if I copied the Popes' schemes plant for plant. But this border of mine does have a unifying theme: it's made up of things that kindly came my way.

DON LEEVERS OF VENZANO INVITED ME TO VISIT A garden. A new and expensive one.

"For your edification," he said.

Arabella Lennox-Boyd, the garden's designer, is prepaid as much as $30,000 for a site visit—a wave of her hand, a glimpse at her extraordinary vision. It's said that the garden here at Ornellaia cost more to complete than the small, though stately, recently remodeled farmhouse it surrounds.

Ornellaia, one of the leading red wines of Italy, is named after this Bolgheri estate where it's produced. It's the home of Marchese Lodovico Antinori, the younger of two brothers whose family has been making wine for more than six hundred years. In his early fifties, he must be one of Italy's most eligible bachelors. His private turbo jet with its American pilot attends his travel needs on a windswept airstrip in the moors at the bottom of his six-hundred-acre estate—it's a fifteen-minute flight to Corsica, to yesterday's luncheon party given by Marella Agnelli, who arrived from Sardinia by helicopter just as Valentino's yacht pulled up to the garden-side dock. (I think I've got that right.) I didn't witness any of this; I heard.

Perhaps this way of life demands a world-class garden—all of the above mentioned international party goers have them. But for Lodovico Antinori the garden is far more than just another inevitable by-product of wealth; though he doesn't tend it with his own hands, he takes an active role in maintaining its good health, in planning its ongoing expansion.

At the Aurelia in San Guido, I entered Viale dei Cipressi, an undulating, five-kilometer-long avenue of towering cypress trees. They were planted in 1801 by Camillo della Gherardesca, whose ancestors' feudal holdings once stretched from Livorno to Populonia, a city of the ancient Etruscan Confederation. The poet Giosuè Carducci spent his childhood in these hills, at Castagneto Carducci, the town that would respectfully take his name. The Bolgheri cypresses must have been already imposing in 1874 when, as an older man passing through the Maremma by train, Carducci looked out and penned the immortal lines that would be memorized by every Italian school kid for years to come: "The cypresses at Bolgheri, honest and tall,/ Leave San Guido in a double row,/ Almost running, giant and childlike,/ They came right up and looked at me." Carducci was awarded the Nobel Prize for Literature in 1906.

I was early for my ten o'clock appointment. It was late July, and yet there was no traffic here, even at the height of this the tourist season; I'd passed only a few power walkers along the great avenue, whose grandeur seemed to suggest that I'd be somehow transfigured by the time I'd reached its end.

I drove into the town of Bolgheri for a brief look around. Entering by way of an arched medieval gateway at its west end, I parked in front of a café in a narrow *piazzetta*. There were hand-painted signs tempting tourists with snack suggestions: *bruschette, panini, torta di mele*. The streets were empty but for a few vacationing Italian families, their minds and conversation focused on what they'd next eat. I went into the bar and ordered a *cornetto* filled with apricot jam, my second breakfast.

I'd collected the *Herald Tribune* with the rest of my mail as I left the house. In "Italy Daily," the new Italian insert, I read:

> Tuscany continues to attract an international crowd of moneyed vacationers. Even Hollywood heart-throb Leonardo di Caprio is heading for the Tuscan hills. He is expected any day at Castagneto Carducci. Antonio Banderas and Melanie Griffith have bought a house in Asciano, away from prying eyes. Other glitterati in arrival: Mel Gibson, Barbra Streisand, Malcolm McDowell, and Richard Gere.

I folded up my paper and sighed. What kind of a house could I buy here if I were—who? Burt Reynolds?

"Is there a real estate office in town?" I asked the barman. I'm an inveterate window shopper.

"Sì sì," he said. "In Donoratico, down the road."

I ate my pastry, stood up, and paced. Against the wall was a display of local wines. There was a bottle of Ornellaia, 1994. The price was L75,000: fifty dollars. I read the barman's mind as he saw me eyeing it—if he can afford to buy real estate, he can afford that bottle of wine. "*È grande, quel vino lì*," he said, a nod and a wink. He had no idea that I was about to drink from the very hallowed source.

From Ornellaia's main gate a straight asphalted road runs upward towards the hills and disappears at a distant low rise; Don Leevers was standing at the foot of it now, waiting for me, a cigarette cupped in his hand. Wisely, Lodovico has hired Don to look in once a week on his garden and its staff of six full-time gardeners. Dressed in khaki shorts, sandals, an unraveling straw hat, and sunglasses, he looked more a far-flung geologist (his previous career) than a gardener. Lodovico instructed him never to handle any tools or do any physical work; Don is here with his guiding authority. Without him Lodovico feels—and rightly so—his beautiful garden would quickly fade and die.

I parked near Ornellaia, the first farmhouse built on the land. There are few historic villas in this part of Tuscany; the masters of these vast landholdings lived in the civilized world, near Rome or Florence, far from the infamous roving brigands who promised to spoil the gentry's fun of a summer weekend. The engraving on the exquisitely embossed Ornellaia label shows this farmhouse as it looked shortly after Lodovico was made a gift of it by his mother in 1980: a plain structure with two matching lean-to wings, two pairs of cypress trees setting the understatement off in quotes. Virginia creeper covers one wing only, and there are fruit trees and a meandering vineyard in front. Don explained that this building now served as the Marchese's offices. The similar-shaped house, a later addition, sitting perpendicular to Ornellaia, is where staff live: the British head gardener, the American chef, the Irish private secretary.

Arabella Lennox-Boyd, whom Lodovico has known since childhood (her husband's surname conceals the fact that she's Italian), was
given the very first commission of her extraordinary career when asked
to lay out this farmhouse garden in 1980. Lawns, hedges, a series of
roughly set walkways, there isn't much to it; no comparison could be
drawn between this, the designer's early effort, and what I'd soon see.

We boarded Don's minivan—so dusty in and out it looked as
though it had just been driven from Paris to Dakar and back—and
made our way more deeply into the estate. The paved road, crossed by
speed bumps, was lined with vines whose grapes had already begun to
turn color. The *Herald* claimed that this summer is the hottest in
recorded history, but I doubt it's true. The vines are planted densely,
French style. I noticed that there were no more than five bunches per
plant: they're after concentration here, prizes, notoriety, high prices,
the right to be counted (at least for quality) among the greats,
Margeaux, Latour, Mouton—Ornellaia is a Bordeaux–style wine.

A few minutes later we'd come to "Bandiera" (flag), Lodovico's
house. Approached via an avenue of ancient olives set in a clipped,
irrigated lawn, the brick-colored stuccoed building has the clear lines
and symmetry of a sixteenth-century landowner's *casa padronale*, but as
are most of the farmhouses here in the Maremma, it was built in the
1930s.

A courtyard in front is flanked by a matched pair of ancillary
buildings that stretch out to your arrival like the forelegs of a seated
sphinx. The scheme is classic, grandiose, but the scale is human, unassuming. The courtyard's paving plan is complicated; geometric, varied,
changing, it's a catalog of masonry options. Planting beds, filled with
various species of lavender, are crossed by narrow walkways that open

to wide crossroads. Fixing the courtyard to a cultural motif, quietly
expressed—folkloric, pastoral, Tuscan—is a giant olive oil jar at its
very center. I thought of Wallace Stevens' poem "Anecdote of the Jar":

> I placed a jar in Tennessee,
> And round it was upon a hill.
> It made the slovenly wilderness
> Surround that hill.
>
> The wilderness rose up to it,
> And sprawled around no longer wild.
> The jar was round upon the ground
> And tall and of a port in air.
>
> It took dominion everywhere.

But this jar will soon be replaced by a fountain, I was told. Don
felt that this front courtyard was the only part of Lennox-Boyd's oth
erwise brilliantly realized plan that seemed to lack something. For him
it was movement, sound. Water! Hence, with another symbolic crux,
this courtyard will soon take on new meaning. Don drew up a design
for a simple stone fountain and presented it to Lodovico. Yes, was the
answer that would lead to a series of high-speed races to the quarries
north of Naples, where the fountain was now being built. It had to be
a new fountain, Lodovico felt; after all, the house was new, and so was
the white stone, from that same southern Italian quarry, that framed
Bandiera's elegantly simple front door.

We'd left the entry courtyard to make a wide loop around Arabella Lennox-Boyd's grand scheme. The sun showed no mercy, but there were two or three attractive local girls bearing cans of water about the terraces and to the single distant plinth-mounted urn, a focal point at the edge of the garden's more formal parts. Water was a problem this year, but so far so good.

The opposite of Lodovico's likely garden tour, Don's loop began at the outer limits, then worked inward, towards the house. He showed me his new "dry border." Thirty meters long, it follows a line of old olive trees beyond which is farmland, more olives, vineyard. The border's white *Iris Florentina*, a species which once dotted Florence's April fields, were neatly clipped back by a third; I was reminded that I ought to do the same to mine. *Agastache rupestris* demonstrated, by its mere presence here, that this was a very smart border; this plant isn't even listed in most plant encyclopedias. Among the more familiar phlomises, rosemarys, and santolinas, native to the Mediterranean islands and mainland seaside, was a globe thistle, *Echinops ritro*, with its stiff, spiny leaves and hairy, white stems. I was drawn to the purple mop-head blooms with their air of dried-flower permanence. Except for the occasional yellow California poppy, this was the only plant in flower; now, in mid-summer, most of the dry border was dormant. "I wish you could have seen it in April," Don said regretfully, committing one of the great gardeners' no-nos.

He pointed to a vineyard beyond. "That's the swimming pool site," he said. "We're moving the vineyard rights farther up towards the hills." I understood what he meant. Wine grapes are overplanted in Italy, the largest wine-producing nation in the world. Strict laws prohibit the construction of new vineyards. You can, however, replace an old vineyard with a new one, and it doesn't have to be in exactly the same place on your land. I asked, "You mean, these laws apply even in the case of a wine like Ornellaia?"

"Oh, yes," Don said.

We continued to the new cutting garden (Don's design) by stepping over a low hedge of dwarf box. My first impulse was to look around for the proper entrance, which I spotted at the far end towards the house—why does it make me uncomfortable to enter a garden where you were never intended to pass? I had the feeling that I wouldn't feel right about being here until I'd gone out and come back in right. This is a rectangular, hedged-off room of straight gravel paths. The beds in between were thinly planted at this young point in the garden's life, but there were orange Mexican sunflowers, *Tithonia rotundifolia* "Goldfinger," and other hot-colored plants in flower. Don said, "The Marchese wanted reds and oranges; 'men's colors' he calls them." There were English roses in bloom: "Gertrude Jeckyll" and "Graham Thomas"—ladies' colors? Don planted the Mexican bush sage, *Salvia leucantha,* in two or three places, a recurring theme. Impressive, full clumps of Peruvian daffodils, *Hymenocallis festalis,* with their extravagantly ragged aromatic white blooms, flank a teak bench.

The head gardener appeared, jumping in the back way over the same low hedge. Nick. Straw hat, grass-green Ornellaia T-shirt, secateurs strapped to his belt in a leather holster. He's very happy here in the Maremma sun, I'd been told, far from his native chilly English Midlands. He took a moment to greet me, but he soon got down to business, telling Don, "I want you to have a look at something in the citrus room."

I followed to a roofless wattle-walled house on the opposite side of the garden. Pure structure and formality reined within; the young

lemons and oranges were installed like sculptures in a gallery. This garden was built just a month ago to Don's plan. "Look here," Nick said.
"It's getting burned." He held a yellowed lemon leaf in his hand, turning it, examining. I looked up at the glaring July sun; not a cloud
approached with its offer of a moment's respite; citrus likes a break
from the midday heat, but these plants weren't getting it today. There
were Valencia oranges here, those tangy, acidic ones, and kumquats.
There was a single *Citrus myrtifolia*, which is sometimes used to make a
spiny, defensive hedge; on its own, as in this case, it's a curious specimen plant, so different in appearance from its neighbors. Don
explained that the wattle wall, a protection from cold winter winds,
would eventually be replaced by a masonry one. I liked the austerity of
this space with its white gravel floor and sparse planting, the bright
delimitation. "In flowering season," Don said, "it'll be a room of
sweet scents that welcome you at the door."

We came to the edge of the Lennox-Boyd domain. Adrenaline
rising! I'd been dying for this. But I approached it quite the skeptic:
most things so talked up sadly disappoint you in the end.

"Her plan is composed of three terraces," Don explained. "The
lowest one here has borders of pink with gray. The middle one, blue
with gray, and the upper one, by the house, white with gray. Essentially, it's a scheme of reflowering roses mixed with plants that like a
hot, dry summer."

The most striking element in this part of the garden is the lawn.
Perfect and weed-free as a putting green, it gave me pause to walk on
it. It's amazing that it was grown from seed, but more remarkable still
is that it's here in the Maremma, thriving even in this relentless sunshine. On staff is a man who does nothing but lawns; still, it takes a
special skill and vigilance to keep grass looking this good. It's almost

unreal, too-good-to-be-true condition is a very dressy finish. This house wears its garden like a tailor-made suit that's not only of the finest cloth but impeccably brushed and pressed.

We walked along the immaculate borders, looking in. There's symmetry and repetition, giving a sense of security. Don pointed out the olive trees, which threw their nonexistent shadows to the roses. "The Marchese said to Arabella, 'Olives? What? But those are everywhere you look!'" She won out, of course, and rightly so, I feel. Why relegate such a magnificent tree, so full of epic implication, to the faraway sun-baked terraces you never visit? There are some rare attention getters here as well: *Salvia dorisiana;* tuft-forming *Cistus x skanbergii;* deep-toned, cascading *Ceanothis* "Blue Mound"; late-flowering lavenders: *L.* Ariele and *L.* Grappenhall. Lennox-Boyd obtained many of these difficult-to-find plants at Venzano—where else?

We climbed three stone steps to the highest terrace. The stairway's wide handrails are fashioned of rosemary hedging. There are two "lime rooms" at the far corners of this uppermost part: the pleached young trees make three walls; the fourth, the open side, faces the house. A pair of green peristyles, through whose tree-trunk columns you can gaze off towards the distant sea, recalls the twin pavilions of Varro's aviary at his villa near Cassino, or those of Frederick the Great's Sansouci—is this Marchese a similar sort of man, I wondered, one who, as a child read forbidden books and played the flute with his servant? *Hebe pinguifolia* "Pagei" and *Potentilla alba* lend their summer blooms to the all-white scheme at the wide-open patio doors. The view from here is to the west: olive trees in mown grass, lavender fields laid out in rows, vineyards, the horizon of pine groves along the beach. Nothing jars the eye; everything contributes, respectfully refers.

At the kitchen end of the house, there's an intricately knotted garden within a hedged-off room: potted junipers and lemons are surrounded by spiky irises, young basil plants, and other aromatic herbs. At the opposite, south end, there's an open-air summer dining room. There are cushioned wicker chairs, blue flowering *Scaevola aemula* in terra-cotta pots, pendulous datura blooms with their sweet, romantic scents.

"He eats very simply," Don said, gazing at the ceramic dining table big enough to accommodate a party of eight. "I've had lunch with him here several times, just lovely simple things from the garden."

I'd fallen into the spell any good garden casts. In the silence following Don's comments, I turned my head from side to side; everywhere I looked my peace of mind was reassured. The floor-length white curtains in a doorway turning in the breeze, the glimpse of a white cotton slip-covered chair, the crystal hurricane lamps on the terrace buffet. The American painted copper weather vane, a trotting horse, the only sculpture present, evoked for a moment my childhood summers on the New Hampshire coast. Nostalgia, retreat; the garden is a vehicle; destinations, known or unknown, always unlimited.

This is a "pleasure garden" in every sense of the word. It's interesting to think of its genealogy.

The Greek Xenophon visited the estates of the Persian satraps as he rode to victory in the East; these were the very first gardens the West had ever seen—*pairidaeza*, they were called, the word from which our "paradise" is derived. Xenophon took this exciting new idea home with him and discussed it in his writings: a *dimora*, or temple, whose surrounding grounds are laid out and planted for beauty's sake alone, a "pleasure garden." He designed the garden called Actemis, at Scillus, fruit trees laid out in a symmetrical plan, an ordered wooded park beyond. This enthusiasm was passed to the Romans, along with so many other aspects of the venerated Greek mother culture, by way of Campania with its strong Hellenistic links. The greatest Romans of the Republic, Caesar, Cicero, Lucullus, all had gardens fashioned in this new way. Augustus Caesar's Villa di Livia at Prima Porta in Rome, Plini's seaside Laurentum, his Tuscan villa near Città di Castello, these are the precursors of what I'm seeing now. The garden, the highest expression of civility, implies love of nature. It symbolizes the will to shape it, tame it, as culture makes sense of life's raw material. Francis Bacon said that the garden offers the purest of human pleasures. Without a garden, he claimed, a house is a mere pile of crude masonry. How heartening it is to see that there are still people, like the man of this house, who share that view.

"Let's see if the Marchese's around," Don whispered. "He'd like very much to meet you."

We went back to the kitchen door looking for the maid, who'd announce us. In a walled-in service patio, a rack of laundry dripped to the terra-cotta terrace floor. One of Lodovico's two Rhodesian Ridgebacks, used to loving human beings, gently greeted us in silence, then sat at my feet and gazed at me with his brown, earnest eyes.

The maid opened the only screen door in the house—screens are rare in Italy, where in summer one lives with the freely passing air, as the ancients did, treasuring that essential contact. She had close-cropped hair and youthful, shiny cheeks. "Oh, Donald," she said, delighted. Behind her on the table was a basket of fresh garden vegetables—peppers, eggplants, zucchini—awaiting her uncomplicated treatment at the chopping board. On the white wall beyond was an array of mounted roebuck antlers, each one dated and signed on the chalk-white cranium, their small size in fitting scale with this diminutive, recreated hunting lodge.

"He's gone to the office," she said, apologizing for Lodovico's absence. I had the sense that he'd ducked out knowing I was here, that the garden is something he's chosen, consciously or not, to avoid discussing, that the response to it of passing visitors, however praising, might somehow diminish its beauty for him, lessen the import of its untranslatable message.

Suddenly the maid's eyes brightened. "Have you seen the magazine?" she asked. This house, its interior and a few tiny photos of the Lennox-Boyd/Donald Leevers collaboration, had just been published in the British *House and Garden*. She showed the article to us, turning pages proudly. She smiled glowingly at Don as she pointed to a photograph taken from one of the upstairs windows: the twin cypress trees, the distant Mediterranean beneath a cloudy June sky, the coarse wilderness tamed—this house's dominion, all that was seen or unseen. "We owe our thanks to you, Donald," she said, coloring with admiration, "truly. *Complimenti! Bravo! Veramente!*"

I visited the *cantina* (winery), got the tour, and tasted Ornellaia. Dante Scanavino, the dapper, linen-suited manager, spoke yearningly of this wine's future, withholding comment about its present excellent quality—yesterday's wine, after all, is made. A celebrated New Zealand winemaker had recently come on the advisory staff with his courageous new methods that promised still greater success with the sauvignon. "Our *cantina*," Scanavino said, "is fine; little room for improvement there. It's the vineyard where great wines are made.

Every year we learn a little bit more." The 1995, a massively structured mouthful, rendered me winespeakless.

I left Leevers and Scanavino discussing the estate's water crisis. Scanavino's directive: "Have them water English style!"

Driving away, I wondered what "English style" watering could be; did he mean generous (after all, soaking rains are frequent there), or might he have meant stingy? (Italians are apt to think the Brits quaintly parsimonious.)

Only a very good lunch could complete my visit to Ornellaia, a garden that both taught and inspired me. I knew a place to take my inner dialogues of response to all this beauty. I knew *just* the place.

I drove back down Viale dei Cipressi, five cooling kilometers in the shade. Turning left, heading south, I passed Tenuta San Guido, where Sassicaia is made, one of the most successful of the new international-style Tuscan red wines. After fifteen minutes across the moors, where only the occasional farmhouse interrupted these broad flatlands by the sea, I'd come to San Vincenzo, a small coastal town. Though the built-up beaches to the south are a madhouse in high summer, the town's neoclassical streets are shady and still. A narrow right turn led me, descending, to a little port of bobbing small craft; in all my many visits here, I've never had trouble finding a parking space. There are a few cafés along the quay, a couple of inexpensive restaurants serving simple seafood spaghettis and *frittura mista*, fried squid and shrimps and *calamaretti*, lemon-bright Tuscan white wines in sweating clear bottles. The usual midday breeze had kicked in by now, and there were low, spindrift-topped waves on the stone-blue sea. Visible in the distance to the south were the rising, forested, slate-gray hills of Populonia, and beyond them, several miles off its coast, lay those of the cloud-capped ancient island of Elba: Virgil poeticized about it, Napoleon was exiled to it, Conrad imagined it in his last, unfinished novel, *Suspense*—he'd never actually been to Elba.

To the north of town is a seaweed-strewn, coarse-sanded beach where a few local bathers were stretched out in the sun, their children and dogs playing at the water's tideless edge. In the distance beyond is Gherardesca, the far more beautiful Antinori beach with its raked shoreline and it palm-roofed cabañas (members only), a shimmering mirage of privilege in the curve of a wide, undeveloped bay. There, and at Bibbona further up, the sea is deep and buoyantly salty, and the beach is lined with groves of maritime pines, giant green-black umbrellas that generously shade their maquis undergrowth of cistus, myrtle, and santolina.

Gambero Rosso is entered via a set of stairs that connects the port to the higher shopping street above. Its few wide, round tables have views of the sea framed by arched, awning-shaded windows facing southwest. The simple white-walled dining room is a neutral context for the extravagant blooms of a potted *Medinilla magnifica* with its pink pendant panicles, a rain forest plant of lush, cheerful beauty.

Winter Sunday drives bring Gil and me often to San Vincenzo, to a portside stroll, lunch here. But the discreet headwaiter, in his formal way, didn't seem to recognize me now. That's all right; I prefer the anonymity, really.

The very talented owner-chef, Fulvio Pierangelini, took my order. A curly-haired man with a stern gaze, he was wearing elegant suede loafers and tailor-made trousers below his chef's whites. He'd just come from the only other occupied table here, a French father and son, to whom he showed well his language talents, his knowledge of the diverse wines he lists.

I removed my napkin from the *sottopiatto*. ITALIA, the steamship line's engraved emblem, appeared in front of me on a silver dish, salvaged, so to speak, from the first-class dining room of the S.S. *Rex*. At the bottom rim, the chef had added his own initials, F. P.

A wine was about to be served the two Frenchmen, who must have just come from the far north—the son had a cashmere sweater over his shoulders even though the windows were open to the port and the outside temperature was pushing close to ninety. Their wine choice was Masseto, the highly praised merlot made by Lodovico Antinori at Ornellaia. I'd never tasted Masseto and was curious about it; this morning, alas, it was withheld, as were samples of the estate's other wines, Le Volte, a San Giovese–based "Super Tuscan," and Poggio alle Gazze, the sauvignon with which I'd hoped to begin my complete and thorough *degustazione*. The tuxedoed waiter corked the Masseto with great dexterity and rinsed out two huge Riedel crystal glasses with the first few drops of it—it's a custom I've never seen practiced in France, yet all the better Italian wine stewards seem to do it. By the time the wine reached the Frenchmen's table the bottle was dripping in condensation. The older man reached out and felt it. "Is it too cold?" he asked. "*Temperature de la cave*," the waiter said with airs and a long-suffering shrug—confident service; the Frenchmen must have felt very much at home.

I ordered a half bottle of En Chailloux, Didier Dagueneau's Pouilly-Fumé. Scanavino at Ornellaia had told me, "It's a good idea to try wines from other countries; so many of us here make the mistake of drinking only Italian." I'd fallen into that trap myself over the years.

My antipasto appeared, a surprise: a tiny red mullet, one of the tastiest fishes of the Mediterranean, filleted and served as a warm salad with two young lettuce leaves. A drop of Balsamic vinegar and a dribble of olive oil framed the simple composition. Despite the French-style elegance, the food here is clearly Italian, as our chef chooses fresh ingredients that need no complicated overlays to make them flavorful.

Pierangelini looked in on his other clients. The father had recognized the label of the wine I was drinking. "What year is it?" he asked the chef.

"Ninety-six," Pierangelini said.

He was outraged. "What do you mean, ninety-six? *Mais qu'es que vous dites?* So young? Don't you age your wines?"

Witholding comment of my own (who asked me?), I thought about the fact that just a couple of years ago I knew almost nothing about wine. In restaurants I'd randomly open a list to choose by price wines that were seldom better than just so-so. Now that I subscribe to a couple of wine periodicals, I'm in much better shape; it's amazing how a little newly acquired knowledge and tasting experience can so enhance the table, even without one's spending much more than before. I knew now, for instance, that unlike Pure Sange and Silex, Dagueneau's top-of-the-line Loire whites, his En Chailloux, my selection, was made to be drunk young. At two years old, the '96 was exactly right, full of honey, ripe melon, and wild herbs; I was hitting it at the height of its age arc.

The specialty of the house was served. *Passatina di Ceci con Gamberi* is a creamy-smooth puree of chick peas with lightly steamed shrimps afloat. Decorating this sensuous conceit was a simple red flower fashioned of tomato coulis. The honesty of the ingredients, like the fresh scent of the sea on a breeze, came through above all else, artifice only a vehicle.

I'm lucky to have grown up with a mother who cooked. Her mother, a French Canadian, valued the table as I'd been taught to do. My mother's favorite seafood was lobster. She knew how to prepare it in lots of different ways: baked, stuffed, gratinéed, or cold in a salad, a frothy lemon dressing. But vegetables were her passion. She longed for summers, when every morning she'd drive down the road in her bright red Buick convertible to Garabedian's farm stand, where she'd load up on green beans, string beans, butter beans, fresh potatoes, and sweet corn, especially "Butter and Sugar." All her summer dinners involved three vegetables prepared in different ways. I can remember how they tasted now, sweet and earthy as the August thunderstorms that blew across the Garabedian's cornfields to later pass, perfumed, through our screened-in porch with its wicker chairs and Chinese red cushions—my mother loved red.

But I knew nothing of the real art of food until the late seventies, when Gil and I found ourselves one September night at Troigros in Roanne, France. The glass-walled kitchen was a theater of toqued chefs in a stage set of silver and white. I remember *Composition de la Maison*, every fresh berry known, dribbled over at your table with a runny *crème fraiche* in an energetic grid pattern, a Jackson Pollock of a dessert. It was the evening that changed my gastronomic life.

Today seafood ravioli was my *primo piatto*. They were shaped like little wontons; half were of white pasta, half of pasta blackened with squid ink. In the center of the plate, shreds of sautéd squid sat in a pink chervil-dusted tomato sauce that spread to the edges of the dish, moistening all. Afterwards: turbot with a *ragù* of crayfish—salt water/fresh water—on a thin cushion of pureed potatoes. I passed on the exquisite desserts, but indulged in the fresh baked bite-sized tarts and gelées.

I was regretting the hour's drive ahead of me, however beautiful, as I sighed and drank the last drop of my En Chailloux: an elegant finish to a unique morning.

The Frenchmen rose to leave. The father stopped cordially at my table and asked, *"C'était bon le vin?"*

"Very," I said. "Didier's wine. He's great!"

"Yes yes," the man answered, "but you should be drinking that in ten years' time."

No no, I thought to myself, now.

Instead I said, "But today's the day I'm here."

He smiled and almost bowed. *"A oui,"* he said, *"ça c'est vrai."*

chapter eight

THE SPIRIT OF THE SPOT

"HOW FUNNY THAT YOU DREAM ABOUT GARDENS,"
Gil said.

"Well, if I were making semiconductors," I said, "I'd probably be dreaming about that."

I was telling him about the garden I'd visited that night in my sleep, a sunken, hedged-in room of green. The feeling I had within this serene, lush space was curiously uplifting even though I stood happily, protectedly, just a little bit lower than the rest of the world.

My dreamed-up garden, I'd soon realize, was a version (highly altered) of Lawrence Johnston's White Garden at Hidcote. A nearly square space with shoulder-high walls of yew, his garden is entered on one side by descending a short flight of steps. The room isn't entirely sunken, as you can exit on its three other sides at ground level via arched green doorways; it's a garden built against a slope. Still, the presence of that staircase, the memory of having entered descending it, and the perceivable ground level above where an old cedar of Lebanon throws wide its thick, feathery umbrella, all make you feel as if you were tucked away in a low bunker of safety.

I pored through my books to find photographs of the White Garden at Hidcote in England's Cotswolds, a place remembered far better by my sleeping mind than by my daytime memory.

It's divided into quadrants with an open circular intersection at its center. The four resulting flower beds, framed by dwarf box hedging, are planted out in white tulips and a mix of white perennials. Within these four beds, towards the paved center circle, stand four box columns, each topped with a perched topiary bird facing inward, in whose mythic, almost Mayan posture you might read the riddles of fable. You can't help but feel that there's a lofty wisdom beneath this garden's fictions, in its masterful ordering of shapes and forms, a marriage of geometry and fantasy. Such places (like my grotto, for instance) have only one role in life: to give focus to the imagination.

I wanted nothing more, just now, than to make that kind of secret garden here in Massa Macinaia, a destination within. But where?

While we were having lunch that day in the *serranda*, Lionel Fielden's conservatory, the new garden's site suddenly suggested itself. There it was, right before my eyes, the plot of ground upon which I'd erect my allegorical, open-air temple.

If any part of my garden had been crying out for total restructuring, it was this wide passageway between the house and the stairway that leads to the shepherd's cottage and the pool. Never having considered its potential until now, I'd always thought of this dismal lot as little more than an unpleasant distance you walk, like a dull hallway between the garage and the kitchen. Ziggy's cage was there, long abandoned, as he'd sadly passed away leaving his young widow, who proved to be considerably less lovable than he—we gave her to a breeder with cocks aplenty and she must have been a happy woman in the end.

The garden site is walled off on one side by the best-built retaining wall we have. Fourteen feet high, its flat-fronted field stones are set in old mortar that wears a rich patina of lichen rosettes and moss. It was constructed in the eighteenth century by Count Sinibaldi, whose ancestors had built this house as a hunting lodge. (I know the wall's date because the count included detailed records of all the improvements he'd made to the estate in a will which left the property to his nephew, the Marchese Massei.) There was a very tall *Magnolia grandiflora* in the center of this space, surrounded by a multicultural mess of plants grumbling among themselves over elbow room. A high-pile carpet of *Vinca major*, whose blue blooms in spring all too quickly bend and fall, spread its cover far and wide, while the rest of the garden was a lumpy, ratty lawn. Sure, there was the *Viburnum x carlcephalum*, with its huge popcorn-ball blooms and opulent fragrance in spring, but most of the other plantings here were charmless: the inverted witch's broom of a pomegranate tree, a rangy white spirea, an entanglement of wisteria tentacles with nowhere to go but snakingly sideways.

At the far end by the steps stood an ancient plum, *Prunus domestica*. More than fifteen feet tall, it was probably a sparrow's gift to this garden, as the hills from here to Ticino are patchy with frail white plum flowers in early spring. This poor old tree was suffering from a killing fungus, but it still put out its tart, cherry-sized fruit each summer, a nice snack as you climbed the steps to the pool.

All through lunch I plied Gil with the vague images of my dream, and my instant, outlandish, much less vague plans for the garden we now looked at through the glass conservatory wall—I was selling the project as I developed it, both to him and to myself.

Later we walked the site. Waving my hands about and talking fast, I remembered what I liked most about the garden I'd visited in my dream, that great feeling of comfort, of protective enclosure.

"We'll take everything out," I said, encouraged. "I don't want my new garden to have anything to do with what's here now. Let's go back to the garden's origins, capture the spirit of the spot."

"Everything out?"

"Well, not everything. We'll leave those three cypress trees. I wouldn't take those out."

"But the magnolia?"

"Chop it down."

Even though his chin would briefly drop, I knew Gil wouldn't object. In the Olivers' day this *Magnolia grandiflora* was pruned into the forced shape of a narrow cone, a shiny Christmas tree. It's a kitsch gardenesque growing method that's still employed at all the nurseries in Pistoia: they raise them to be planted in Victorian formality, seemingly unaware that passing years and styles have rendered such cruel methods anachronistic. (On second thought, here's an idea for one of our celebrated visionaries of the "urban landscape": a zigzagging stainless steel paved *allée* of *Magnolia grandiflora* cones in individual planters of tractor tire tubes painted white!) We decided early on never to prune our magnolia again, hoping that it might recover its natural form, and after ten years it was well on its way to some semblance of normality. But one winter, while we were in New York, a well-meaning project gardener pruned it back to a tight cone at his own initiative. Gil was furious. It would take another ten years before the magnolia looked like a magnolia and not a monkey puzzle tree.

"Well, I wouldn't miss that stupid thing," Gil said about the magnolia, "but the plum?"

"Chop it down," I said.

"Never."

He'll get over it, I thought, changing the subject.

Paper, pencil, triangle, ruler; I worked out a plan at my desk. The proposed garden was perhaps twice as large as the Hidcote model I'd reimagined in my dream, and so I wanted a layout that went far beyond Johnston's simple cruciform with a circle at the central intersection.

At the Giardino Buonaccorsi near Potenza, the Renaissance terrace garden is composed of a grid of L-shaped flower beds that are bordered by knee-high box hedging. Each group of four such beds is anchored at the intersection of crossing walkways with a terra-cotta pot on a stone base. As I thought about adapting this scheme for my own garden, I remembered having seen the very same layout somewhere else. But where? I pored through my green thumbed books, the endless memorized images, and found it. Harold Nicholson had used the Buonaccorsi geometry in his design for Vita Sackville-West's White Garden. But instead of placing pots within the framing groups of four L-shaped flower beds, he planted box cubes. Very clever, I thought.

I decided to steal a little from both the Buonaccorsi and the Nicholson plans. In my two central groups of four hexagonal flower beds I'd place terra-cotta olive oil jars (chosen for their modesty; every old Tuscan farm has cellars full of them). All other groups of four flower beds would be interposed with box cubes as in Harold Nicholson's scheme.

I came up with the idea of building each of the four outside garden walls of a different material. Given that one of the walls was already there and of stone, it might have made the garden seem U-shaped—off, somehow, from a design point of view—if I'd built the other three walls out of a single type of hedge. The wall through which the stairway passed I'd make out of sweet bay, the mainstay of Italian hedging plants. It would be the same height as the stone wall, and it would be trained to form an archway over the stairs. On the valley side I'd plant a hedge of box, trimmed at shoulder height; from most parts of the terrace you'd be able to look over it to views of the distant Apuan Alps, to the pine-forested mountains closer in, to a neighboring villa on a hilltop in a crown of cypress trees, but you'd not be able to see any other parts of my garden from here. On the new garden's fourth side, closest to the house, I'd plant a high yew hedge with a passage cut through at the center. This doorway would be the only other entrance to my now secret space, a garden not unlike the one I'd visited in my dream.

At Buonaccorsi the *vialetti*, or walkways, are laid with river gravel. But at the Sackville-West garden they're paved in red brick. I felt that paved *vialetti* would be easier to maintain than gravel-covered ones, as they'd require no weeding. And I liked the look of them better: more finished—beautiful in the rain, when they take on the deep red gleam of a waxed floor. The central path, a straight boulevard that links the two access doorways, was already there, made of thick, irregular slate slabs; I'd leave this just as it was, as variations in paving methods are common in Italy's formal gardens.

There, that was my plan.

What would my co-commissioner think?

"It's an excellent drawing," Gil said. "But where's my plum tree? Where's the viburnum?"

"Oh, they're gone," I said.

"No no," he said. An ironic laugh. "This *won't* do. I'll call out Greenpeace! I'll go on a fast, I'll chain myself to that old plum!"

Back to the drawing board.

Well, it wasn't as pleasingly symmetrical as it had been in the original plan, where everything came logically together. The new limitations offered challenges to the fledgling designer, challenges he'd have preferred not to have faced. But in the end the project still had its garden-worthiness. Life is a compromise; in gardens it's that of nature and the gardener's vision. Perhaps our new garden was even more interesting a bit botched up in this way; there was the cruelty of the aging process between its irregular lines, the touching subtext of imperfection, of decline, of passing time—"Let not a monument give you or me hopes,/ Since not a pinch of dust remains of Cheops." That's the way I'd look at it whenever its irregularity jarred me.

It was spring by the time we got to work. Justin, the British gardener we hire for bigger jobs, started in with his nimble, bright red backhoe just as Rupert and Lillian Meade of East Eighty-second Street, New York, and their three-year-old daughter, Clarissa, moved into the shepherd's cottage (right above it), which they'd rented for a two-week stay in beautiful, peaceful Tuscany.

I suppose I hadn't timed that well, but it was too late now. The ground was broken, work was in progress. The last thing you want to do (not just in Italy, but anywhere in the world) is stop construction on a building site; you'll never get the crew back again.

In the deepest corner of the new garden, where the wall meets the stairs which lead to the guest house and pool, the ground level was six feet higher than everywhere else. Perhaps it had been a convenient place for the shepherd, Lionel Fielden, and the Olivers to dump their garden refuse—my theory. The new garden had to be level, at all cost. I was sure that the space I was working with had been flat when the wall was built and that this corner mound had risen with the passing of time. I was convinced that the great wall's base was buried under there. Others of us doubted it.

My hunch proved right. Half a day's digging unveiled the wall in its original dimensions: just as level at the bottom as it was at the top. Still, it took close to a week to fully dig the corner out, and it took all of the following week to spread the removed dirt throughout the proposed garden site, filling in lower dips, scraping the entire surface to a good working flatness. Eight hours of bulldozer work a day, five days a week. The poor Meades; the noise must have set their teeth on edge. Oh well, the job was getting done.

But let's go back a minute, back to when the "digger," as Justin calls it, first started in.

One morning after making my rounds about the farm and garden site, I found Ottavia in the kitchen looking a bit perplexed. She has a pleasant little insecure smile that she tones down in the presence of her *padroni* (perhaps she thinks we find it common, or somehow inappropriate), but when she sees me inevitably responding to her little insecure smile in kind, out comes all her blushing laughter, the hell with decorum. So there we were, the two of us, laughing with each other in the kitchen—it was quite a while before it occurred to me that she was the only one who knew what was so damn funny!

"Aren't you gonna tell?" I said.

She had all she could do to hand me a rumpled piece of paper (obviously torn from a child's scholastic lined notebook). I looked at the paper, turning it this way and that—which way was up? It was a drawing of a bug! A big bug. A bug under a microscope. Here were the bug's antennae, its stelets, proboscis, and pedipalpi, all those contemptible bug members you can't see with the naked eye and yet you know they're there.

"What *is* this?" I said.

Beet-red, Ottavia couldn't speak for the laughter.

"I don't want this for dinner," I said, "if that's what you have in mind."

"The signora from the guest house . . ." she said, pointing to Al Pastore lest there be any confusion. "The *signora* came down earlier this morning and handed me this drawing. She says they're in her house."

"They're in their house? These things? What on earth are they?" I don't know an insect's mandible from its gaster, but I was sure we weren't talking about mosquitos.

"I think that's what she was trying to say," Ottavia said. "She speaks Italian very badly."

"I wouldn't know about that," I said, "she hasn't spoken to me in any language." Lillian Meade seemed to think I was the bellman or something—I made the mistake of helping Rupert with their bags.

Ottavia and I studied the drawing together. Someone had put a lot of work into this hexapodal study, and I knew it couldn't have been the three-year-old Clarissa. Ottavia turned the paper over to show me what was written on the other side. BEDBUGS, it said.

"Bedbugs?" I said.

"What is that?" she asked.

"*Quelle bestie che vivono nel letto,*" I said.

Ottavia put her hands to her face. "*Ma, non è possibile!*" she said.

"*Ci penso io,*" I told her. "Leave it to me." As I recalled, Rupert Meade last evening had said that he was taking the whole family off to the market in Forte dei Marmi the next day, and that they wouldn't be back until after lunch. This would give me more than enough time to investigate.

I trudged through the grinding clay of my new garden site, the backhoe's engine ringing in my jaw, and climbed the steps to the shepherd's house. I want to make something very clear at this point should anyone hesitate before renting my adorable guest house for a brief pastoral visit to Lucca. We've since completely restored the facility to Relais et Chateaux opulence, but in the days of my little narrative here, the house was . . . rustic. I prefer that word to my niece's description of the place: "poopy." Because the house in those days wasn't poopy at all, it was just . . . rustic.

Crossing the shepherd's sweet little cottage garden of a pear tree, a persimmon, and a pomegranate, I got a whiff of the most gaggingly offensive smell conceivable—and it wasn't the diesel fumes of Justin's bright red "digger," and it wasn't the stinking gladwyn everywhere you looked. It was far worse. It was the smell of, what? Dead meat?

Maybe this place is every bit as "poopy" as Abigail says, I thought.

I walked straight into the house (it was unlocked) and right away tracked down the source of this contemptible stench. The Meades had left out on the kitchen table the remains of their very unconventional breakfast: a greasy salami, a wedge of Gorgonzola, and half a big red onion, already going dry and shrunken at the cut. I thought, Should I wrap it all up in plastic and put it in the refrigerator for them? And then I remembered that poor Rupert Meade had that funny disease where if he doesn't eat a whole three-course meal every thirty-seven minutes, his wife ends up having to call him an ambulance. Perhaps the Meades' thinking was this: Forte dei Marmi is a thirty-minute drive. If Rupert had a pizza in Forte, got right into the car, and drove here, that would give him exactly seven minutes to park, walk along the farm road to the cottage, and make a ravaged, headlong dive for the salami. But what if the salami, thanks to my fastidiousness, had inconveniently found its way back into the refrigerator? Just that slight delay in his precisely planned schedule could have killed him.

I left it out. Pew.

I don't know why I felt like a burglar, all ajangle, climbing the stone steps to the bedrooms. After all, it was my house, and I had the same right to enter its occupied rooms as a chambermaid might have, had we offered chambermaid services in those days (at present we do).

Well, *of course* there were bugs up there! The Meades had left all the windows wide open and it was spring and this is the country. Bugs are part of it, part of that forgotten, forested, ivy-tressed life most city people have only read about in *Mill on the Floss*. Bugs are everywhere (except in genetically altered fruits and vegetables), though to tell you the truth, that particular bug, that which Lillian Meade had rendered so chillingly lifelike in a fine, conscientious hand, didn't recall any of the local bugs I knew—but maybe it was just its size that confounded me.

I would never insist that people on vacation make their beds, pick their wet bathing suits up off the floor, or return bathroom towels to the appointed racks, but the Meades had seemed such the model American family to me: Mr. and Mrs. Everything-in-Its-Place—besides, they had a young lady to bring up here. Suffice it to say that I chose not to close armoire doors or dresser drawers even though there wasn't a single one of either of the above that didn't gape as if an African wind had just blown through, and I really wished it would soon—that smell! I went to their half-stripped bed, calling up all my courage to bring my face down close to its matted surface, and then I thought to myself, You idiot! You can't see bedbugs!

But how did Lillian Meade get one of them to pose so nicely for her?

Gil and I were bending over the dictionary. Oh, my God! There it was, illustrated. It didn't look exactly like Lillian Meade's drawing, but it didn't look *unlike* it either. I compared the two, holding both. "Hers is skinnier," I said.

"Well, of course it's skinnier," Gil said. "No one's slept in those beds since last summer."

> bed•bug (bed'bug') *n.* Also Bed bug. A wingless, bloodsucking insect, *Cimex lectularius,* that has a flat, reddish body and a disagreeable odor and that often infests human dwellings.

"*Often?*" I said.

"Well, you went up there," Gil said. "Was there a disagreeable odor?"

"No no," I said, "it was the very breath of spring in that house."

"Then there are no bedbugs. How could there be? Bedbugs live in flophouse hotels with a high turnover, not in places like that."

"Oh," I said.

"I mean, think about it. Who last occupied those beds and when was it?"

I tried to remember. "Oh, my God! Last September. Your brother Steve and his family! No! And they're so clean-looking. Who'd have thought they have *Cimex lectularius*."

"Oh, Paul! You think Steve and his family have bedbugs? They live in Pride's Crossing, for heaven's sake."

"I'm only kidding," I said. "Of course they don't have bedbugs." Afterthought: "But Julia goes to boarding school!"

"Oh, Paul. Where's your head?"

"I don't know," I said, "but I'm gonna have it shaved in a minute, Jeesh."

"Bedbugs can't survive without sucking human blood," Gil said. "How could they have gone a whole winter up there without a body?"

"*Cimex lectularius* are cannibals," I said. "You didn't know that?"

"ALL RIGHT! Look. Here's what we'll do. We'll get a can of bug spray, and Ottavia can give the mattresses a good disinfect. OK? Let's not argue with them. They're the guests. The customer's always right. We disinfect and hope they feel better about it."

Not a cloud in the sky; a Mediterranean day. Justin dug and dug. Ottavia got Ugo to give her a hand dragging the guest house mattresses outside to give them a good biological shelling in the open air.

It wasn't until late afternoon that I ran into Rupert Meade giving Clarissa an airing in the meadow. He was wearing a Yankees hat and a terry-cloth bathrobe with the word EVERGLADES embroidered over the pocket. To tell you the truth, I'd been avoiding him—not because of bedbugs; because of the backhoe noise.

"Lovely weather," he said.

"Isn't it," I said.

"What's this interesting plant there?" he asked.

"*Cimex lectularius*," I said.

Clarissa danced "down the green hill athwart a cedarn cover"; I wanted to put a little wreath of *Gaura lindheimeri* in her hair.

"Something's very disturbing . . ." Rupert said.

There it was: the foreseeable shift of mood. Suddenly I was a landlord again. Bye-bye, Justin and your nimble red backhoe, see you next . . . year?

"I'm very sorry about that noise," I said. "We're . . . ah . . . building a new garden here you see, and—"

"No no," Rupert said. "The noise is fine. I mean, we live on East Eighty-second Street, for cryin' out loud. This place is like, utter tranquility to me. I don't even hear it."

Lillian appeared, making a dash for her daughter as if she hadn't seen her since they'd left New York—I was amazed that she'd let her out of her sight for as long as it took for Rupert to walk her out here to the meadow (perhaps, for career motives, she'd had her only child a bit late in life).

"Hi," I said.

She diverted her eyes and said nothing. I thought about how often in hotels I might have completely ignored the bellmen. I'd make it a policy from now on to always smile and sat hello to them as if they were human beings and not hotel chain automatons.

"The disturbing thing is this," Rupert said. "Some animal came into the house while we were out and carried off my salami and a wedge of Gorgonzola."

In the corner of my eye I saw Riga and one of her friends, both looking very stuffed, bouncing heavily down the stairs.

"Must have been a badger," I said.

"A badger?"

"Oh yes," I said, "they can be quite pesty."

"Perhaps I should put my food away from now on," he said.

"Oh, I think that would be a good idea," I said. "How about in the refrigerator?"

"Yes," he said. "The refrigerator. Brilliant. I'll try that!"

THE MEADES WERE GONE AND SO WAS THE *MAG-nolia grandiflora*. "Clean Slate with Viburnum and Plum," the not-quite-empty canvas might have been called.

Finding the right builder to lay the *vialetti*, the walkways between the plant beds, wasn't easy. The brilliant Gabriele, job foreman for all our restorations here, would have overbuilt it with foundations strong enough to sustain a steady traffic of three-ton Isuzu pickups. It was a *garden* I was making, not an *autostrada*. Gabriele no. Justin suggested an English friend of his, Peter. "The English are very good masons, you know." Peter had a free month. He could start tomorrow. He was a nice guy, honest and serious.

We hired him. Working with a Moroccan laborer who hand-cleaned hundreds of old painted-over terra-cotta ceiling tiles with acid, Peter got the job done in twice the estimated time and for twice the expense. Part of this overrun was my fault; I can't hold myself back. When the work was almost done, I came up with the idea of including two stone benches like the ones I'd placed along the front hedge. I installed one of the benches at the foot of the old plum, where the view off to the Apuans was best. I imagined myself, summer evenings, sitting there with a glass of Sorbus, watching the swallows circle in a waft of nicotiana. The second, smaller bench I placed at the base of the cypress tree, the only other full-sized tree that falls within the garden's geometric plan.

How funny the site looked with this new network of walkways that made no sense without the filling box plants in place. But it was July and no one in his right mind plants a garden in the summer sun. We'd have to live with the nasty hot mess until the autumn.

The plants were furnished by Andrea Mati of Pistoia. In that we'd known his extraordinary grandmother (she slid down banisters in her eighties) and had met him when he was just a boy, he's always given us good prices. But several hundred box plants, a dozen yews, and just as many sweet bays go for a stinging price, especially the good-sized plants I wanted—why wait ten years for results if you don't have to? The garden at this point had been dubbed by Gil, "Paul's Folly."

All winter long I thought about what I'd plant within the fourteen open flower beds I'd created in my new secret garden. Vita Sackville-West's White Garden is planted in a scheme that negates the garden's intrinsic symmetry. Iceberg roses, *Rosa longicuspis, Argyranthemum foeniculaeum,* white Regale lilies, delphiniums, eremurus, and foxgloves, are all planted without the expected repetition or common concerns for height that form other such gardens everywhere. My garden would not be all white, but I wanted that same kind of irregularity, so sophisticated-seeming, every bed different from the next in texture, height, and color.

The Terrace would be a summer show of flowers. It was common at Italian Renaissance villas, such as Villa Medici at Castello, to have geometric flower gardens like mine off to the sides of the house. Cosimo de' Medici personally cultivated his collection of exotics in these showcase gardens, which were handy to his private apartments. Though not endowed with endless good qualities, Cosimo was a great plant lover. He founded the School of Botany at Pisa and developed the municipal herb garden in Florence by importing medicinal plants from America. At home at Castello he grew violets, columbines, irises and lilies, tulips from the Near East, and marigolds from Africa. There was no poverty of choice; as early as the sixteenth century there were already several thousand identified cultivated species of plants in Italian gardens.

I did what Cosimo de' Medici had done, and planted everything that came into my grasp. Nowadays, however, there *is* a poverty of choice—Italians don't grow perennials with the same enthusiasm as do the Brits. I put in lupines, delphiniums, *Solanum rantonetti*, and echinacea, and I planted white violets under the viburnum. From seed I grew *Nicotiana sylvestris*, *Mirabilis jalapa*, and *Tithonia rotundifolia*, the Mexican sunflower. In a spirit of bold all-inclusion I tossed in a few bright dahlias, whatever monstrous bulbs the nurseries had left after all the mamas of Lucca had bought off the sensibly less showy ones. I thought I was being playfully outrageous. Wrong. I was like a toddler with fingerpaint; I had it all over my bib and the walls too.

In spite of my intensive spring efforts, only a few of the garden's fourteen beds were planted out; most spent the summer as roughly formed polygons of weeds. September brought despair. A garden isn't like a soufflé. If a soufflé fails, you break more eggs and try again; if a garden goes wrong you have to wait an entire year before you can give it another shot. It could take me the rest of my life to get this garden right.

Almost everything I'd planted there was wrong. You can't grow lupines in Italy—why hadn't I believed Iris Origo on that point? And delphiniums are so English in style that they undermined my garden's delicate sense of place.

But in all this failure there were one or two successes. The tithonia's orange, daisy-like blooms looked good; they had the right height and reflowering habit. Mirabilis did an admirable job of filling out space, and so I decided to build upon it. I added mirabilis of every imaginable color—yellow, cream, pink, white—all of it grown from seed I'd gathered from roadside gardens while mama and her family were inside having lunch. My expanding mirabilis collection even included a two-toned cultivar; Gil called it the "Harlequin."

But then, one summer day, came a visitor.

"Oh no," the visitor said, "Mirabilis! That sucker just *ruined* my garden. You'll never get rid of it. It's got rhizomes like burrowing moles." As soon as he'd left I got out my fork and had a look. He was right; mirabilis holds onto the earth with an iron grip.

This year I'm taking it out (I hope I can get it all). Not just the mirabilis, but everything else too. I've had it with all these flowers. It's time I came to terms with the fact that I'm much more a leaf man that a bloom man. I'll be filling my terrace's fourteen beds with *Caryopteris clandonensis* "Heavenly Blue." I love its fine gray-green leaves. Easy weeding, no staking up. In late summer we'll walk among geometric cushions of cool blue. How refreshing.

The other day Gil came to me and said, "You want to hear a funny story?"

"OK."

"Chris and Draper were visiting when we were finishing up work on the Terrace. Remember?"

"Yeah."

"Well, they thought you'd lost your head. They couldn't get over it. They couldn't imagine doing such a useless thing as building a gar-

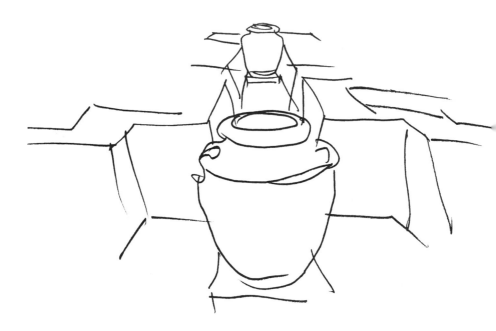

den like that. What for? Is he crazy? Spending all that on a garden? They were worried, not just for you, but for me. They kept saying, 'He's out of his mind.'"

"Oh, really?" I said.

Long pause. "I thought you were crazy too," he confessed, daring a grin.

"Oh, you did, did you," I said. "And now?"

"I love it. I think you really captured the spirit of the spot."

chapter nine

GODLINESS AND GRACE

HE WAS AT THE GATE. CLAUS SCHEINERT, ONE OF the leading new garden makers of Europe, had taken me up on my impulsive invitation. He was coming to see my garden.

I'd been to visit his garden, after all. I was pretty bold. I'd read about his exquisite La Casella in Vivian Russell's book *Gardens of the Riviera*. I remembered that it was in Opio, near Grasse, and so while visiting a few gardens in the South of France last year I looked him up in the phone book. "I'm staying in Eze," I said. "Would it be all right if I came by to see the garden?"

La Casella isn't open to the public. But Claus must be used to such calls—his garden has been published far and wide. "You can come on Monday at two-thirty," he said.

"Oh," I said, "tomorrow would be better."

"Tomorrow it's impossible," he said. "And Sunday too. And Monday morning it's impossible. Only Monday at two-thirty."

All right, I'd extend my stay.

I was on time. I got to the gate just as his luncheon guests drove off, leaving it wide open for me—what had it been, savory garden chat over a warm *chevre* salad and a bottle of *petal de rose*? I was envious.

Claus seemed to have got wind of the fact that I'd entered the grounds; he met me at the top of the driveway. "There you park," he said, pointing. And then, "My goodness, what a big car. I've never seen such a big car." Well, it's no bigger that millions of other cars you see on every road everywhere. Still, thinking about its intrusive volume in this rarefied setting made me suddenly aware of the fact that I was already in a garden, that I'd been in a garden ever since I'd come through the gate; there were happy, healthy plants everywhere, artfully positioned, not a single stone out of place.

Claus is a former Munich businessman who, in this leisurely phase of life, is always in garden clothes: grass-stained chinos, faded Lacoste shirts with split seams—he's living out the dream of half of Bavaria. He's big-boned and sturdily built. He has pale blue, light-filled eyes and silvery hair.

He led me on a hurried tour, as he had an appointment and would soon be running off.

It was one of those situations in which none of the compliments you try out in your mind sounds quite right.

This is the lap of luxury!

No.

Boy, does this garden put mine to shame!

No.

Why, if this place isn't waxed in godliness and grace!

Definitely not!

Claus has the only lawn that's ever given me pause—shouldn't I have golf shoes for this?

"It's perfect," I said, finally breaking my awkward silence.

"No, it's not."

I knew I'd say the wrong thing.

"Look here," he said, pointing. There was a yellow spot.

He was right. But why was I looking at this yellow spot with the splendors of Athens all around?

"The dog," he explained.

I said, "I would never turn a dog loose in a place like this."

Why didn't I just keep my mouth shut?

There wasn't a corner of this sizable piece of land that wasn't worked out to maximize its garden use. Theme after established poetic theme, Claus's breadth of imagination is inexhaustible. It was all very daring for its scale and the inventiveness of its finishing effects, no quality embellishment spared: sky-high arbors of whispering hewn beams that cover wide formal terraces, walls of cypress hedges with green finials and windows cut through, long rose walks paved with river stones, climbers arching, ramblers clinging to festooned chains. And pots! Extraordinary pots everywhere, giving you the sense that every one of these countless terrace rooms, many with statues and water features, was equally lived in.

Claus took a moment to chat with me. "Lucca? You live in Lucca? Then you must know Camilla."

"Of course," I said.

"I go there every summer," he said. "To Marlia."

"Then you'll have to come and visit me." What largess!

"Do you have a garden?"

"Ah . . . yes," I said. "But, ahm, not like this."

"No, of course not."

"But come and visit anyway," I said. "I'd love to see you."

Claus very generously left me alone in the garden to look around as he drove off to the airport to pick up his companion, Tom Parr. What an opportunity—I studied every trick, the equivalent of looking in the cupboards and behind curtains when you're a house guest and your host is in the tub. I went to school on that airport appointment of his. It was inspirational.

I met him at the top of my driveway. "Park there," I said, pointing—I was quite practiced at greeting garden visitors at this point. Then, "My, what a . . . beautiful car." It was the car Gil's been dreaming of, in fact. If we ordered one now, in a year and a half we'd have it—if we could somehow manage to get these Italian car dealers to talk to us.

"It's the last car I'm going to own," he said.

"Oh, come on, you're not that senior."

"No no, but I'm fed up with buying cars. This will do fine for years."

We were at the side gate, where the August sun came dazzling through the leaves and flamed upon the stones underfoot. This dry season takes no prisoners, but the grapes adore it. Only my sky-blue plumbago was in bloom and the cascade of pink geraniums above the ficus-covered wall. Not the best time for a garden visit perhaps.

"The first thing I would do is plant out that *allée*," he said. "I would plant a double row of cypress trees all up and down that *allée* there, a distance of five meters between each. Why is it you have never thought of this? To me it is so obvious."

How did he know I hadn't thought of it?

"It isn't that I never—"

"It's what it wants, that *allée* there. It wants to have cypresses."

"Well, it's just that they're so expensi—"

"Oh, hang the expense. Go without other things. The garden is more important." An avuncular smile.

Sage advice, I thought.

I led him across the front terrace with its new bordering hedge and evergreen filler plants, some merit-worthy for their rareness. It all looked pretty good to me at this point, but I knew that Claus would never have stood for a lawn as poor as mine. A *tappeto verde* is what it is, in fact, not a lawn; it incorporates every weed known to horticulture. Still, it's right for Italy and a house like this; I need not apologize, and so I didn't.

Claus was very speedy. "*Ja ja*," he kept saying, on the move. He had a list of other gardens to visit before lunch. Funny, I'd seen him only twice and both times he was running.

"*Convolvulus cneorum*," I said, flashing a potted plant whose white, yellow-centered flowers, now finished, I love.

"*Ja ja*," Claus said. "That was one of the plants that got me started in the garden. I put so much water on it that it died, and then I understood. I needed to apply myself, study these things. A Mediterranean plant is not the same as a plant from the mountains of Bavaria."

I was going through a plant name-dropping phase at the time (repetition helped me learn). "*Anisodontea capensis*," I said, pointing, happy to see that the cited plant held an unexpected pink bloom or two.

"*Ja ja*." Claus was gazing elsewhere. "It's more beautiful over here than on the other side of Lucca where Marlia is," he said. "What marvelous mountains, all this green. Let's sit down there a minute." He gestured to my wicker ensemble, four armchairs and a table under the cedar of Lebanon.

It's a kind invitation, I thought. "But don't you want to see the rest of the garden?" I asked.

"There's more?"

"Well, ah, yeah," I said. Did he think I'd have dared to have him in just for this? I mean, it's very nice, the front. But there's all the rest. The Terrace. The pool. The grotto. The parterre.

"What are you thinking of doing with that field there?" he asked. He was talking about my meadow with its path mown down the center.

"I have an idea, in fact—"

"Ja?"

"I'm thinking of making a chestnut room. Pleached chestnuts underplanted with chestnut bushes. If—"

"No no. Chestnuts no. They get too big."

"But I'd pleach—"

"No no. Not *le marron*, no. Too big, even pleached as you say. It would all go dark in there."

"But they're native to these hills, in—"

"No no, not *le marron*. I don't care if they're native or not. And they get a disease. In summer the leaves go brown. And then you're spraying them, and for God's sakes, *marron* no. I would plant the mulberry. This too is a good tree for here. Better size, better leaf. Mulberry is what you plant."

We'd made it to the terrace. I couldn't wait to hear the usual remark: But of course, this garden was already here. I was all puffed up with my ready response: Oh no, I planted it. Only three years ago. Isn't that amazing? Unbelievable, no?

"And so when did you plant this garden here?" he asked.

It still looks new to me too.

When he saw the grotto he said, "How old is this?"

"It was done in two periods," I said. "The niches with the masks are from the Renaissance, but the facade, with all these columns and Ionic capitals, is from the nineteenth century."

"Marvelous," he said.

"You'd be amazed how many people ask if we built it."

"Are there still people around here who can build such things?" he asked. All at once I saw a spiffy new grotto at the top of Claus's garden.

"I doubt it," I said.

End of tour. "Very nice, very nice," Claus said, "but I really must go along, as I have to get back to Marlia for lunch. Camilla said she'll invite you one day this week, so I'll be seeing you again."

"Oh, good," I said.

We were standing on the front steps. "Yes yes," he said, "very nice. But listen to me a minute. First I would plant that *allée* there, a double row of cypresses up and down, a distance of five meters between each. And that field over there, mulberrys. Never mind the *marron*, forget it. Mulberrys is what you want. OK?"

"Mulberrys," I said. "Chestnuts no. Got it."

"And that *allée*, don't forget."

"Cypresses."

"All right, then," Claus said. "*Au revoir.*"

MARLIA, LUCCA'S GRANDEST GARDEN, IS AT THE foothills of the Pizzorne. Villa Reale has a matriarchal history, and so it seems fitting that it's now in the hands of the sisters Pecci-Blunt: Letizia, Viviana, and Camilla. They've just invited me to lunch as Claus said they would. I'm all eyes when I'm there; Marlia has inspired numerous other gardens, great and small—in France, England, and even in America.

Napoleon slept here at his sister Elisa's "Villa Marly," as he called it, the center of the divine realm he created just for her. Elisa Buonaparte Baciocchi, Princess of Lucca and Piombino, then later Queen of Etruria, bought Marlia, by a forced sale, from Lelio Orsetti in 1806, paying 150,000 francs in silver coin. The indifferent, or perhaps resentful, Orsetti had the coins melted down and forged into bars, then sent word to the princess that at a certain time and date she should look out the window of her city palace to watch the "Villa di Marlia" passing on an ox-drawn cart.

Elisa was almost masculine in appearance, but at times Napoleon regarded her even more highly than he did her delicate-featured younger sister, Pauline. Elisa had her brother's straight, imperial nose, the same sturdy, assertive chin, his dark, swelling lips, his deep black eyes, at once capricious and firm. Napoleon remarked that she was especially talented at cracking the whip; it's true that she sent many a court official running in desperate dread of his lady governor, "half soldier, half woman," as the poet Labindo put it, "and wholly despotic."

Elisa's administrative skills were evident all about these enviably large territories that not even the Medici, with all their power and means, had managed to get their hands on. Talleyrand would call her "the Semiramis of the Serchio," referring to the legendary founder of Babylon and wife of Ninus of Nineveh.

Elisa's "Committee for the Encouragement of Agriculture, Arts and Commerce" would have far-reaching effects for Lucca's economy and the self-esteem of its people. She was full of fresh ideas and had the courage and wherewithal to see them through. She opened factories, in the public interest, to accomplish such extraordinary tasks as the extraction of sugar from chestnuts, and mastic from Pistacia lentiscus, the fragrant sap-derived gum that's used in dentistry, medicine and in varnishes. She founded a cotton industry of some success, and she developed methods to employ the fibers of hemp and other plants in fashioning innovative fabrics that were tough enough to be used for the sails of Viareggio's marina. She ordered the planting of

saffron out of which dyes were made for use in Lucca's already boom-
ing silk industry, which exported its gossamer weaves everywhere, and
she doubled the plantings of mulberry trees at the silkworm farms.

It was Napoleon's wish that Elisa act as a kind of French cultural
ambassadress here, and this she did in great trend-setting style,
appearing in Lucca's sumptuous salons wearing the latest Parisian
fashions by Leroy. On a higher cultural note, she founded libraries
and schools, and with her husband Felix's participation—he devoted
the better part of his life to playing the violin—made Lucca a vibrant
music center headed by Paganini, whose strains coming from behind
salon screens made her literally swoon with the vapors. In a passion
for the arts and anything that was white, she focused her interest on
one of the region's greatest resources, the Carrara marble out of which
Michelangelo had sculpted his *David,* and Jacopo della Quercia his
Ilaria del Carretto. She took control of the ailing quarries in 1806 when
its financial failings had already caused the emigration of most of its
best artists. In Lucca's Palazzo Bernardini she founded the Accademia
Napoleone l'Appiani after the French model, where even the great
David occasionally assisted. Napoleon appointed as its director
Lorenzo Bartolini, sculptor of *The Battle of Austerlitz,* one of the great
reliefs of the Vendom column in Paris. A native of Prato, it was he
who lured Canova to Carrara, where he'd procure the stone for his
monumental statue of a nude Napoleon that might have won the
hearts of its subject's art-loving admirers everywhere, but highly
embarrassed the emperor.

It was the Orsetti family who commissioned, a hundred years
before Elisa acquired them, Villa di Marlia's formal gardens, a series of
enclosed green rooms among *boschi* of ilex and sweet bay. Elisa was
quick to apply her insistent, reordering touch; nothing that fell into

her hands ever remained quite the same. She called in French engineers to channel the waters of the Fraga to her grottos and pools where, as she put it, they would "sing their perennial songs." She enriched the villa's farm activities, planting potatoes, never before seen here, new cultivars of corn and grain, and French vinifera grapes, merlot and Rousanne. She filled her villa's stables with luxurious imported pure-bred horses, and its rolling south-facing meadows with Spanish merino sheep in order to supply local spinners with her favorite wool.

In her ambition to enlarge the villa's already sprawling park in such a way that she could ride for miles and miles about her own valleys and reforested hills, she commissioned a plan that incorporated large portions of the estate's surrounding territories: upper Marlia, San Pancrazio, and Matraia. As for existing major villas in the way of her advancing grand scheme, they were to be razed, their formal gardens replaced by a mannered wilderness. Because her water resources were already exploited to the maximum, it was doubted that the extensive new woodland plantings could survive the harsh, dry sunshine of Tuscan summers, and so the project was abandoned. Perhaps Elisa and her architects finally came to understand that this proposed fragment of fake naturalism in the midst of rigidly cultivated countryside would stand out as the gratuitous intrusion it surely would have been.

In the late eighteenth century many Italian gardens, Baroque or Renaissance, were reforged in the English manner as *giardini all'Inglese*. It was the new preferred mode, and it came with its own compelling philosophy that captured the imaginations of landed gentry far and wide. Marie Caroline of Austria, queen of Naples, with her "landscape garden" at Caserta started the trend on this peninsula and in her noble set. The "landscape garden" was inspired by the mid-seventeenth-century idyllic depictions of the Roman countryside as painted by Claude

Lorrain and Salvator Rosa. Joseph Addison and Alexander Pope, for whom all art was about the imitation and study of nature, took up the landscape garden cause in their literature. By the end of the eightenth century some tenets of the landscape garden philosophy had been applied to most of Europe's great estates, sometimes successfully, sometimes with ruinous results. Elisa Baciocchi, a woman of fashion, had no need or desire to escape the prevailing trend. She'd seen the Marquis de Girardin's naturalistic garden at Ermenville, near Paris, where the tomb of Rousseau sits upon its Isle of Poplars in the middle of a romantic lake. She'd visited Désert de Retz, the garden of Baron de Monville designed by Morel, whom she'd eventually call upon for the plan of her landscape garden interventions at Marlia.

But the ideally laid-out landscape garden was perhaps far easier to realize in England than in Italy. England's already natural-looking meadows became incorporated into an estate's private universe by virtue of the ha-ha (a dry ditch, unseen from the house), which replaced the fence and its spell-breaking constraint. In Lucca, great estates like Marlia were always enclosed by high stone walls, as just beyond these lay geometrically divided fields plowed in rows, busy villages, and roadways. At Elisa's Marlia a successful compromise was reached. The lower gardens, adjacent to the village, were converted to the landscape garden style with new curving lanes and thick plantings of tall trees, while the upper gardens surrounding the house and to the east of it were left in their original Baroque state. In this way Elisa provided herself with the best of both worlds.

The estate's main house was of course completely redone for the highly refined demands of a Buonaparte. It was somewhat dull and flat in Elisa's eyes, much less interesting in design than the house she'd had her heart set on, Villa Torrigiani in Camigliano—alas, no amount of imperial coaxing could acquire it. She added a third floor plus a rear portico whose Doric columns supported a marble terrace. Most of the furnishings came from the Baciocchi hunting lodge in Livorno; these and other neoclassical pieces, some French, some local, in cherry and walnut, sat well in the provincial airy rooms of white and gold.

The approach to the villa is the same today as it was in Elisa's time. A wide sycamore-lined avenue brings you to the twin gatehouses Elisa built, *le palazzine gemelle*. With their gray stone facades embellished with urns and arches and columns, they're fully Napoleonic in style. In the gatehouse to the right lives Romano, the custodian. It's he who answers the villa's single phone line, intoning, with his dignified voice, "*Chi la desidera?*" and "*Attenda, prego.*" On occasion Romano has driven Camilla Pecci-Blunt to dinner in Massa Macinaia, and so he knows Gil and me well. In the off seasons, once the sisters' standard is taken in, he lets us wander the garden with our out-of-town visitors without the usual obligatory guide and without our having to pay the modest entry fee—I guess we're family in his eyes.

I remember how intimidated I felt my first visit here when the great iron gates opened just for me in their boding, slow silence. I'd only visited such grand palaces, always in the hands of national trusts or government agencies, with a ticket in hand and hoards of tourists with the same idea all around. I wonder how many properties of this scale are still in private hands, and how many of these are as well kept as Villa Reale, as it eventually came to be called. The driveways are immaculately tended, their white gravel raked free of intruding weeds, and the hidden gardens beyond are always in perfect shape.

After a moment's drive within *la chiusa*, the villa's walled inner domain, a long view opens up. In the distance to the right is a free-form lake with swans afloat against a backdrop of *boschi*, which in

Elisa's time were stocked with roebuck and goats in the landscape garden spirit; to the left lies a huge rectangular expanse of lawn, the great house at its far end. In the original seventeenth-century plan the lawn was to be a *ménage*, framed by high clipped hedges with towering cypresses forming regular, periodic pinnacles. But Elisa, in making it new and hers, added specimen trees and bushes along its edges, their blowsy, irregular growth softening the geometry, achieving that contemporary look. Today this part of the garden is turned out in Victorian style. As the naturalistic dream inevitably dissipated in the early part of the nineteenth century, a revivalist interest in order suddenly appeared out of the burgeoning boredom of it all. Humphrey Repton, one of the leading landscape garden practitioners, had already broken the ice for this harking back when in 1803 he wrote that his followers might, in moderation, allow an element of the "regular and artificial." Even the odd flower bed was OK, even up against the house—previously unthinkable. In the 1820s John Claudius Loudon invented what he called the "gardenesque" style. Suddenly it was desirable in his eyes to introduce the odd object, folly, or shaped flower bed into the pure landscape gardens of the already old order. Pauline Buonaparte, at her Villa Paolina in Monte San Quirico near Lucca, would lay out her mansion's grounds in this new gardenesque way; period watercolors of the estate show a donkey tethered to a round plot of mown grass beneath the villa's front stairs, circular flower beds here and there with their fiddly white bent-iron borders. At measured intervals along the edges of Marlia's great lawn there are gardenesque rectangular flower beds punctuated by sculpted hedges. Providing cheery dots of park-like color, each bed contains the same gorgeously flowering annuals and bulbs in the same precise cascading arrangements of dahlias, cannas, and marigolds.

I parked, as instructed by Romano, by the Villa del Vescovo, the long-abandoned summer residence of Lucca's archbishop. Elisa, upon arrival here, annexed the archbishop's lands, forced him out, and installed him in another, albeit finer house, in San Colombano. It wasn't long before she'd completely destroyed the sixteenth-century garden surrounding his Renaissance villa in order to make way for her new *giardino all'Inglese*.

I was to meet Camilla and my other hostesses by the pool, but I snuck a moment to admire the Villa del Vescovo. Though it's obvious when you look at its flaking casement windows that the rooms within contain only the old musty air of long ago, the garden is maintained as if the archbishop might come back any minute for a much purloined summer vacation. It makes me think of Nymans in Sussex, where the garden is perfectly preserved even though the house burned down years ago, leaving only its external walls. The inner courtyard of the archbishop's old house is divided into four grass quadrants crossed by paths, but the Renaissance geometry is broken by an asymmetric grouping of grown-up trees. A deep terrace looks out across the rolling naturalistic park where Elisa's merino sheep once grazed. Today there's a lake in the view, but that was built by the Pecci-Blunt. The sisters' father, Cecil, didn't like the villa's view of the village rooftops, and so he excavated the lake and piled the dirt beyond, concealing it behind a wooded hillock. I draped myself over the iron railing and looked down. Twenty feet below lies a small geometric garden room, a gardenesque touch, meant to be admired from this vantage point. I might never have known it was here had not Letizia, showing around some French visitors a few summers ago (I was along for the ride) pointed it out with "*E ça c'est un petit chose extra!*" Then the complicated knot garden of dwarf box was bedded out with summer GMAs of various primary colors; today it's filled with colored gravel, a far more tasteful, less fussy treatment.

I could hear the distant voices of a crowd by the swimming pool. I passed the clay-surfaced tennis court along hedge-walled walkways and came to the old bathing center built by the sisters' parents in the 1920s. A polychromed Victorian summer house of changing rooms, a bath, and a bar, it's like something out of *They Shoot Horses, Don't They?*, a charming fragment of an old Adirondack bathing club. The paint on the filigreed eaves is dulled by sunshine and time, but the building is otherwise in perfect shape; it's as if it's known no winter life.

A few guests were seated with their hostess, Camilla, in the shade of the pavilion's low-hanging roof, all gazing off towards the sun-filled pool, whose border began at their feet. The pool was full of floats as usual; each year new, wackier, crazier floats replace older, dimpled, faded ones that get sent out to pasture at season's end. Just now Viviana, who has the best sense of humor of the three sisters, leaned on a huge chop-licking alligator, counting to herself as she completed her regimen of underwater scissor kicks.

Camilla is a woman of quiet, natural confidence. Her perennially youthful core (she's an artist) has an inveterate hold on her raised cheeks and focused eyes. She's married to Earl McGrath, who has a well-known contemporary art gallery on Fifty-seventh Street in New York, but he usually doesn't appear here at Marlia until much later in the season.

Camilla introduced me around as Claus Scheinert's bronzed torso just now emerged from the pool.

"Why are these plumbago so full of blooms?" I asked him— terra-cotta pots of plumbago were everywhere; their pale blue flowers, hanging masses of them, were like little airborne fragments of the pool's light-filled water.

"Because they're fertilized well once a month. All the pots need it, once a month you give it to them." Claus seems to understand the garden here far better than anyone, though he regrets that not speaking Italian he hasn't been able to get much information out of the head gardener.

"Paul," Camilla said, "help yourself to a drink."

The bar was spread just as Camilla's parents, Cecil and Mimi, must have done it. There were bowls of American-style cocktail nibbles, pretzel rounds and chips. The tumblers, which seem to intone "gin and tonic," come with their own individual color-coded thermal coolers designed to keep your fingers warmly away from the iced drinks they contain. They're from the fifties, and their chrome trim's a bit dented and scratched by now—a patina—but they're treated with the same reverence one has for the great house's antiques.

Letizia (the Princess Buoncompagni) appeared in a bathing suit from out of one of the several changing booths, whose doors, one next to another, all alike and therefore numbered, would lend themselves well to a staged comedy—how long will it take for the husband and wife to notice that they've found themselves in the same unlikely place with young dates? These doors are framed by a never ending collage of black-and-white photographs of all the Pecci-Blunt, their family and guests, beginning with their earliest years here and ending in the forties, when the war drove them temporarily abroad.

I have the sense that Letizia's the villa's curator, and what a masterful job she does! I'll never forget seeing her bedroom one night (it's part of the after-dinner tour, as it was Elisa's apartment). Most of the furnishings are original, arranged just as in the villa's previous princely days. Elisa's Empire-style bed, where a white nightdress was carefully laid out, stands, true to style, with its length against the elaborately painted wall. The Napoleonic desk, where Letizia tends to the business of her international foundation work, is by the window for its natural light. On a small Empire table near the bed, which was made up in crisp white linen, lay Letizia's reading glasses, her book, a candle in a gilded bronze candlestick, a crystal pitcher of water. Beside this, on the floor, her white immaculate slippers awaited her bedtime feet; they might have been fashioned by Leroy, out of fine Lucchese silk. White reins here even now—the legacy of white.

More guests arrived: Francesca Antinori, Letizia's daughter and wife of Piero Antinori, head of the great wine dynasty; the Brazilian ambassador to Italy and his wife; the Italian ambassador to Spain and his—there are always lots of ambassadors around. The guest roll at Marlia is unsurprisingly distinguished: world leaders and famous movie stars whose names I won't presume to list. Henri de Beaumont arrived, widower of the late Graziella Pecci-Blunt, the fourth sister (there was also a brother, Dino, who recently passed away)—interestingly, an ancestor of Henri had been one of Napoleon's chamberlains. With Henri was his daughter Gaia, the novelist.

When lunch was announced we moved, by now eighteen of us, a brief walk away to the eighteenth-century grotto of the Villa del Vescovo, a folly of the old lower garden which Elisa chose, fortunately, not to destroy. Summer afternoons one dines in the grotto's airy alcove, to which prepared cold trays of food are delivered in huge wicker hampers carried by pairs of butlers in blue and gold livery. Camilla is in charge of the villa's kitchen; its cuisine is at once simple and sophisticated—she's not afraid to include the odd bean sprout or a *sauce Tailandaise*.

In this, one of the most photographed garden follies of Italy, the window-shaped light burns across the several round dining tables in arch-topped shafts. Deep niches in the walls contain *trionfi* on plinths, urns brimming over with sculpted peaches, bananas, grapes. The wall's colors are muted and complex, a thickly woven mosaic of stones from different sources forming classic patterns that are repeated everywhere about the garden, in its stairways and terraces, on its walkways, in its several grottos.

The lunch proceeded. I loved the crabmeat salad. Viviana spoke perfect Portuguese to the Brazilian ambassador. "How do you know Portuguese?" I asked. "I lived in Brazil for eighteen years," she said. We talked about our various activities of other seasons, about cellular telephones, computers, fax machines, about opera, music festivals, movies, cities, people.

By four lunch was through, and it was nap time for house guests. A procession formed and headed to the villa along the shady park lane with its sky-high walls of tapestry hedge. Claus invited me to walk the garden with him. When he asked Camilla if she cared to join us, she said, "No, *thank* you," assuredly; after all, she tours it with her coffee mug every morning while compiling the day's menus.

Gardens are best seen through skilled eyes, and Claus Scheinert has them. He pointed to a pair of plant beds that flank a side walkway to the grotto. "Those are marvelous!" he said. I'd barely noticed them. I looked again. They were essentially two rectangular puffs of monkey grass (or mondo grass), *Ophiopogon japonicus*, with three large, equally spaced pots of fuchsia-colored bougainvillea in each. The elements: gravel ground, monkey grass, outsized terra-cotta pots on stone bases, brilliantly colored flowers in opulent profusion. Not one of these ingredients was important or unusual in itself, but together, in this way, they were perfection; it was a scheme that spoke of place and history, of habits and manner and shared graces, perhaps even of Elisa herself. I thought about Claus's having said that he had very few plants in his garden, and now understood what he meant. The garden is bigger than the sum of its rare or endangered parts. It's enough that plants be the *right* plants; how common or uncommon they are is of minor concern when in the end the garden's magic is measured against the height of a visitor's soaring spirits.

I followed Claus straight to the heart of the matter, to the *Teatro di Verdura*. Green upon green, this is the quintessential Italian garden; its fanciful interpretation of a Baroque theater is unique in all the world. Its terra-cotta actors, Columbine, Harlequin, and Pulcinella enter center stage from niches carved through a towering yew drop, an infinite fly space of sky above. The firmament is this theater's proscenium. Ovations might be the rain or a thunderclap. Standing here in the orchestra lawn, you're in a green audience behind green box ball footlights and a green box prompter's hole; for all practical purposes, you're a plant.

We walked back out to the *peschiera* by way of the round fountain room that serves as a kind of foyer to the green theater. You'd expect to see smokers flipping through their programs at the entr'acte. The rotunda's entertainment is a low pool in its center. A single jet of water rises twenty feet or more; we circled it on the dry, upwind side and found a bench to sit on.

"And so when did you first start working on your garden?" he asked.

"Just a few years ago," I said. "I don't know that I'd ever really looked at gardens before then. I mean, I looked, but I didn't see."

"Well, this is true of me too," Claus said. "But once you finally see, off you go. There's no stopping us. Before I bought my house over there, I knew nothing, like you say. I didn't know a tulip from a petunia."

"Story of my life," I said.

"We had our friend Russell Page come by to give us ideas after we first moved in, but off he went and died, and so there I was with no one but myself to do it."

"He did you a favor," I said.

"What's that?"

"Not by dying. I didn't mean that."

"No, of course not."

"What I mean is, he launched you."

"Oh, perhaps," Claus said. "Anyway, at this point, I'm doing other people's gardens as well—this I never could have foreseen in a million years, doing other people's gardens. But you'll see. Soon they'll be coming to ask you things as if you've always known them. Soon you're making gardens for all your friends and who knows, even giving lectures."

"Lectures?" I said. "Me, no."

"But you're doing very well, I must say. Your garden is lovely. You just need to come to places like this once in a while and look and see. There are a million lessons here for the gardener, there is genius, and it's all free for the taking. Come."

We opened an outsized, creaking iron gate and entered what is undoubtedly one of the greatest garden rooms in the world. Its centerpiece is an enormous reflecting pool surrounded by a gray stone balustrade upon which stand more than a hundred terra-cotta pots of lemons. A pair of swans breaks the water's surface in their slow back-and-forth glide; I'm sure that the occasional *cristiano* (Italian for

human being) snuck a capricious swim here in the hot summer afternoons of Elisa's day.

"These lemons, for instance," Claus said. "Do you see how brilliant it is to have lemons like this. And they're only little ones, but
they're marvelous. They cost nothing when they're this small, but the
effect is great. I am thinking about such lemons these days, you should
too."

No one builds gardens like this great room anymore. Even with
the biggest corporate budget, the modern need for instant gratifica-
tion would never allow a planting that takes a hundred years to complete its task of framing out a space that is meant to be autonomous.
This garden, the subject of a series of watercolors by John Singer Sar-
gent, is especially impressive for its walls of Holm oak, which for
most of the Orsettis' years here stood chest high or lower. Now,
twenty feet tall, precisely pleached and underplanted with clipped
yew, the ancient trees keep back any and all intrusion from the imper-
fect outside world, momentarily forgotten.

In a *ninfeo* (a grotto) at the top of the garden a statue of Leda
and her swan, with three water-spewing dolphins at her feet, is
enveloped in Baroque architectural splendor. Claus was particularly
interested in the design and execution of the terrace floor within this
grotto's arc. Squares and diamonds are drawn out in cut stone slabs;
the paving all around is fashioned of *spugne*, sponge-molded simulated
lava rock.

"I just built a new terrace at La Casella inspired by this paving
scheme," Claus said. "It replaces that lawn you found so perfect."

"Oh no," I said, "that was one of the most stunning lawns I've
ever seen in my life."

"Yes, but you don't know what it was like to have to weed it.

Never mind. It's gone. I built a paved terrace there instead, inspired by this one here."

"And how did it turn out?" I asked.

"Well, this one's ancient and so more beautiful. But mine's very nice as well. In fact, I'll *love* it in a hundred years."

Maybe these farsighted gardeners do still exist.

chapter ten

THE VISIT

IT WAS MARCH. THE RAINS CAME ON IN A WEEK-long downpour. Having momentarily put aside my trowel, I made some progress weeding the endless stacks of papers that force their way into my study while I'm out gardening. At the corner of my desk lay a piece of priority correspondence:

Jas des Eydins
Route de Pont Julien
84480 Bonnieux
Nov. 28, 1997

Dear Paul,

Subject: Gamble Garden Tour, May 1998

At long last I find the time to get some work done on my garden; we were caught unprepared by some extremely heavy frosts end of October which caused overnight disaster among some plants.

I hope you have had a most enjoyable summer. We spent another three weeks in Italy after seeing you in May, visiting more gardens around Viterbo and south of Rome. I was much impressed by La Landriana, which needless to say has been added to my programme.

Down to business. The dates of the Gamble Garden Tour have finally been confirmed and the hotels reserved, not without difficulty, and I am now trying to arrange appointments to see the gardens. Do you think we could visit your garden at Villa Massei on Wednesday, 13th May at the end of the afternoon. I am asking to visit Villa Reale at 15:00 and we would like very much to drive from there to you, arriving at about 16:30. We will be 22 persons, plus myself. I have to warn you that this tour is a ladies' affair, largely; but don't worry, they're seekers of respectful ends one and all.

I was wondering if, after our garden stroll, you might offer a wine tasting of your own production, at our expense, of course. I shall look forward to hearing from you.

Kindest regards from us both,

Shirley Kozlowski

No sooner did I finish (for the fiftieth time) reading (very apprehensively) this letter than the phone rang.

"*Pronto,*" said the unfamiliar voice. "*Sono Maria Luisa Madonna. C'e Paul Gervais?*"

"*Sono io,*" I said.

"*Paul, ti ricordi di me?*"

Why couldn't I remember who that was? Maria Luisa what?

"I visited you last September, you don't remember? With Maria Giusti?"

"*A sì,*" I said. Now I remembered. Of course.

Maria Giusti is head of the *Soprintendenza per i Beni Ambientali, Architettonici, Artistici e Storici di Pisa,* the fine arts commission. It's her awesome responsibility to faithfully protect, as architectural authority, the historic monuments of the provinces of Pisa and Lucca. In fact, all antique buildings here—leaning tower or palace, farmhouse or barn—are listed in her active files: nothing can be done to them, alteration or restoration, without her written consent. Proud of our architectural conservation on the home front, Gil had been trying to get her out here to Massa Macinaia for years, but given all the countless sites that dot the map of her jurisdiction, she'd never had time until that September evening last year, the evening Maria Luisa Madonna just referred to on the phone.

It started out as a less than ideal occasion. There were two other carloads of friends who'd stopped by at the very same time for drinks and a garden walk. Gil busied himself as host with Maria

Giusti's group, while I entertained another party who'd got here first. Poor Carol MacAndrew, who'd brought the third group ("I've-got-some-people-I'd-like-you-to-meet") had to wing it on her own for a while—oh well, she knows her way around here better than we do.

When the confusion cleared an hour or so later, I was surprised to find Maria Giusti and her friends sitting under the cedar tree at the far end of the lawn. I brought them a chilled bottle of Sorbus with which to fill their cloudy warm glasses, and we sat there for a while and talked and sipped and gazed into the sunset.

Maria Giusti's friends, Maria Luisa Madonna (my surprise caller) and her husband, Marcello Fagiolo, turned out to be garden people. Marcello is vice president of the National Committee of Historic Gardens, and Maria Luisa is a professor at the University of Siena, with a chair in Garden History and Landscape. She's delightfully *simpatica*, a voluptuous Roman, all silks and chunky jewelry that clatters with her breathless repartee. Her huge blond lion's mane bounces on her padded shoulders, and her wide reddened lips part in a constant smile, riding a giggle she can't help. Marcello's quite the opposite. He removed himself by several feet and lay Manet-style *sul'erbe* behind our backs; if he was following the conversation he didn't lead on.

"I'll never forget our evening with you," Maria Luisa said, just now on the phone. "It was the most extraordinary experience to see that piece of paradise you and Gil have made. It's unique, I feel. I've visited lots of gardens here in Italy, but yours is special; it's that English touch, or something. I've been talking about it for months."

"Oh, thanks," I said. "But I'm American."

"Did I say English? American, I mean. That *American* touch. *Scusami, è?*"

"*Niente.*"

"Listen, I've called with a favor to ask of you."

A pause (mine). Long pause.

"*Sì?*" I finally said.

"I'm organizing a conference for the province of Arezzo on behalf of the *Facoltà di Lettere e Filosofia* at my University of Siena. It will be called 'The Garden: History, Myth, Reality, Perspectives.' " Full stop.

"Oh?" I said worriedly.

"It'll run from March tenth until May twenty-sixth, eleven evenings. Some impressive people will be speaking, Giorgio Galletti of the Boboli Garden, Monique Mosser of Versailles. . . . In other words, it's an important event involving many of Europe's leading garden authorities."

"Wow," I said, working up an enthused tone, "sounds great."

"Listen to this, OK? May twelfth, OK? Ready? 'Paul Gervais, writer. The resurrection of Villa Massei in the Lucchese Hills: a Modern Commission.' There. *Ecco.* What do you think?"

"Ah . . . what is that?" I said.

"That's the title."

"Oh," I said. "The title of what?"

"Your presentation."

"Oh, my presentation." Try to be nice.

"That's right. I discussed it with my committee and we all agreed. It'll be magnificent. An American writer with a garden in Lucca is just the sort of thing our audience would love to know about."

"It is?"

"You don't think so?" She giggled. I could hear her chunky jewelry clattering. In fact, she'd been giggling pretty much all through this—she's a Roman fountain. "You don't think they'd be interested in what you've got there?"

"Oh no, I mean, it's just that . . ." I giggled. We were both giggling.

"Most of them have never seen a garden like yours, you know. Certainly they've seen Lante, Caprarola, all of that. But a garden like yours? No."

"You mean, they're coming here?"

"Oh no! You're coming *here*. I mean *there*. I'm in Rome. You'll show them slides and talk to them. You're used to that sort of thing, aren't you?"

"Well no, I mean, sort of. I've talked about my writing in public, but never about the garden."

"Come on. It's all the same."

"*A, sì?*"

"*A, magnifico,*" she said, "I knew I could count on you."

"Well, I—"

"You'll be introduced by Maria Giusti. She's already agreed to it. She thinks it's a magnificent idea."

I guess I'd just said yes.

"You'll be our guest at a five-star Arezzo hotel, of course. Perhaps a dinner party for you at one of the villas; I'm working on it. They'll treat you well there, believe me. And by the way, we'll pay you a three-hundred-thousand-lira honorarium. *O magnifico!* I'm so happy you've agreed to this."

"I'll be looking forward to it," I said automatically.

"So we'll be in touch, OK? *Ciao* for now. *Ciao.*"

As soon as I put down the phone Gil appeared in my door. "Who was that?" he asked.

"Maria Luisa Madonna."

"You look a bit crazed."

I told him the whole story: blah blah blah, May twelfth.

"May twelfth?" he said.

"Right."

Shirley's Gamble garden tour letter lay in front of me on my

desk. He picked it up. "That's what I thought," he said. "They're coming on the thirteenth."

Whoops.

My camera is ancient, its leather case all cracked and buckling. The
ascoted man in the photo shop gave its innards a quick cleaning and
said it shouldn't present problems. I told him about my project and he
recommended an appropriate film. "Use a tripod," he said. "If you
have any trouble I'll come out there and give you a hand."

Things were still a bit wintry-looking, but that afternoon I got a
brilliant shot (I felt): the house from the front gate, framed in a sun-
filled, golden corona of flowering mimosa. Purists feel that the
mimosa, *Acacia baileyana*, is out of place in our Tuscan landscape, and
so I'm quick to admit that I didn't plant it there; the Olivers did.
Mimosa comes from New South Wales, where it's called "Cootamundra wattle," but by now it's all over the Mediterranean, Gibraltar
to Malta. On Women's Day, March 8, it's customary to give a little
nosegay of fragrant mimosa blooms to the woman in your life, tied
with a length of red ribbon. But some women are married to unsenti-
mental men and are thereby committed to procuring their own
mimosa sprays for the occasion. Looking out my study window on
March 7, I'm apt to spot these lonely ladies twisting the hell out of
my lower-hanging mimosa branches, filling their cars—couldn't they
at least use proper secateurs? But what a great image to open my lecture with: the sloping *viale* newly planted out with forty-four cypress
trees (thank you, Claus), the afternoon sun on the villa's warm facade,
green shutters open wide, all viewed through a golden volute of
Cootamundra wattle—I can hear the gasps now.

And my field of crocuses! That's a good shot. *Crocus etruscus*, I like to think, but really I have no idea which species it is. Our "Crocus Meadow," walled in on one side with a stand of bamboo and on the other with a bank of Indian cane, is covered with them in late winter, tens of thousands, a silvery lilac *moquette*. A few dozen crocuses pop up by the *lavatoio*, a stone basin along the stream where the village women still wash their clothes, their elbows immersed in the icy cold water that rushes down from Monte Serra—Gil, in his broken Italian of years ago, used to call it the *lavatroia*, "whore wash" (the local priest had all he could do to keep a straight face). I got a good close-up shot of these crocuses by the stream, their yellow-orange styles, all the purple veiny details. First I'd show my audience the glorious meadow, then click off to a closer look. Isn't that the way it's done? Overview. Specifics. Sure, they've all seen crocuses before, but a pretty picture's a pretty picture.

Let's see, I wondered, walking along with my camera. Everything was poised for a burst of bloom, but poised doesn't make for good visuals. Where are you, Spring? ". . . all our longing eyes are turned/ Up to thy bright pavilions: issue forth,/ And let thy holy feet visit our clime" (compliments of Blake). The *Viburnum plicatum* f. *tomentosum* was covered with warm, juicy-looking buds, its lace-cap blooms months away from happening. And Gil's birthday *Davidia involucrata*—Italians call it the *fazzoletto* tree; in April it pulls out little handkerchiefs of leafy, snowy-white bracts, then drops them like a lady qualifying gentlemen. It was planted with ceremony for Gil's birthday a few years ago. All of us threw in a shovelful of dirt, Gil, Ugo, Ottavia, and I. But the Davidia's hay fever hadn't kicked in yet this year—not a sign of a handkerchief in sight.

Just inside the upper gate was a neat bed of *Crocus vernus* "Purpureus Grandiflorus*," the "Dutch Crocus" that's native to Italy (I suppose it's Dutch because the Dutch took it and ran with it: there are twenty or more vernus cultivars listed in my encyclopedia of garden plants). I got a nice shot of these handsome deep purple flutes, still shy in the cool late-winter sun. I have to say, I really love crocuses; I'd like to put together a collection, in fact. *Crocus biflorus* with its striped outer tepals tempts me, or the tulip-like *C. chrysanthus* "Ladykiller," the two-toned white and purple one (I'm not averse to cultivars). *C. cartwrightianus*, from Greece, is elegant; its long, curving styles sit like fine juliennes of pimento and yellow pepper on a white, six-petaled plate, a Japanese *amuse bouche*.

The camellias were still putting out their bursting blooms, though many of them were a bit wilted at this point. I got a good, tight picture of a single red flower with two bees abuzz, and then I took some distant views from a few different angles. The wild plum in the front border, a white celestial sphere in an angled shaft of sunlight, like one of love's many laid snares—that made for a splendid shot. Up at the pool, *Euryops virgineus*, a native of South Africa's eastern Cape, put on a golden smile for the camera, and the "Corsican Blue" rosemary dangled its tender, flowering crossed legs over a stone wall. The *Bergenia cordifolia*'s persistent winter blooms are a welcome cliché— everyone in the world seems to have it, but so what? My *Lavandula dentata*, of the Baleric Islands, seems to bloom all year round here—not everyone has *that*. For sentimental reasons, I love anything from the Baleric Islands; it was on Formentera that I had my first real taste of the Mediterranean. I was twenty-three. I'd never experienced such dry, light air, a sea so crystalline and calm. The island was virtually undeveloped. It was April—or was it May? There were no clouds; the nights were cold; mornings, the heat came on. The cove-like beaches were empty; I swam and strolled the dunes among the most extraordinary sun-loving plant life—but I took no notice. I knew nothing of rosemary. I didn't even realize then that the Mediterranean would soon become the home port of my spirits: the farther away I stray from it, the less happy I seem to be.

As for flowering photo subjects, that was pretty much it for now. Earthly pride hadn't yet begun to challenge the majesty of heaven. It was even pointless to take general shots so early in the season, as none of the borders were filled in and the lawn in front was still winter worn and spotty with yellow moss. I'd have to wait until late April and take all the pictures in a blitz. Scary thought.

I developed my first roll of film to find that the slides hadn't come out badly at all. My technique wasn't great, but it was good enough. I'd make up for visual shortcomings with talk.

Talk? What would it be? How much can I say about a crocus? I asked Lindsay and Don, of Venzano, for advice. "They want a two-hour lecture," I said.

"My heavens," said Don.

"Let's see," said Lindsay, "you could do an hour and fifteen minutes on the grotto, I suppose."

What panic ensued with *that* supportive quip!

The days passed, the weeks, the months; nothing to photograph.

Spring is the longest season here. That pregnant abeyance framed by the dead of winter and a surge of bloom—in New England it lasts about thirty seconds—goes on for four months in temperate Lucca. We were well into April and my slide library was minuscule, hardly enough to inspire twenty minutes of lecture, never mind two hours. I was getting nervous.

I was getting on a plane, in fact.

It's a bad habit of mine not to look over my diary before saying yes to things. I was off to New York and wouldn't be back until May 4. My lecture was on May 12. This would give me eight days in which to tidy up the garden, take the needed slides and get them developed. Only eight days. And I'd still have to go through them all, putting them in some sort of order. And supposing those were eight rainy days? With wind?

"Oh, don't worry," Gil said. "You can shoot five or six rolls in one afternoon. Good heavens."

I left for the States and tried not to think about it.

"What a mess," I said when I brought my eyes to the window that first morning back. Things were in impeccable shape when I left, but the destructive advance of nature over the last two weeks had muddled my garden's message. Ugo had mown the lawn and swept up under the camphor, but my borders were weedy, my edges were ragged, and only some of the roses were in bloom.

I put in twelve-hour days weeding and clipping things into shape; carrying around my camera as if it were another garden tool, I fluffed up the flower beds and snapped. A friend stopped by and gave me a few technical tips that promised to give me more interesting shots, and so I jiggled the f-stop just like he said and hoped for bigger and better success.

My fourth day home. The weather was ideal for a photo shoot. I took close-ups of the earlier roses: Frau Karl Drushki and Ville de Bruxelles. I got panoramic views of the whole domain taken from the top of the olive grove: the elongated rectangular meadows accented with cypresses, the church at San Giusto in the distance against the sloping green backdrop of Monte Serra. I sighted my garden through a lens from sunrise to sunset, when the house lights came on through a bluing dusk—it was like an *Architectural Digest* cover (you've just pulled up for a candlelight dinner). Five rolls of film. There wasn't a single aspect of my life here that I hadn't captured, for the garden art lovers of Arezzo, in the eye of the 35mm cyclops.

I rushed my film to the processor. Ready tomorrow afternoon, said the ascoted one. That night I slept (except for when I lay awake worrying about Shirley's Gamble group, the believers and mystics of Palo Alto, hungry to plumb my garden's myths).

What a funny look he had on his face, the film store man. "Something must be wrong with your camera," he said, his voice all irony.

I must have looked like chalk. My tongue felt like chalk when I said, "Wrong?"

"Black," he said.

"Black?"

He held up my five boxes of slides fastened together with a navy blue rubber band. "Black," he said. "That'll be fifty-six thousand lire."

I paid him and he handed me the boxes. I opened one and poked through. Black. Unerringly black.

"Would you like a bag?" he said.

Poor Gil. When I go nervous, I go nuts. I watch all rationality disappear behind a luminous horizon, and woe is anyone who stands, backlit, this side of it. Black.

"Don't worry," Gil said, "you still have two more days."

"TWO MORE DAYS?"

I arrived in Arezzo the afternoon of the twelfth. It really didn't matter to me that it was only a three-star hotel, or that the previous guest in my room had smoked Toscani uninterruptedly for twenty-four hours prior to my checking in, or that there was no BBC World, no CNN, just RAI 1, 2, and 3: old Zorro reruns or half-naked Folies Bergère long-legged women in plumes kicking up in the faces of game show contestants—"Name the country where Nelson Mandela is president . . ." kick, kick.

My little red plastic phone rang. "*Ciao,*" she said. "*Sono Maria Luisa. Come stai?*"

"*Io, bene,*" I said. "Where are you? Is that train noise I hear?"

"Yes," she said. "I'm on a train."

"Where?"

"Pulling into Arezzo station. *Ecco,* the brakes."

I heard them squeak.

"I'm up out of my seat, OK? I'm going down the steps. *Grazie, molto gentile.* I'm crossing to the station house. You know it's right across the street from our hotel. Is it all right? The hotel?"

"Oh yes, fine," I said. "There's a bed here and there's a bathroom there."

"I'm crossing the street. Look out your window. Do you see the street?"

I stood up and looked. There she was in the traffic. I could hear it in both ears. "So you don't believe in crosswalks," I said, "traffic lights and stuff."

She looked up and waved, all smiles. Cars screeched to smoky halts or wove their way recklessly around her; she took no notice; she's Roman. "Meet me in the lobby," she said. "Bring the slides."

It was the reunion of dear old friends (with kisses, of course), even though we'd only seen each other once before.

"This is Stefano," Maria Luisa said, introducing a clean-cut young man who looked like he could have been a law student—he'd been waiting for her by the reception desk. "He's my assistant," she said. "He'll make everything effortless for you, as he does for me every day of my life." She gave him a big, devouring hug. "Oh, my Stefano," she said. His blushing head emerged from between her breasts. "I hate to think of what a mess I'd be without him."

The hotel lobby was a seventies lounge of serpentine bank seating, but there was a note of luxury in the chromium bar, the white-jacketed barman, the blown-glass pitchers of bright-colored fruit juices (unquestionably sweetened) in silver bowls of ice. We sat amidst the sprawl of the professor's manuscripts and research materials and perfumed silk scarves—Maria Luisa occupies space like a cabbage rose shedding its endless outer petals. "*Vuoi un caffè?*" she said.

"Oh, no," I said, "just one a day for me, and I've had it."

"*Io, invece, sì,*" she said, raising her gaze to the barman, who caught the implied order like a pro.

In a force of unpremeditated professionalism, she welcomed me on behalf of the *Comune di Arezzo*, the *Assessorato Centro Storico e Qualità Urbana*, the *Biblioteca Citta di Arezzo*, and the *Associazione Museion e di Italia Nostra di Arezzo*. "Whew," she said; she gasped, then fanned herself with a scholarly journal.

"I'm very happy to be here," I said.

Her coffee arrived and she sipped, the saucer by her chin. Her nails were the red color of her lips. "Promise you won't be mad at me?" she asked.

Oh no, I thought.

"Maria Giusti won't be able to introduce you after all. She's under a deadline, but she sends her best. *I'll* introduce you!" Up came her padded shoulders with a swagger as her assistant nodded as if to say, Don't worry, you're in great hands.

"Oh, it's all the same to me," I said. "Well no; in fact, I'd have preferred your introduction anyhow."

Maria Luisa smiled broadly and threw one arm around me. "What sign are you?" she asked.

"Cancer."

"*O Dio, un Cancro!*"

"Not good?" I said. Paranoia.

"Your qualities are hot-dry," she said, "your conditions are gaseous, your humors are yellow bile, and your temperaments are choleric."

"Oh," I said disappointedly. I wouldn't tell her that I'm a *double* Cancer.

"That notwithstanding," she said, "I'll let you in on another secret disappointment."

"Another? Disappointment?"

"The ladies of the villa set haven't come through for us. There won't be the noble dinner party I promised."

"Oh, that's all right," I said. "Really."

"But they had *grand* ambitions for your evening, really they did. One baronessa—well-meaning girl—wanted to commission an Eiffel Tower out of roses for the occasion, three meters tall—"

"An Eiffel Tower? Three meters tall? Why?"

"Why three meters tall, or why an Eiffel Tower?"

"Why any of it?"

"Don't ask me!" Maria Luisa said. "I told her, 'Baronessa, you don't need to go *that* far.' But never mind, the baronessa's off to the Maldives instead."

"I guess it's just as well."

"I can't imagine giving up an evening with you for the Maldives, but what do *I* know? I've never been to the Maldives."

"I might have opted for the Maldives," I said.

"*O amore,*" she said, and gave me a squeeze. "Are those your slides?"

"Yes," I said. "One hundred and three of them."

"*O Dio,*" she screamed.

"Too many?"

"No, that'll be fine."

Stefano took the box, and it sent a worried shock all through me. Supposing he got broadsided by a bus between here and the Palazzo Pretorio. He had no idea what I'd gone through to produce them—up until yesterday they didn't exist. "I'll stack them in the projector for you," he said. "You won't have to do a thing."

"*Grazie,*" I said.

"All these pressing matters so resolved," Maria Luisa said, "you don't mind if I retire for a while. I have all *this* to read," She pointed with her chin to the flood of papers spewing out of control all around us. "Shall we meet at Palazzo Pretorio at five?"

"Perfect," I said.

I was glad to have a chance to see *Legend of the True Cross,* by Piero della Francesca, one of the greatest fresco cycles of Italian painting. The last time I came to Arezzo—was it ten years ago?—the masterpiece had been covered by blind scaffolding.

But wasn't it just my luck to find that the scaffolding, all these years later, was still in place (this was far worse than any of Maria Luisa's so-called disappointments). They must be doing an awfully good restoration job.

But Vasari's house, in Via Venti Settembre, saved the day. Its lugubrious frescos, full of pagan references, are movingly grandiose, in provocative contrast to the modest building that contains them. What passion possessed him! His newly restored garden, a *giardino pensile* of rose-covered arbors, was surprisingly well planted. I left on a note of optimism, almost having forgotten what I'd come here for.

My talk was scheduled for five, but I decided not to arrive at the lecture hall until five-fifteen. I'd just been to a conference at the American Academy in Rome on the subject of Russell Page, and no one, neither participants nor audience, arrived in the hall on time. I'd go native. I'd spare myself that long, ominous wait with only my nervousness for company.

On either side of the main entrance of the fourteenth-century Palazzo Pretorio, which now houses the city library, stood easels displaying huge posters. Below a full-color illustration of the Medici garden of La Petraia my name appeared, and below it, Maria Luisa's extravagant lecture theme: *La resurrezione di Villa Massei nelle colline Lucchesi: una committenza moderna.* Gulp; talk about the Eiffel Tower!

Just as I'd thought: empty hall. A hundred chairs, a slide projector rising on a pedestal in their midst like a hollyhock. But suddenly the hall filled up, Maria Luisa leading my pageant of an audience in as if they'd all got off the same bus.

At one end of the room stood a long table, two chairs, two microphones; I tapped my finger on one of them: bump, it was on.

A very mixed group: some students with books, some ladies with shopping bags, some single gentlemen in bow ties, some well-turned-out couples. Thirty or so people?

"Shall we start?" a very serious Maria Luisa said.

"Why not?"

We sat. Maria Luisa opened. A lot of descriptive praise, building rounds of context, fadeless blooms of language, the syntax of a golden age of rhetoric that's never ended here in Italy. Economy of phrase, the beauty of English, is just a pity, isn't it? My attention waned, then refocused, but Orpheus, in unbound eloquence, went on singing. ". . . and so it is with great pleasure that I present to you now . . ."

I was on. Finally. My well-rehearsed opening acknowledgments and thank-yous out of the way, I told the little story of how I came to be a gardener: this entire book reduced to a five-minute synopsis.

The mood palpably brightened when I called for the first slide. I stood and stepped to the side. Maria Luisa took a seat in the front row, and the lights went down in the great hall with its gilded ceiling *a cassettone.*

And there it was, here in Arezzo: my house in Massa Macinaia seen from the gate in a golden frame of mimosa. I said, "An Italian friend once remarked: 'It's the quintessential house of a foreigner in Italy. Not only for what it is, but for where it is.' "

"Muuum," said the audience in agreement.

I raised a finger for Stefano. He clicked the clicker and a new slide appeared.

What's this?

The murmuring grew louder. I didn't recognize the image. I felt like I'd been picked up by a crane the size of a tornado and dropped in another hemisphere.

"Oh, yeah," I said, "this is Gil and me having a sunset drink at the Eden Rock in St. Bart's." How the hell did that get in there? You idiot, I said to myself, one finger raised. Idiot!

New slide.

Oh no! What in the world?

Laughter.

"Oh yeah," I said, "that's the family picnic in Gloucester, Massachusetts. My niece Abigail and me running the three-legged race." Oh shit! Abigail and me stepping out of the same burlap chamise—these Arezzo esthetes had never seen anything like it in their lives.

What a slob!

I turned to the audience, rows of dark faces. "You're not in any hurry," I asked, "are you?"

MAY 13. I DIDN'T GET BACK HOME UNTIL TWO. NO
time for my usual afternoon nap. Garden open today. There was even
a wine tasting to arrange.

The lecture had gone pretty well in spite of my having bungled
the slides. Maria Luisa said, "The odd irrelevant image lent a cute
dose of *follia* to it all. Don't worry, they've suffered crazier speakers
than you." In fact, the garden lovers of Arezzo were generous and
understanding. I spoke for more than two hours and only three of
them left early. I did have some pretty pictures of flowers to show; so
what if they were interspersed with a snapshot or two of Gil and me
looking a bit irascible among the holiday makers of Nerha?

But for good or bad this distraction of a lecture to give had taken my mind off the scariest thing of all: a visit from the Elizabeth F. Gamble Garden Center of Palo Alto, California.

The day was dull, unfortunately, overcast and still. In England they call such weather "bright"; here in Tuscany we call it "dark." Dark doesn't bring out the best of a garden, I'm afraid. I thought, Let's hope they're as forgiving as the garden *appassionati* of Arezzo.

But, miracles of miracles, the heavens widened just as the gate bell rang—exactly on time, by the way. What must they have thought at the village *bottega* when a big bus pulled up to the *piazzetta* and twenty-two Californians got out in all their beribboned, straw-hatted splendor, pens poised over notebooks, yakking away in a foreign tongue?

The double hedge of Pinkerton roses just inside the gate bowed to the advance, and the garden visitors bowed back to them and sniffed. They seemed to be all over the place at once: some came out of the bottega, some had taken a peak at the church, some had made themselves comfortable by the babbling, fig-shaded *lavatoio*.

First ones through the garden gate: three men. So it wasn't an *all-lady* affair. They came to me, shook hands, introduced themselves. Would I have to remember twenty-two names?

And then Shirley.

A whole year later, imagine! It could have been a week ago that she and Jan came into our lives on their ardent quest for beauty which brought them so surprisingly here. The other day Ugo said to me, "My, how time flies, Paolo. *Veramente.* It seems like I just took out the Christmas tree." (It's a potted, living one.) "Time flies so fast, Paolo, it makes no sense that I haul that Christmas tree all the way over there by the garage. Next year I'll just leave it by the front door; in a blink of an eye it's time to take it in again."

"So nice to see you," Shirley said. She looked beyond me, off towards the meadow. "And the garden! The garden looks divine!"

I turned and had a look for myself. The light was golden, the time of day propitious. The shadows of the great twin cypresses crossed the lawn and made their ripply way up the facade of the house. Green sculpture, hedges and topiary, stood starkly geometric, and the roses bloomed and the nepeta held forth. There was color everywhere: the blue ceanothus, the lilac *Phlomis Italica*, the pink *Papavero vivace* "Princess Louise." A breeze came up off the sea; the herbaceous plants nodded in their border under La Folette—they went crazy for that rose in Arezzo.

I gathered my visitors around and made a few welcoming remarks. But they weren't here for a lecture. One by one they fell off to different beckoning garden features.

I followed a few of them to the niche where a stone dolphin spews water to a basin of aquatics. Along the front was a thick drift of moisture-loving plants.

"That's not *Lythrum salicaria*, is it?"

Who said that? An elderly woman with a baseball hat and an aluminum, rubber-tipped walking stick.

"Yes," I said. Wow! I had some real gardeners here.

"Oh *no*," she said. "You know that plant's the bane of Canada, don't you?"

"No," I said, "I didn't know that, actually."

"Oh yes," she said. "They're having to napalm it, it's gotten so bad."

"But this isn't Canada, Genevieve," someone kindly said.

I looked at the lythrum's showy magenta blooms, which I'd artfully mixed with *Echinacea* "White Luster." I remembered sending away for the seeds on the basis of a catalog description and a photograph. How carefully I cared for the seedlings, misting them three times daily. It seemed like just the right plant for the apron of a water feature. When it bloomed that first summer, I recognized it: purple loosestrife. It's all over Massa Macinaia, by the roadsides and along streams; it's all over my own land, in fact. But this was a different cultivar at least: "Roseum Superbum."

"They've made it illegal up in Canada," the woman said. "Scarcely wonder why; it's a menace; it's choked out untold species of native plant life." She *tsk*ed and shook her head.

There were six or eight of us impertinently staring at the poor plant with suspicion as if at any moment it might turn on us and pounce.

A hand on my shoulder. I jumped! It was Gil. "What do you call that gray thing with the yellow?" he said.

"*Phlomis* 'Edward Bowles,' " I said.

"Oh, right."

I heard my words "*Phlomis* 'Edward Bowles'" echo about the garden on the wings of nature's breath. To think that only a couple of years ago I didn't know what a phlomis was, had never even seen one before. I visited a garden in England that had a full-mantled *Phlomis fruticosa*, but when I asked the young gardener what it was, he said, "*Santolina chamaecyparissus.*" Not even the English are infallible.

Shirley joined me by the mouth of the *viale*. "It's such a relief to come to a personal garden," she said. "I mean, Villa Reale was marvelous, of course. But some of these others! Here the lamps of heaven flash with a softer light. Don't you think so, Deborah?"

"It's all a matter of touch," said a woman in jeans and a straw hat. "A living touch. The world of these old gardens is irrevocably detached from our own. They're an enchanted isle certainly, but lost, invisible. You go there thinking you'll see things. But you don't. What I really love are gardens of the moment. Like this one."

"Well, thank you," I said, "but I don't think you can compare my little effort here to the great gardens of Italy. Let's be reasonable."

"I'm talking about how a garden makes me *feel*," Deborah said. "You, as a gardener, surely know what I mean."

Me? I thought. A gardener?

We walked on. We passed the little *salottino* of wicker furniture, a table and four armchairs in the shade of my cedar of Lebanon. By the time we'd have made our loop and come back, we'd find a tray on this table, several bottles of chilled Sorbus, twenty-five glasses, some olives and locally made bread crackers, *crespini*—Ottavia would invisibly deliver them once we were out of sight.

To the meadow.

Its mown central strip, straight as the gate, was Albertina's idea. All these years later we're still doing it, still mowing that *viale* with stakes and string to get it right, still walking there among the waist-high wildflowers. Pepperwort or pickerelweed, pigeonberry or poor man's weatherglass, I have no idea what these delicate blossoms are called, so busy am I studying the names of plants I *don't* have, ignoring the ones I do. Still, I'll never take for granted the unconsidered planting nature arranged, the pale pinks with the soft blues, the golden yellows, the tender whites. It's a homogeneous scattering; it's perfection.

In the mown part, wild thyme has taken over; when you crush it underfoot its spicy scent rises with your appetite. "This must be a helenium," someone remarked about a tiny flowering plant along the edge. Who knew?

Half the group had already made the turn and were heading

back, single file, along the "Renne de Marché" cherry walk, thirty-six young trees. "Do you eat these cherries?" someone asked.

"There were three this year," I said. "Gil ate the first, I ate the second, and some bird ate the third. In a few years we'll have more. I can't wait."

> VISITOR I: Time passes so slowly in the garden. It's very preserving of the gardener, you know.
> VISITOR 2: Gardeners live long lives. It's the anticipation that keeps us young. Like the Christmas morning that never seems to come.
> VISITOR I: It's the *work* that gives us longevity.
> VISITOR 2: It's the yearning.
> VISITOR I: It's the digging, my dear.
> VISITOR 2: Well, Caroline, it's all of that.

What a sight this was, twenty-two people walking single-file, whole distances between each, along the meadow path, then back through the cherry orchard, all following me. I felt a bit like a bridge builder must feel when he watches those first few cars pass the cut ribbon in a shower of champagne and cross his finished product: that thing he'd spent years making is no longer a mere suspended assemblage of girders and cable and macadam. It's a bridge.

They loved the terrace: all that clipped geometry, the scheme of hedges, wall, and jars. "Of course, this was here when you bought the place," they said. I was pleased, proud.

We were standing under the camphor tree when a breathy cuckoo called as if I'd ordered his participation in the afternoon.

"Hail to thee, blithe spirit!" Shirley said, raising her shoulders.

If I were up to it, I might have added, "Bird thou never wert,/ That from Heaven, or near it,/ Pourist thy full heart/ In profuse strains of unpremeditated art."

I led them to the grotto. This is my garden's destination, and praise be to the end! It seems to me that I've withheld, throughout all these pages, a proper discussion of this, the most important thing here. I don't know why that should have happened; only in the grotto's spiritual-life-giving role does it defy description.

As for its physical state, it's a kind of temple, completely Greco-Roman in style. If you were to thumb through that souvenir illustrated book you picked up at Delphi, you'd come upon a drawing of the treasury of Siphnos; these are its proportions' roots. It has a wide, triangular pediment whose plain entablature is supported by four flat, doubled columns in relief, standing upon a *crepidoma*. The capitals are Ionic, the molding beneath the cornice formed of dentils. The building's entrance is an arch, a Roman touch. High upon the terra-cotta facade, each assembled piece expressly made for this project alone, are tiny lion heads, and below these, at shoulder height, there's a pair of carved stone masks out of whose mouths water trickles into terra-cotta Lebes vases. But this is just the exterior.

The interior is all of the above multiplied by four. Each wall is decorated with four Ionic columns in relief, lion-head accents, and dentils under the cornice. There are three *spugna*-lined, arch-shaped niches where huge, grotesque masks spew water to deep stalagmite-incrusted pools. And the floor: an elaborate composition of hexagonal terra-cotta tiles, narrow bricks, and river stones set in mortar surrounds an oval stone centerpiece that represents the microcosm—

man hemmed in on all sides by the physical universe—expressing the correlation and interdependence of all parts of the cosmos. Whoever put this work of art together was a genius.

The water was softly flowing now, the surface of the dark pools like old rippled glass. As is our tenuous hold on this water, the garden's life-giving force, so is my hold on the loggia parterre which, as soon as I've cleaned it of its weeds, making it somehow perfect in my

human eyes, time (like the wind that picks up and blows the mandala's sands off to eternity) soon causes to revert.

All twenty-two of our garden visitors, having climbed the hill of Delphi and reached the inner sanctum, were there in the grotto with me now, and so I took this opportunity to tell them a little story.

Last December, Gil and I went to the town of Tirukkalukundram, just outside of Mamallapuram in Tamil Nadu, India. It was a rainy morning and our driver turned us loose in a muddy square at the foot of Vedagirishvara Temple, which is dug into the peak of a 160-meter-high mountain. We still weren't used to taking off our shoes at these sacred Hindu sites, but this morning was a real test, as you had to walk up the four hundred steps barefoot. It rained and then it stopped, but the steps were standing water and the dryer parts were grimy with sand and small sharp pebbles that dug into one's tender, Western, lily-white feet.

We climbed and climbed in total solitude, and when it really poured we ducked under the eaves of an overhanging rock—only to discover quickly that it was a halfway pit stop for any and all human needs. At long last we reached a narrow terrace where priests feed two sacred vultures who regularly fly down at midday. But it was too early for vultures; all was calm as the rain fell across a view of green rice paddies that stretched southward for mile after flat Tamil Nadu mile.

At the top of yet another flight of steep steps an ancient, bent, painted-faced priest in a badly soiled dhoti emerged from a door that led to the mountain's core. He was barefoot and topless and wore a string of beads around his tortoise neck. "Come, come!" he ordered with so broad a gesture that it might have been understood beside the water tank at Bhaktavatsaleshvara Temple a kilometer away in the plain. Without a thought as to what lay ahead we answered the priest's beckoning, climbed the steep steps, and entered a temple which the *Blue Guide* describes as "of little interest architecturally."

Once inside the damp colonnade of marble and stone the old man closed the enormous wooden vault-thick door. Clunk!

Oh, my God!

I'm claustrophobic.

Sometimes it seems that I'm only *mildly* claustrophobic—I can drive the seventeen-kilometer-long San Gotthard tunnel provided I do my breathing exercises just prior to entry. Sometimes, on the other hand, it seems that I'm *very* claustrophobic—the last time I unwittingly sank into the London tube I made a beeline to the surface and demanded my money back for health reasons (they gave it to me).

But here I was now in this mile-high temple, conscious of the fact that this interior space of cold marble aisles was dug into the top of a mountain and that a hundred feet of stone peak hung over my head. And as if this wasn't bad enough in itself, the door was *closed!*

I know the telltale signs all too well: accelerated heartbeat, sweaty brow, the feeling that you're about to faint, and that desperate inner query from the psyche: "What are you waiting for? Get us *out* of here!"

Gil was aware of this problem of mine, but he tends to prod (helpingly, he feels). "Oh, come on," he said. "He's telling us to come."

I looked at the old priest. I'm not sure it was English he spoke, but I knew what he meant. "Come."

"Why is he so *insistent?*" I asked Gil.

"Never mind," he said. "It's what they do. Come on."

I followed. Against all instincts. Why do I tend to do this? I've done it time after time, and I know I'll do it again. One never learns.

The priest was interested in conveying offerings on our behalf to the temple's divine figures in the inner sanctuary. Of course I understood this. Of course I understood that this meant money for the temple coffers and that money was very important to everyone here. But none of this understanding helped matters. I'd have given him every red cent I had just to get the hell *out*. But the priest, in line with his commitment, demanded our visual contact with the deities, and he would not rest until this fundamental visual contact was made.

I followed, blood pounding in my ears, along the column-lined axis, through gates he opened and closed. The smell of burning ghee (clarified butter) was worse than Rupert Meade's breakfast.

And there it was, the focal sanctuary, a space of no more than a dozen cubic feet. Another priest, his torso feebly painted in vermilion and white, stood beyond the threshold over a smoking, ghee-glistening idol reciting prayers and singing hymns. "Come," the old man insisted, almost pushing us now. "Come, come." I looked into the candlelit dark hemmed in by the universe and thought about that mountain on top of my head—What, he expects me to step in *there*? Are you *mad*?

"I'm outta here," I said.

"No no," Gil said.

"Oh yes I *am*," I said.

Before I knew it, I'd made it through two iron gates, Gil and the old priest following. As I struggled to open the third gate, Gil apologetically explained. "My friend here is . . . afraid . . ."

The old man knew *that* much English; Gil couldn't have said the word "afraid" more clearly.

"He's . . . *afraid* . . ." Gil said, leaving out the specific nature of my fear.

Well, that old priest had never heard anything so funny in his *life*.

The laughter that rolled out of him could have brought the craggy ancient mountain down on our backs.

I picked up speed. I was headed for that damn door with a vengeance. I have a thing about doors: I never forget how I get into places. I had the floor plan of that temple printed on my retina. I rushed to that vault-like exit as if I'd sprouted the wings of the Furies. The laughing priest helped me with the latch; I bolted out and never looked back, but I could hear that naked priest laughing from the depths of his holy diaphragm all the way down those four hundred steps and onto the muddy plane of Tirukkalukkundram.

"My friend here is . . . *afraid*," I said, repeating Gil's explanation once we were clear of any threat. "Why didn't you tell him I'm claustrophobic? He thought I was, like . . . spooked!"

"I didn't think he'd understand," Gil said, laughing himself delirious.

"Well, you could have tried. You had time. *Claus . . . tro . . . pho . . . bi . . . a*. What the heck's the matter with you?"

Laughter everywhere. Laughter from the mountaintop. Laughter from Gil.

Laughter filled the inner sanctum in which I now stood with twenty-two garden visitors who'd spent so long in the pagan shadows that they were looking pasty as mushrooms.

I made my way to the open air among the exited throng. Ah, the silver light! The outdoors, that's for me.

"Look here," said Genevieve, pointing into my woodland beds under the wisteria with her aluminum rubber-tipped cane. "That's another loosestrife there."

"Genevieve's our plant expert," Shirley said apologetically.

"*Lysimachia clethroïdes,*" Genevieve said as several of her students gathered around. "Gooseneck loosestrife. It was once the bane of my garden, but I've finally eradicated it. Set a flamethrower to it, I did, and don't think it wasn't deserving." She gave the beak of her baseball hat a tweak and knocked away one of my lysimachia's curving blooms with her cane. "It ruined my best border. It jumped the fence to my neighbors, and my relations with them were already bad enough! That plant there, kill it whenever you see it, do you understand? Eradicate it! Show no mercy!"

"But it's so pretty," someone said.

"Young man!" Genevieve said. "Young man!"

Did she mean me? I hadn't been called "young man" since 1981. The satanic delinquent responsible for these border atrocities, I broke my way through a terrified gallery of onlookers and joined Genevieve by my beloved *Lysimachia clethroïdes*—I'd searched far and wide for those fair little maidens. "Yes?" I said.

"Look here," she said, "loosestrife! What are you planning to do about this pest?"

"Don't ask me," I said, "I'm just the gardener."